IMAGES
of America

CHILDREN'S FAIRYLAND

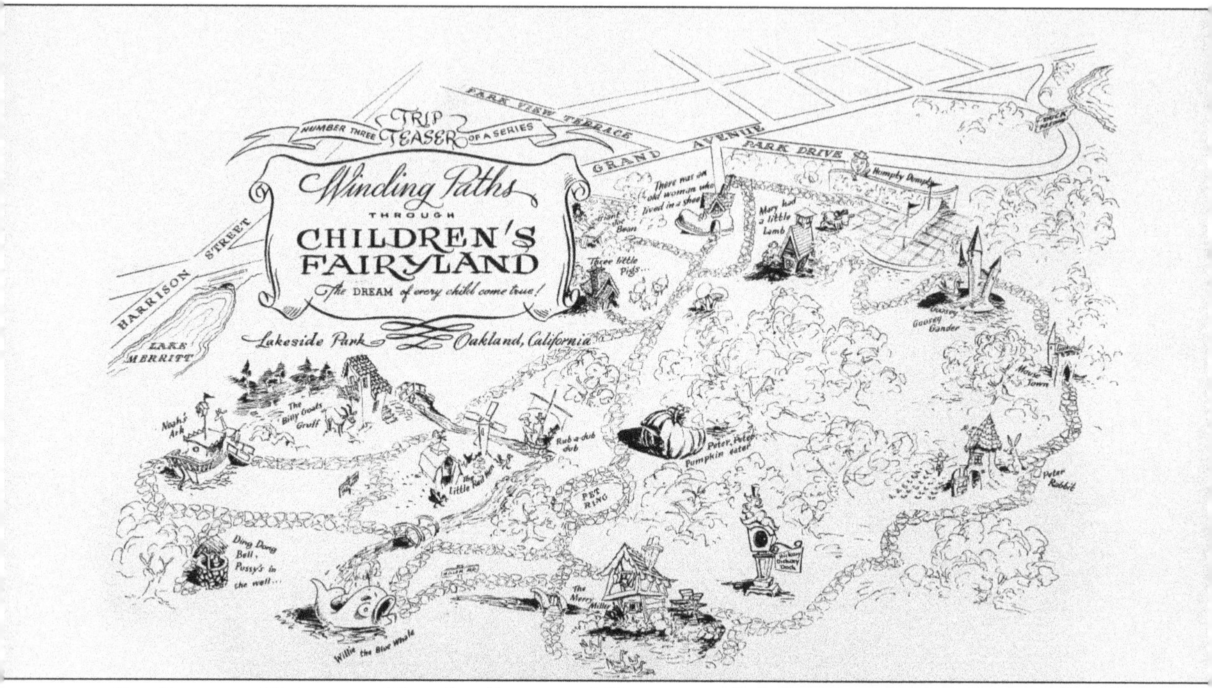

Big Launch. This map of Fairyland's original 17 sets is included in the *Trip Teaser No. 3 Souvenir Booklet*, written by Sven Skaar and illustrated by George Mathis. The 20-page booklet, which contains full-color paintings of the park sets, was published in 1950 and mailed to a wide audience as part of a promotion for Oakland and Fairyland. (Children's Fairyland Archives.)

On the Cover: Presentation Day at Fairyland, 1974. The Lakeside Lark, Fairyland's little train, transports dignitaries through the park to the Emerald City Stage, where the year's new Fairyland Personalities will be introduced. Built in 1959, the Lark also carried visitors from the parking lot to the front entrance; today, a new version of the train is brought out occasionally for community parades. (Children's Fairyland Archives.)

IMAGES
of America

CHILDREN'S FAIRYLAND

Randal J. Metz on behalf of
Children's Fairyland

ARCADIA
PUBLISHING

ISBN 978-1-4671-2416-4

Published by Arcadia Publishing
Charleston, South Carolina

Library of Congress Control Number: 2016945897

For all general information, please contact Arcadia Publishing:
Telephone 843-853-2070
Fax 843-853-0044
E-mail sales@arcadiapublishing.com
For customer service and orders:
Toll-Free 1-888-313-2665

Visit us on the Internet at www.arcadiapublishing.com

This book is dedicated to the dreamers, artists, storytellers, and craftspeople who keep alive the magic that is Children's Fairyland.

Contents

Remembrance

I was born in Oakland in 1951—a year after Children's Fairyland opened. My family believed in taking weekend excursions, and one of our favorite places to visit was right here in Oakland: Children's Fairyland.

The magic started when we walked "through the Shoe": Mom, Dad, and six kids. We began our tour by pulling the tongue of the Talking Dragon, who welcomes families to Children's Fairyland. Then it was off to see Willie the Whale and to venture down, down, down into his scary (to me) mouth.

At the puppet show, we marveled at the marionettes that walked, talked, and danced. Then you would hear "All aboard for the Jolly Trolly!"—Fairyland's railroad, whose track circled the park. As I rode, I would think enviously about the kids who were Fairyland Personalities and got to stroll the park dressed as storybook characters.

Many years passed before I visited Fairyland again. I was a grown-up; I had worked as a paramedic and a schoolteacher and had started an agency called Safe Exchange, which provided supervision for court-ordered child visitations. My office was across Grand Avenue from Fairyland, and one day I had an idea: Why not get out of the office and take the kids to Fairyland? These kids' lives were filled with conflict and stress, but when they entered the fairy gates they could just be kids again. They could run around, explore, and feel safe.

I am retired from social services work now, but I have not retired from Fairyland. I have served on the board of directors, and I record voices for the puppet shows. And since the early 2000s, I have been fulfilling my childhood dream of becoming a Fairyland Personality. Each winter, I put on a red suit and white beard and become Santa Claus during the Fairy Winterland festivities. When kids (or parents) act surprised to see an African American Santa, I tell them we have our own special tradition at Fairyland.

Because that is what Fairyland has always been for me and for thousands of children: a special place with special traditions. I would not have it any other way.

—Ron Zeno

Acknowledgments

Many years ago, following a terrible world war, a group of dreamers set about to create a place where a city's children could create, imagine, play, and learn in peace and harmony. We acknowledge the founders of the nation's first storybook theme park: nurseryman Art Navlet, Oakland Parks superintendent William Penn Mott Jr., architect William Russell Everritt, and the members of the Lake Merritt Breakfast Club, a group of local businessmen who believed in the dream. We are grateful for access to Mott's personal memorabilia.

I would also like to thank a few of the people who have worked tirelessly on this project, checking facts and keeping me on the right track. They include Michael Flores, C.J. Hirschfield, Tony Jonick, Carl LaRue, Lewis Mahlmann, Burton Weber, Annie Wong, Nancy Friedman, and the Fairyland staff.

Unless otherwise noted, the memories and photographs in these pages come from the Oakland Children's Fairyland Archives. Each photograph was taken on behalf of Fairyland by a talented artist to whom we owe a debt of gratitude. Many names have been lost to history, but some have not. They include Yvonne Backman, Diane Brady, Jack Chin, Mike Fittleson, Michael Flores, Richard Haick, Cricket Hamilton, Deborah Io, Carl LaRue, Kristin Loken, Barry Muniz, Maria Rodriguez, Jackie Salas, Lonnie Wilson, and Harold Winder.

We hope you enjoy this story as much as we have enjoyed telling it! Enter the fairy gates with us and discover the enchanting world that is Children's Fairyland.

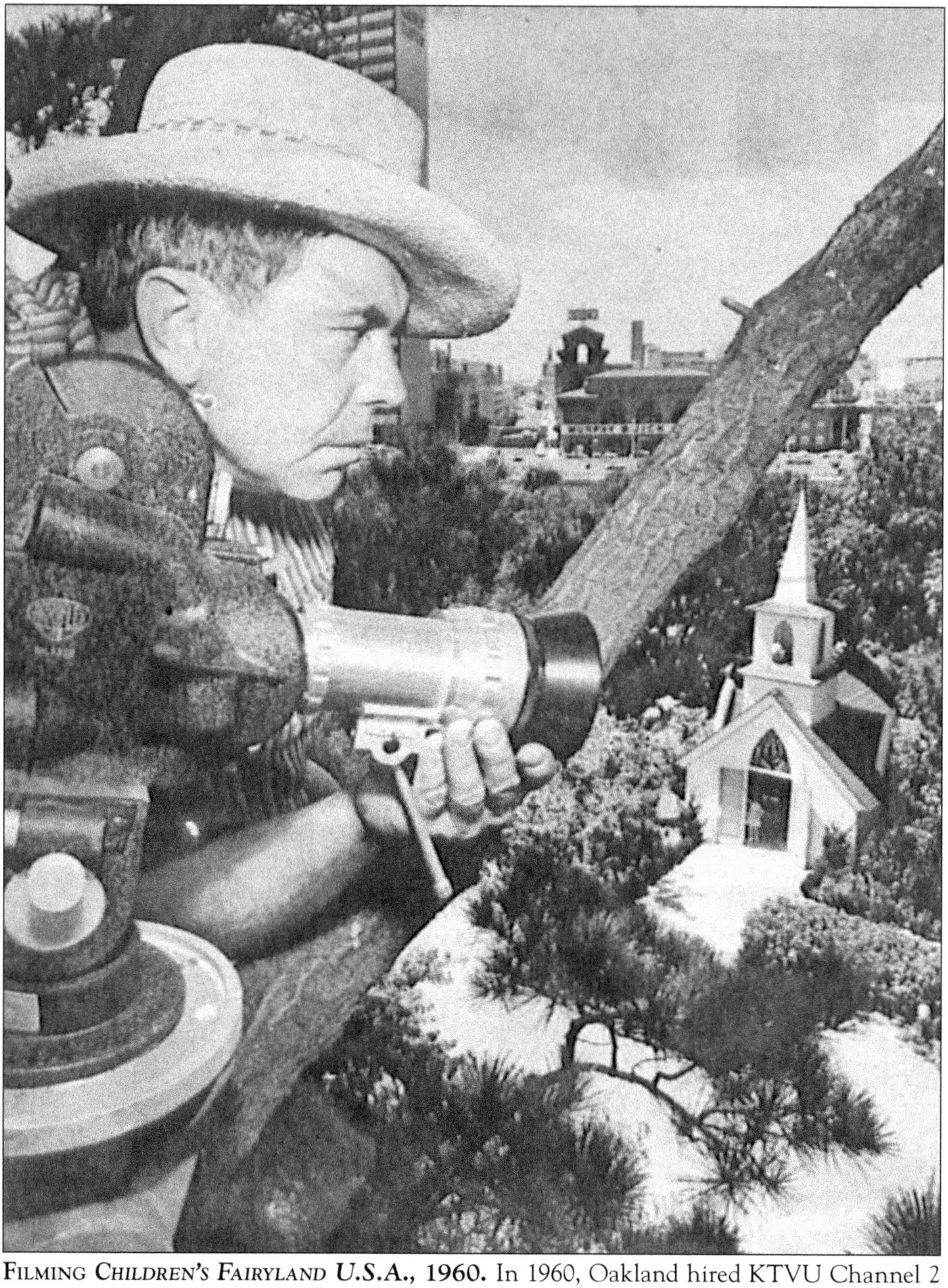

FILMING *CHILDREN'S FAIRYLAND* U.S.A., 1960. In 1960, Oakland hired KTVU Channel 2 cameraman Buck Joseph to make a feature-length documentary. The film features child actors and television celebrities who voice characters from fairy tales; Joseph also put members of his family in the film as visitors experiencing the park. Here, Joseph is perched in the pine treetops, planning his next aerial shot of Fairyland.

INTRODUCTION

This is the tale of how, in 1950, a storybook dream became a reality and of how that reality continues to inspire childhood dreams.

In 1948, Arthur and Alma Navlet, owners of Oakland's largest nursery, visited the Belle Isle Children's Park and Zoo in Detroit. The children's play area in the zoo featured fanciful storybook settings brought to life by the addition of baby animals and exotic plantings. Captivated, the Navlets decided that the children of Oakland, California, should have something like this in their own backyard.

The San Francisco Bay Area and the United States were in a creative mood during the late 1940s. World War II had ended, and families were picking up the threads of their lives. City dwellers found, however, that there was little in the way of organized amusement for families with young children. Vaudeville was dead, and television was not yet a popular medium. There was radio and movies and public parks but few other places for whole families to spend leisure time.

It was in this fertile landscape that the seed of Navlet's idea was planted.

Navlet collected all the information he could on the Detroit children's zoo and headed back to Oakland, where he met with his social organization, the Lake Merritt Breakfast Club. Since 1933, this businessmen's club (which later admitted businesswomen as well) had been dedicated to creating a "better Oakland." Members met once a week at 7:00 a.m. to enjoy breakfast and a lecture.

Navlet had his eye on Lakeside Park, adjacent to the breakfast club. Home to the first designated wildlife refuge in the United States, Lakeside Park abuts both downtown Oakland and Lake Merritt, a man-made lake created from a tidal estuary. Navlet decided that Lakeside Park would be an ideal location for the new family experience he had in mind.

It was in many ways a perfect site. In 1869, Oakland's mayor had declared Lakeside Park a wildlife sanctuary. After the devastating 1906 earthquake and fire, some 150,000 displaced San Franciscans had fled to Oakland and found refuge in Lakeside Park, where the US Army Corps of Engineers installed water and sewage lines to accommodate the emergency tent city. Blessed with an abundance of the oak trees that had given the city its name, the park blended natural attractions with urban comforts.

Navlet persuaded the breakfast club to sponsor the new park, and together they persuaded the Oakland Parks Commission to become involved. The commission was headed by William Penn Mott Jr., a dynamic figure who was revitalizing Oakland's parks landscape and who later played important roles in statewide and national park stewardship. (In 1967, Gov. Ronald Reagan appointed him as director of the California State Department of Parks and Recreation, and in 1985, Mott became the director of the National Park Service, where he went on to create 17 new national parks.)

With Navlet and Mott leading the campaign for the children's park, businesses all over Oakland signed on to sponsor the storybook sets and live animals that would create the landscape of Oakland's

"Fairyland." Very soon, local artist and architect William Russell Everritt was commissioned to design this enchanted world. Everritt's playful, off-kilter designs for the park won many admirers; he is featured in a reference book, *Artists in America*, as a painter, sculptor, photographer, and industrial designer. His work has also influenced the look of many miniature golf courses around the nation.

The last ingredient needed for this fairy-tale recipe was ADMARK, the Oakland Advertising and Marketing Club. For 51 years, this business group extolled the virtues of Oakland and Children's Fairyland. Its achievements include a movie made in the 1950s called *Fairyland U.S.A.*, which was used by the United Nations to promote the United States, and a 1952 article with color photographs in *Life* magazine that presents the park to the nation.

On September 2, 1950, Fairyland opened its gates to large crowds and enthusiastic reviews. Very soon, copycat playgrounds and parks sprang up all over the country. Fairyland's success also drew the attention of a certain animator in Los Angeles. Walt Disney was looking to open his own brand of family park: Disneyland. Of all the parks, fairs, and playgrounds he visited, he found only two worthy of imitation: Tivoli Gardens in Copenhagen and Children's Fairyland in Oakland. Disney was so taken by Oakland's accomplishments that he even hired away two of the park's original staff members—the executive director and the puppeteer—to duplicate Fairyland's success.

Over the years, Oakland has been committed to maintaining the simple charms of its storybook park. Fairyland does not offer the carnival games, mechanical amusements, or fast rides on which most contemporary amusement parks rely. It is instead powered by imagination, using storybook settings inspired by classic tales that in turn inspire children to create their own adventures. Fairyland is intended to be the first amusement park small children experience. To keep it safe for young children, the park established an admissions policy in 1950 that is still in effect: "No child without an adult, and no adult without a child."

Most of the storybook theme parks that opened after Fairyland have since closed or been paved over, but not Fairyland, which has just celebrated its 66th birthday. It survives and thrives—and maintains its vibrant relevance—thanks to a unique civic-private partnership: the City of Oakland owns the land, but a nonprofit organizational model has ensured the park's ongoing viability. Admission fees are deliberately kept low to allow wide access, and a vigorous outreach effort ensures that families with limited means do not have to pay at all. Fairyland's outreach extends into Oakland schools and libraries as well, where young children learn about plants, animals, stories, and the enchantment of puppetry.

At 66, Children's Fairyland could qualify for senior citizen status. But the park retains its youthful innocence—a rare quality in a world of glossy technology and accelerated pace. To watch children stream "through the Shoe" and marvel at Oswald the Bubble Elf is to realize that in the 21st century, as in the mid-20th, the promise of Fairyland's founders—that the park would be "every child's dream come true"—is still being kept.

One

Dreaming the Dream

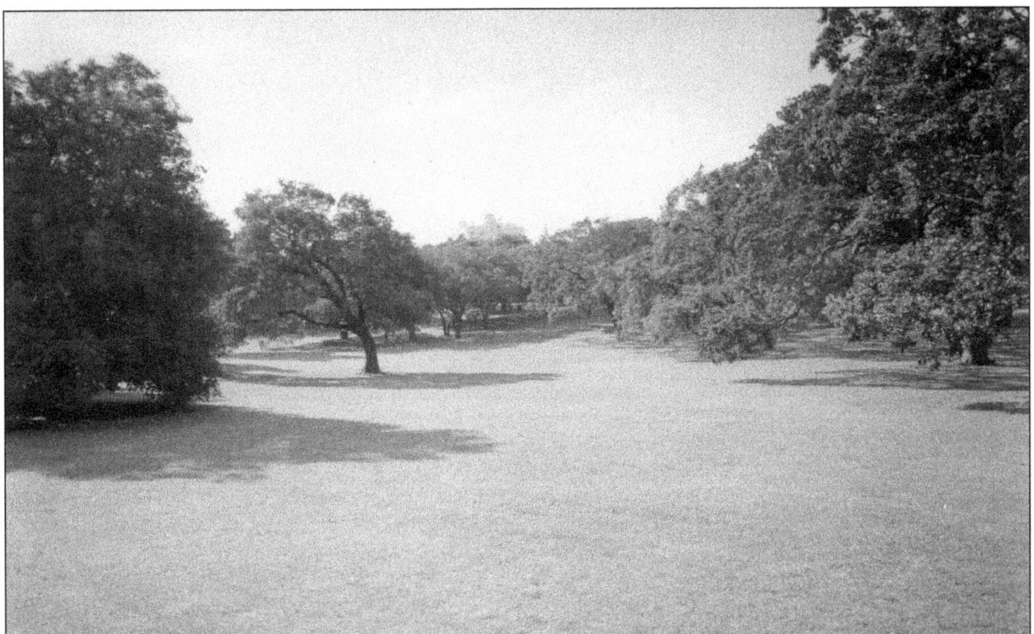

Lakeside Park, 1948. This is the tranquil park chosen as Fairyland's future site. Many of the oak trees in the photograph had to be removed or relocated to accommodate the sets of the new proposed children's playground. The final cost of building Fairyland was $50,000, a considerable sum at a time when the average household income was $3,200.

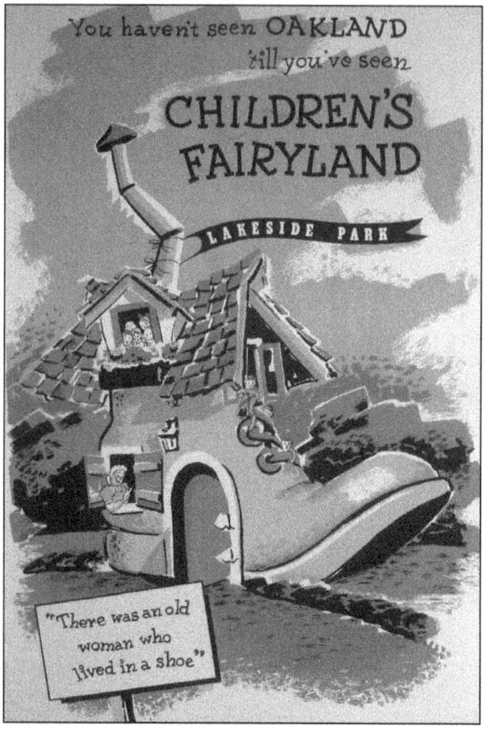

Opening Day Poster, 1950. This silk-screened poster was displayed on local businesses, buildings, and billboards. Fairyland opened to an eager public on September 2, 1950. Admission was 9¢ for children and 14¢ for adults. One amusement park historian pointed out: "Fairyland's significance is unquestionable: It influenced a wave of copycat parks, but more importantly it animated designers, bureaucrats, and citizens to rethink children's playgrounds."

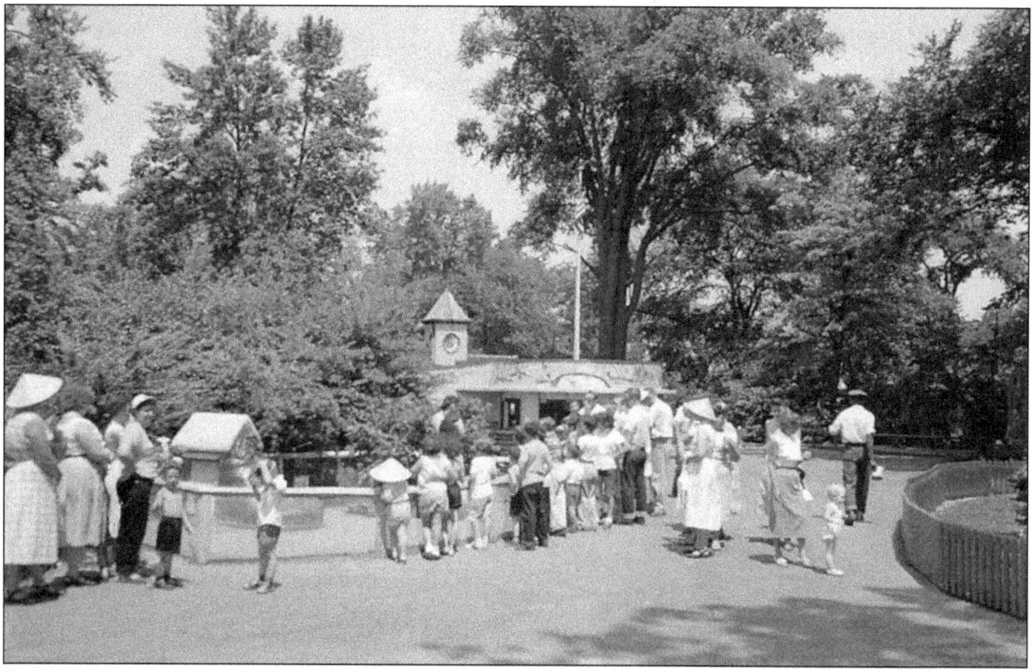

Belle Isle Children's Zoo, c. 1963. Fairyland was inspired by Belle Isle Children's Park and Zoo in Detroit, which opened in 1947 and featured storybook settings with small animals and thematic plantings. The zoo and park closed in 2002 due to lack of city funding, but many of the original small buildings still stand amid the ruins, for urban explorers and photographers to discover. (Belle Isle Archives)

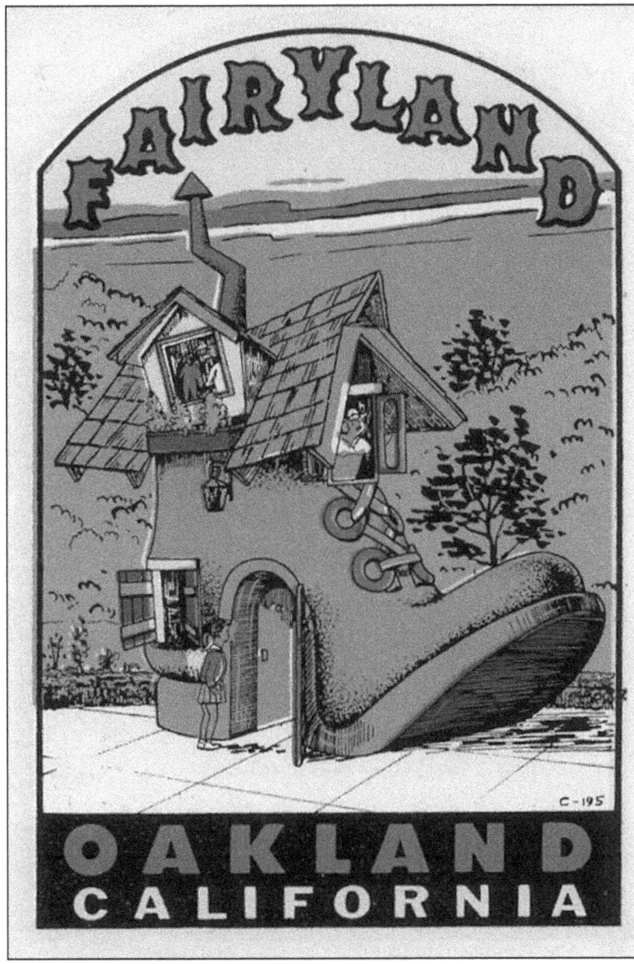

Decal and Bus Poster Advertisements, 1950. When the Oakland Advertising and Marketing Club began to promote Fairyland to the public, it used the image of the Old Woman's Shoe entrance gate as a symbol of the new park's fanciful storybook theme. The image appears in all approved advertisements, pamphlets, and print media, as well as on decals, patches, postcards, and posters. Today, collectors diligently search out some of the rare early images of the park, including decals and posters such as those in these photographs. After more than 65 years, the "Shoe" has become a Fairyland icon and a beloved community landmark.

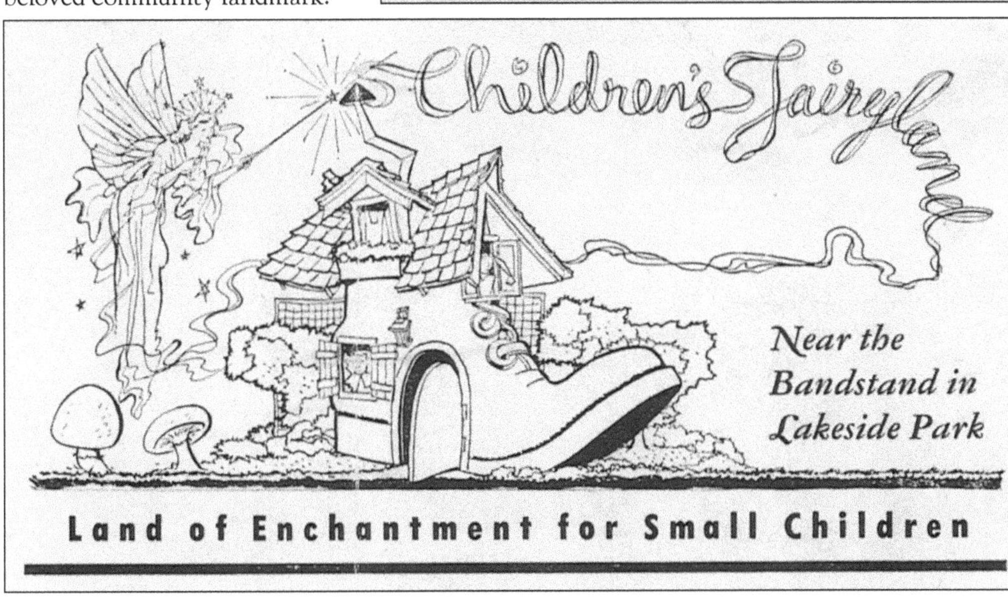

What Is Children's Fairyland — Location, Purpose, Cost?

The object of Childrens Fairyland is to supply diversion, interest and education for Toddlers and Youngsters on a scale hitherto unknown in the West.

Conceived and designed entirely at the Child Level for a beautiful, sheltered glen, under majestic old oaks, just north of the Bandstand in Oakland's Lakeside Park, it will bring the popular Mother Goose Rhymes and Fairy Tales into actual being, in a fantastic and permanent way.

The fabulous, permanent settings, built entirely to Children's scale, in Fairytale design, will draw youngsters and oldsters alike, from everywhere.

The "Three Little Pigs," "Mary's Little Lamb," "Peter Rabbit," "Flopsy and Mopsy Cottontail," "Billy Goat Gruff," "The Little Red Hen," "The Three Little Kittens," "Bambi," and others will all be there, *alive* and in person.

There will be cut-outs of "The Merrie Miller," "Mary," "The Big Bad Wolf," "Farmer McGregor," "Humpty Dumpty," "Simple Simon" and others.

Supervised by Graduates in Education and Child Psychology, Children will be encouraged to be kind, gentle and solicitous for the live baby inhabitants of Fairyland — they will be permitted to caress and feed the pets in a special "Pet Ring."

Adults will be admitted only when accompanied by Children. Youngsters who do not have the price of admission get in when unaccompanied oldsters show up. Conducted groups of underprivileged Children will view Children's Fairyland on certain days, without charge. The admission will be 10 cents.

The first unit of Children's Fairyland will cost $50,000.00 The money is to be raised by public subscription. Many organizations and individuals have already subscribed approximately $13,500.00 as of August 1, 1949.

There is no overhead for campaign and promotional expenses charged against your subscriptions to Children's Fairyland — these are underwritten by the Lake Merritt Breakfast Club and its friends. Thus, every penny pledged goes into the actual building of Children's Fairyland. Your subscription is solicited for any sum.

Make checks payable to "Children's Fairyland." Mail to Mr. David L. Anderson, Trust Officer, Central Bank, 14th and Broadway, Oakland 12, California. A subscription blank and postage-paid envelope is enclosed for your convenience.

(We are advised that subscriptions to Children's Fairyland are deductible from Income Tax.)

What Assurance Is There that Children's Fairyland Will Be a Financial Success?

Basing our judgment on experience at Belle Isle Fairyland, Detroit, ours will also pay its own way and earn a surplus. Detroit operates but five months of the year. Their 1940 census figures give a population of 1,623,450. Oakland will operate 12 months of the year and draw from the six Bay Area Counties with an estimated population of 2,597,500.

Here are the Detroit figures for five months of operation:

210,687 paid admissions @ 10¢	$21,068.70
28,589 Two-ounce bags pet feed @ 5¢	1,429.45
Souvenirs, Mother Goose Rhyme Books, etc.	3,162.55
Total Revenue	*$25,660.70*
Salaries, Federal Admission Tax, Wages, Supplies, Equipment	16,661.02
Revenue above all costs	*$ 8,999.68*

Experience at Detroit is that Children come back again and again. In the City of Oakland alone, some 15,600 prospective visitors to Children's Fairyland are born each year.

Under a Trust Agreement between the Board of Park Directors and the Lake Merritt Breakfast Club, acting for the public, all surplus monies are to be used for completion of Children's Fairyland, which will eventually be a $100,000.00 asset to the community. When there is no further need for development, surplus funds will go into other improvements at Lakeside Park.

Children's Fairyland will be operated under the Naturalist Program of the Oakland Park Department in a manner that will always be a credit to the community. The admission charge in addition to being revenue producing, will serve to regulate and protect the project.

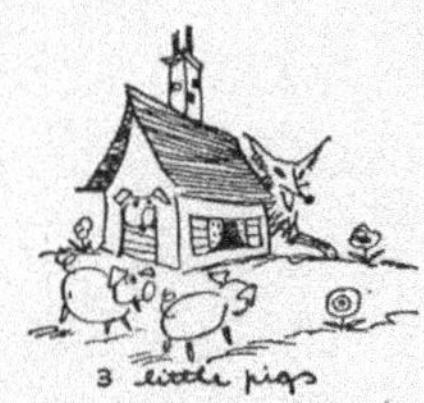

Over →

BUSINESS PROPOSAL FOR FAIRYLAND, 1949. The Lake Merritt Breakfast Club created this promotional flyer using information that Art Navlet brought back from Belle Isle Children's Park and Zoo in Detroit. It was used to raise funds and promote the idea of building a Children's Fairyland in Oakland. This document offers insight into the morals and business practices of the 1950s.

PoPo, Mott, and Navlet, 1976. Fairyland's favorite clown, PoPo, celebrates his 76th birthday with Fairyland's "fairy godfathers" Oakland Park superintendent William Penn Mott Jr. (center) and nursery owner Arthur Navlet. With the help of the Lake Merritt Breakfast Club, Mott and Navlet persuaded the community to build the innovative family attraction.

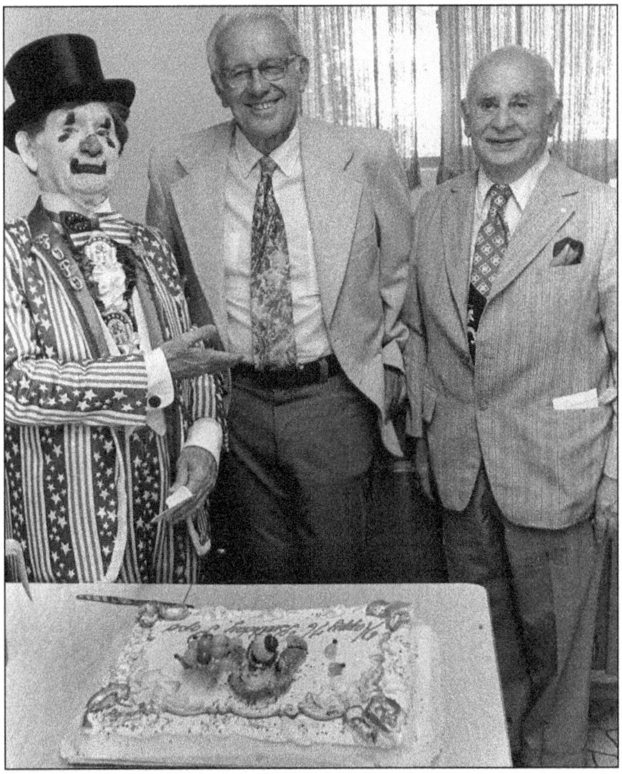

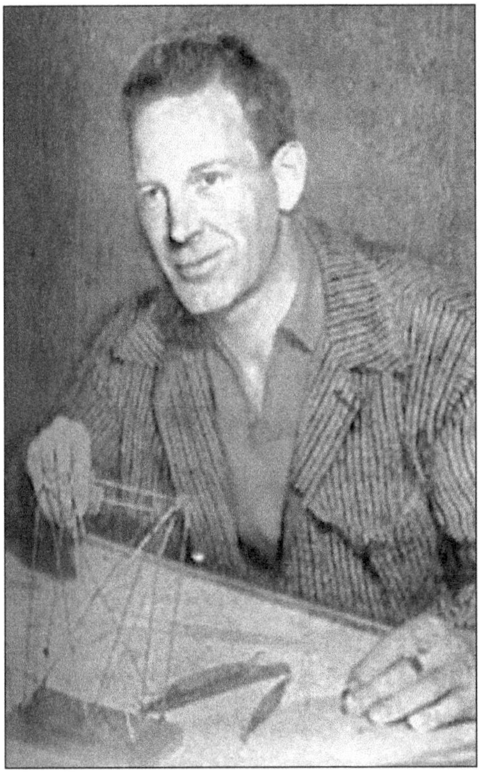

William Russell Everritt, 1950s. This is the only known photograph of Fairyland's architect and designer. Although Everritt was portrayed in the press as either a serious architect or a free-spirited bohemian, the truth lies somewhere in between. Before he retired in 1963, Everritt designed or inspired 30 to 45 of the park's play settings and structures. His three-dimensional models were used to raise capital to build the park. (Courtesy of Oakland History Room.)

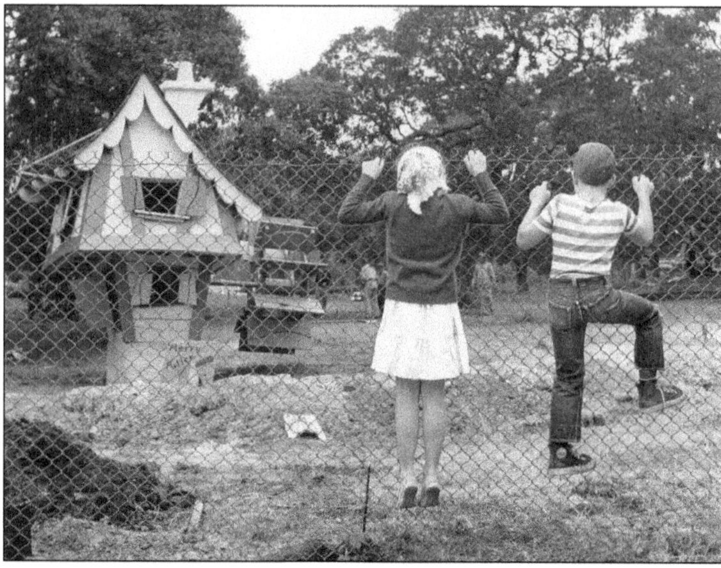

What's Happening?, 1949–1950. The children of Oakland eagerly awaited the construction of Children's Fairyland. After being teased for months with images and newspaper stories about each of the park's attractions, it is no wonder that children were climbing the fence trying to get a view of the new storybook world.

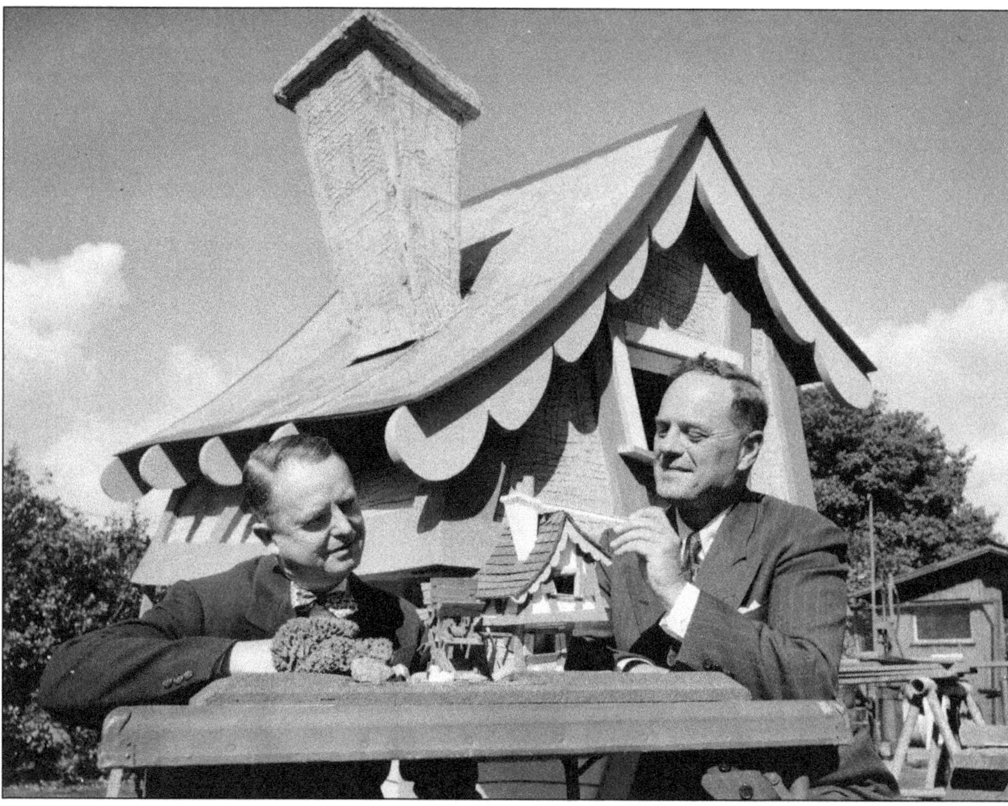

Checking the Designs, 1949–1950. Judge Homer Buckley (left), president of the Lake Merritt Breakfast Club, and Willis Ostrander, president of Oakland's board of park directors, check the accuracy of William Everritt's model against the built Merry Miller set. Everritt is credited with making sure there are very few right angles in Fairyland's design. Both he and William Penn Mott Jr. felt the park needed to look like a child's view of the adult world: a little nonsensical and out of kilter.

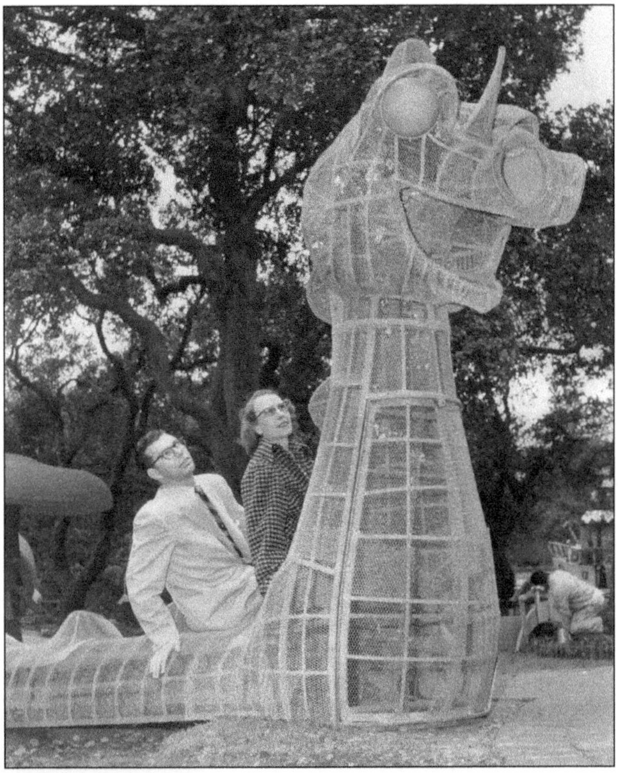

STRUCTURE FOR THE HAPPY DRAGON, 1954. Unidentified members of the Oakland Advertising and Marketing Club approve the structure. Most of Fairyland's original structures, built by the City of Oakland, were metal frameworks covered in concrete. Almost all of the original sets are still standing today, as solid as when they were built.

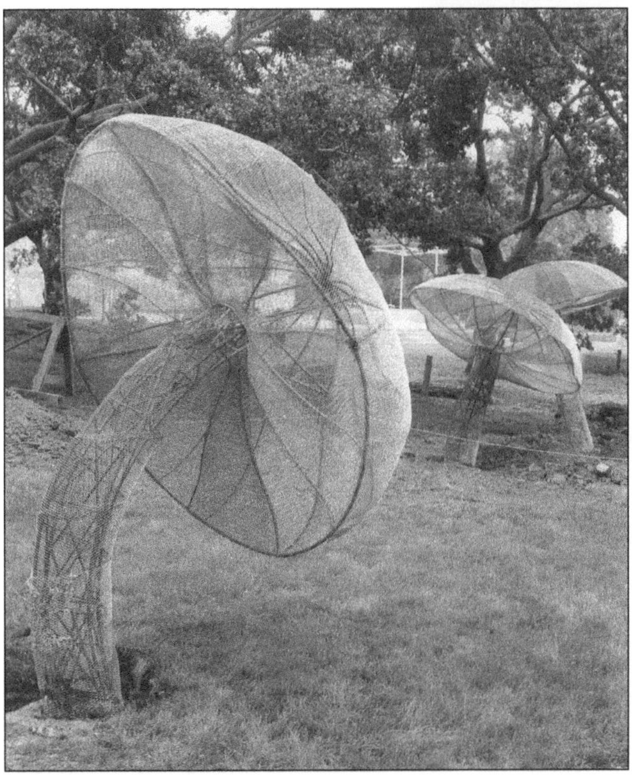

METAL MUSHROOMS, 1949. These metal mushrooms—examples of the park's distinctive building style—bloom throughout Fairyland. All of the play structures were designed to be child size and child friendly. Today, the structures are regularly repainted and maintained by members of the park's art and restoration department with an eye toward preserving their authentic beauty.

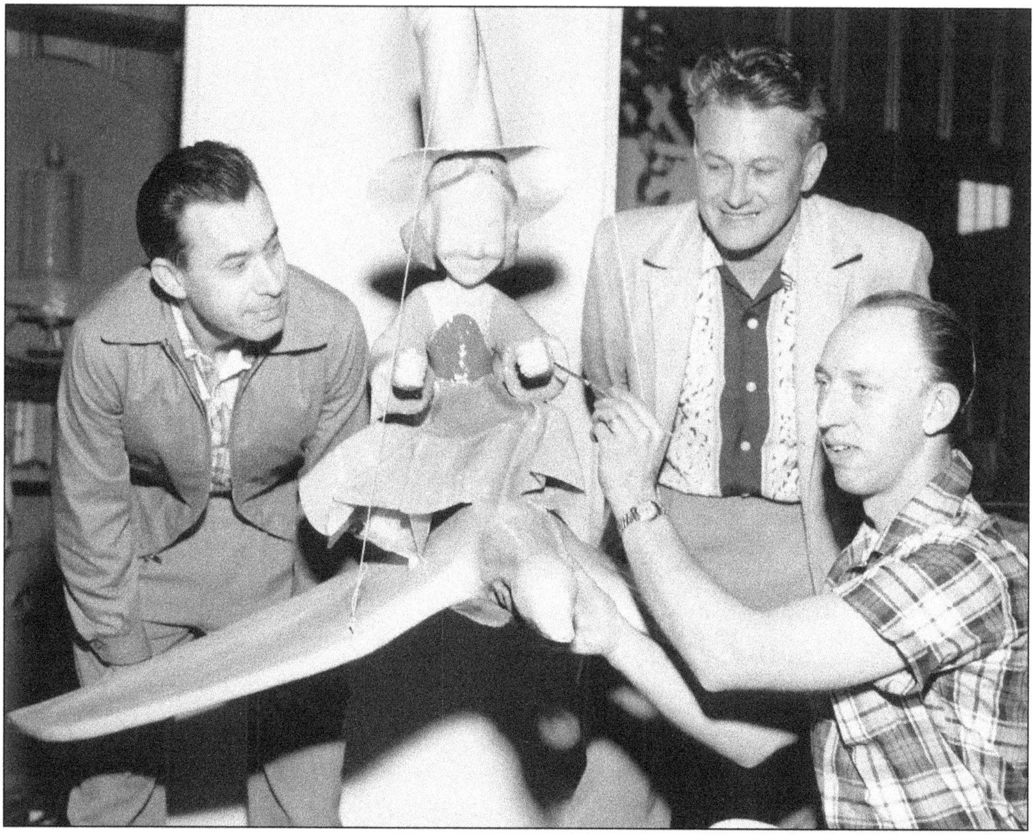

MOTHER GOOSE IN FLIGHT, 1956. Before flying off to a new nest in Fairyland, Mother Goose gets a final paint check from Sam Neft (left) and Dick Merrill (center) of Merrill Sign Company, the set's sponsor. The figure was sculpted by Gordon Mortenson (right), a City of Oakland employee; many of the sets were underwritten by local businesses.

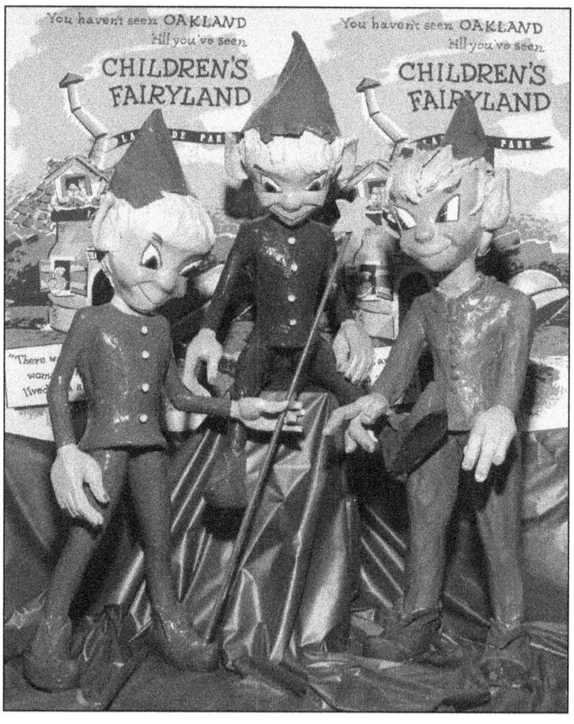

FIBERGLASS ELVES AT PLAY, 1950S. Gorden Mortenson created many elves to live amid the trees and plants of Fairyland. The elves shown here were on display to promote the park at a local flower show. Over the years, the elves have gone missing, possibly victims of a college fraternity rite of initiation. They turn up mysteriously every so often in Berkeley.

FAIRYLAND COSTUME SKETCHES, 1949. The park opened with a staff of five: the director, two guides, an animal keeper, and a gardener. Each was a civil service position that came with strict guidelines for behavior. (Employees were expected, for example, to answer the toughest question a child could ask.) The original design called for elaborate uniforms, including these for host guide (right) and gardener (below), designed by costumers of the Laney College Trade and Technical Institute. Deemed too restrictive as designed, the costumes were replaced by practical uniforms that could withstand the rigors of working in an active children's park. The city had a large costume department located in the Parks and Recreation Department that stored and handled outfits used in community plays, pageants, and special events.

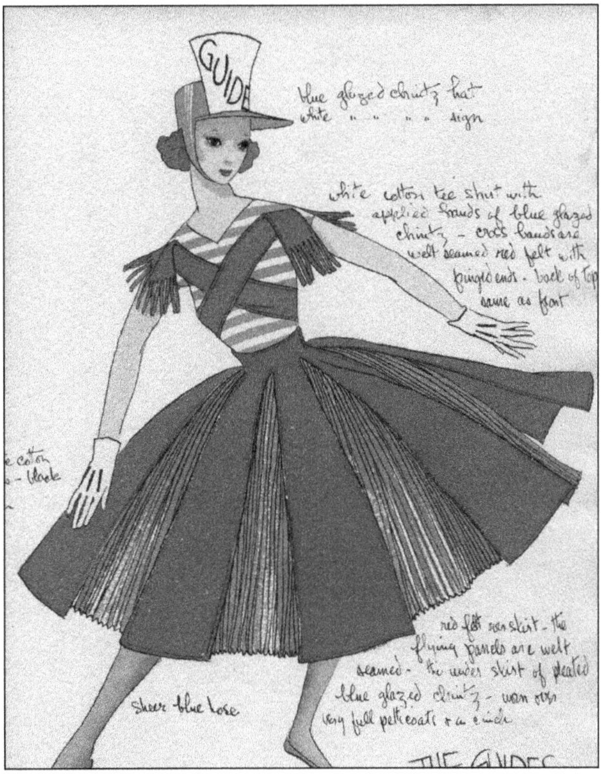

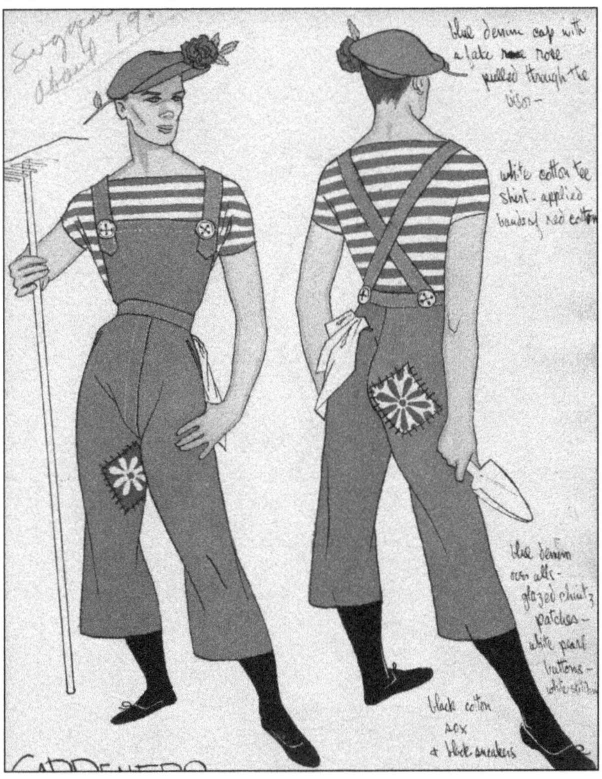

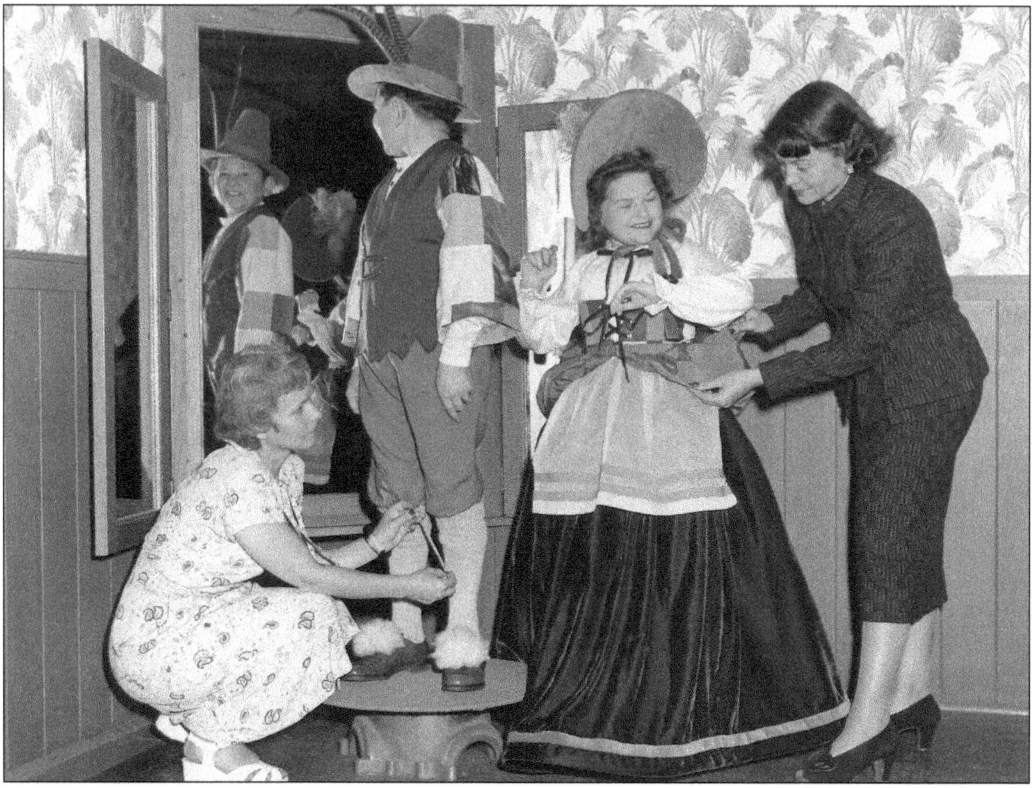

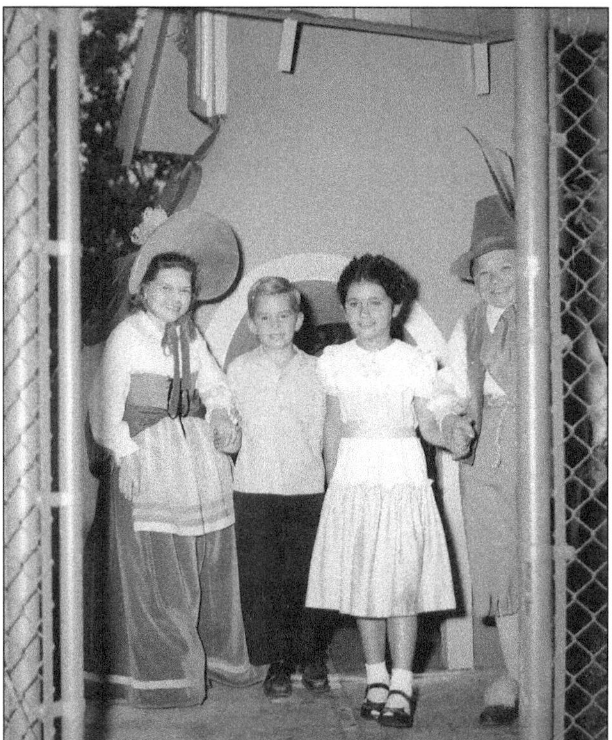

FINAL FITTING, 1950. Fairyland's original host and guides get fitted for their opening day costumes. Lila Johnson (left) and Esther Howard of the Laney College Trade and Technical Institute check details on the new guide outfits for Victor and Edna Wetter, who worked at Fairyland for two years as park hosts. The diminutive couple met in 1936 at the Midget Village of the Texas Centennial Exposition in Dallas.

OPENING NIGHT VISITORS, 1950. Cousins Steven and Diane Russo are welcomed by Victor and Edna Wetter. Victor portrays a Munchkin in *The Wizard of Oz*, filmed before he married Edna and settled in Oakland. One of the original requirements for a host job in Fairyland was "small stature"; after a lawsuit, this restriction was lifted and the Wetters had to compete with taller applicants.

THREE MEN IN A TUB, 1951. An unidentified family enjoys the view along the Merry Miller Stream, as Three Men in a Tub sail past. Over the years, the fiberglass figures became increasingly detailed. Visitors sometimes used the large tub as a wishing well into which they tossed coins.

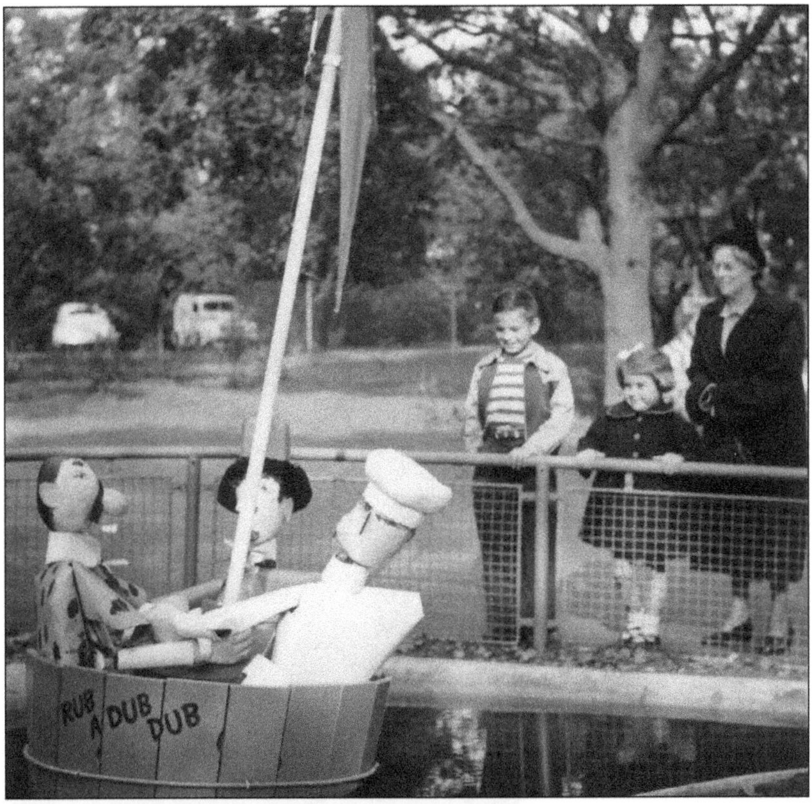

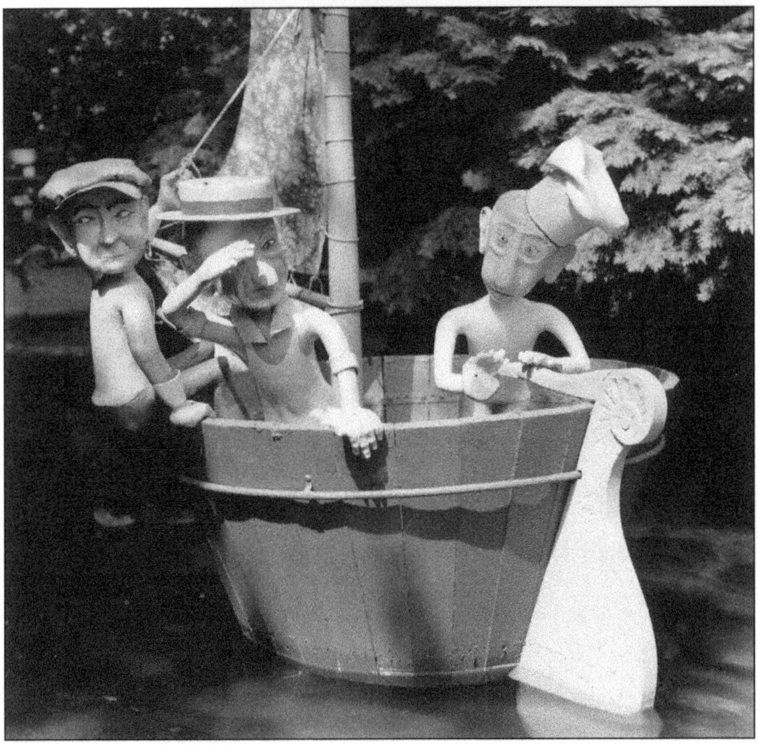

RUB A DUB DUB, 1970S. As the need arises, the park refurbishes fiberglass figures. These Three Men in a Tub, by Gordon Mortenson, sailed the park for close to 40 years. Sometimes, the City of Oakland would repaint a figure and add a touch of whimsy or even satire. This update includes the figures of Richard Nixon (candlemaker), Spiro Agnew (butcher), and Charles de Gaulle (baker) incognito as they travel the winding turns of the stream.

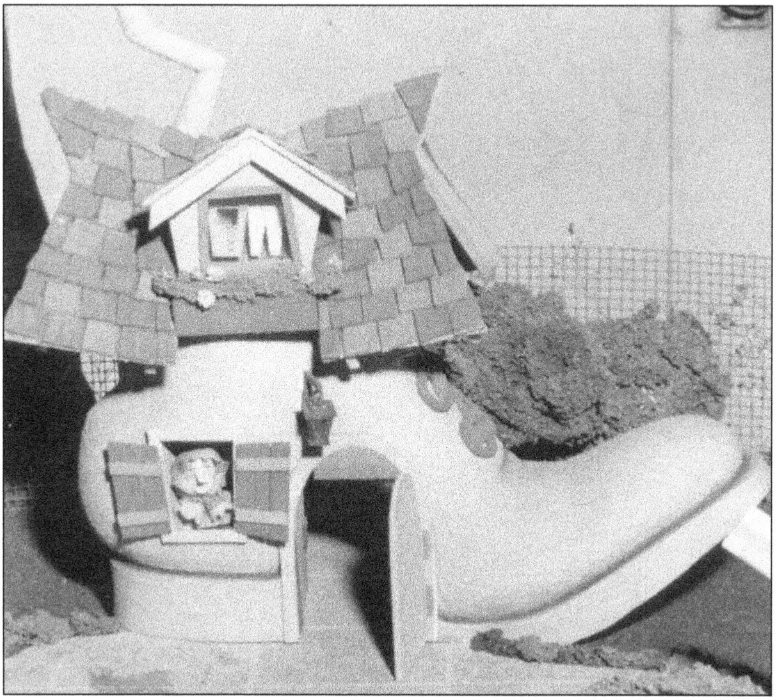

The Old Woman's Shoe Model, 1948. Here, the artistry of the model created by architect William Russell Everritt is visible. These maquettes (model sets) were carted around to local events at which funds were raised for Fairyland. Unfortunately, they have been lost. Everritt also produced detailed blueprints and illustrations for each attraction.

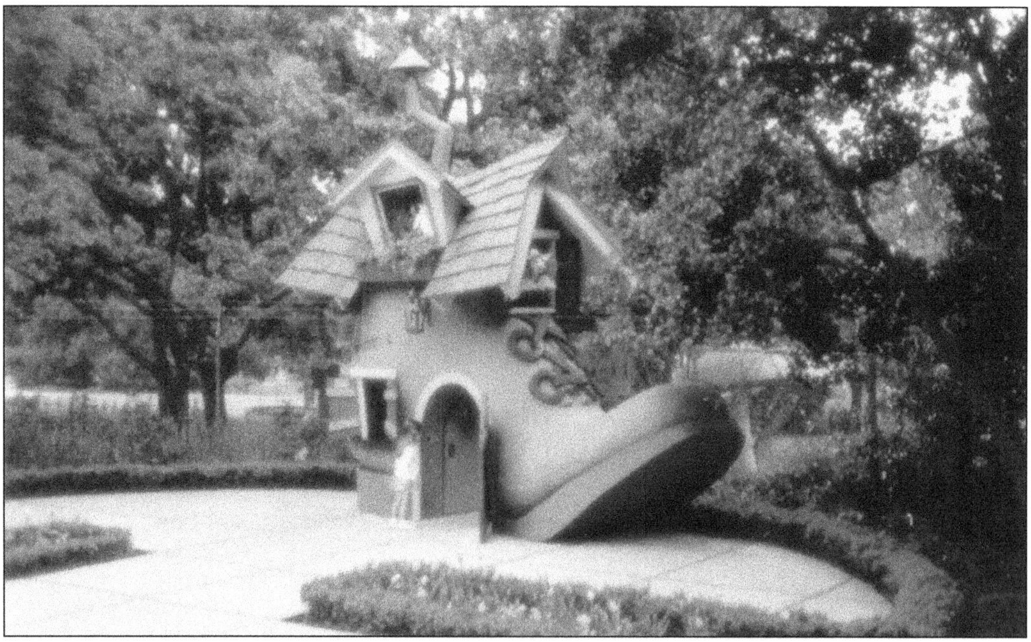

Postcard of Shoe Entrance, 1951. This postcard depicts the finished set that welcomed visitors to Fairyland. Adults had to stoop down when entering, while children could skip through. Jim and Bobbie Stevenson of the Oakland Advertising and Marketing Club photographed and produced the first set of 12 postcards for Fairyland, which today are popular with collectors.

Two

The Original Park

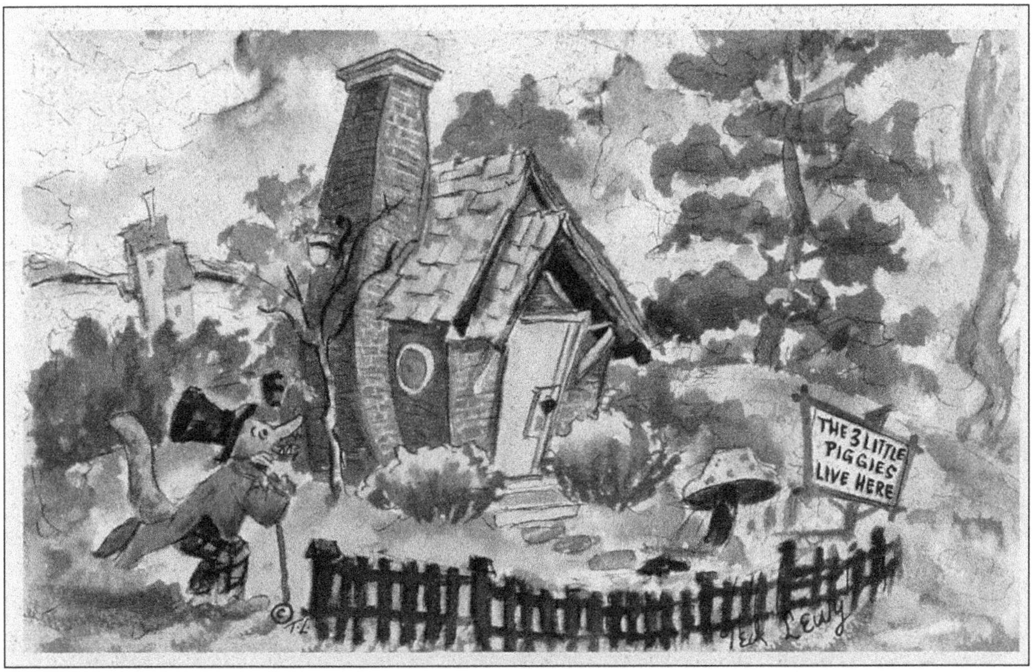

Three Pigs Postcard, 1954. San Francisco artist Ted Lewy produced a series of 12 watercolor paintings that were turned into postcards. Lewy is best known for colorful, whimsical artwork that features the cable cars of San Francisco. Shown here is his interpretation of the Big Bad Wolf trying to get into the pig's brick house. This is the first storybook set children encounter after entering through the Shoe.

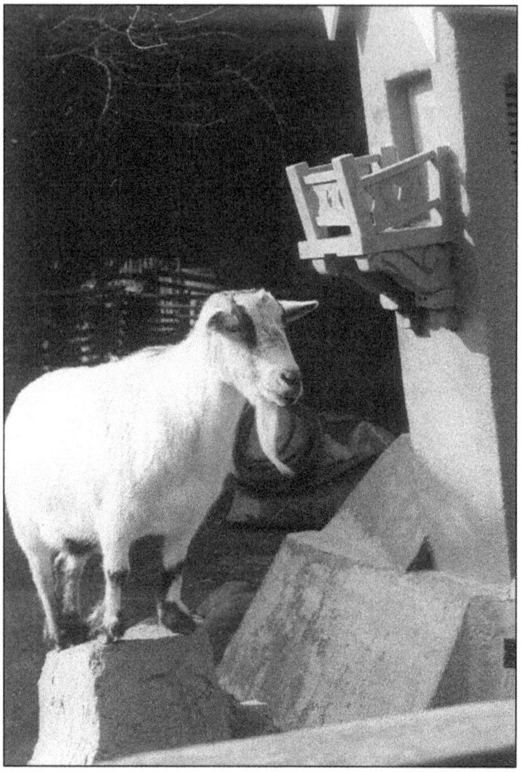

King of the Hill, 1990s. At the Three Billy Goats Gruff set, hungry goats waited for children to hand-feed them goodies from a nearby vending machine. In this photograph, the largest goat is laying claim to the rocks and all he can see. Just behind the rock he is standing on, the Merry Miller Stream begins its route through the center of the park and down to the Merry Miller set. Children love to pretend they are goats, climbing the rocky hills and clip-clopping over stone bridges. This troll, created by artist Larry O'Hare, hides by the stream, waiting for unwary goats and youngsters. Watch out for "troll bridges" throughout Fairyland.

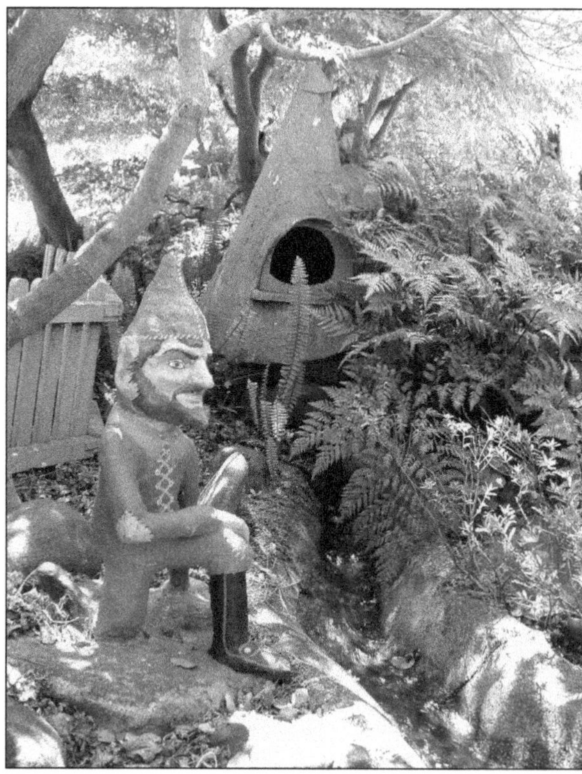

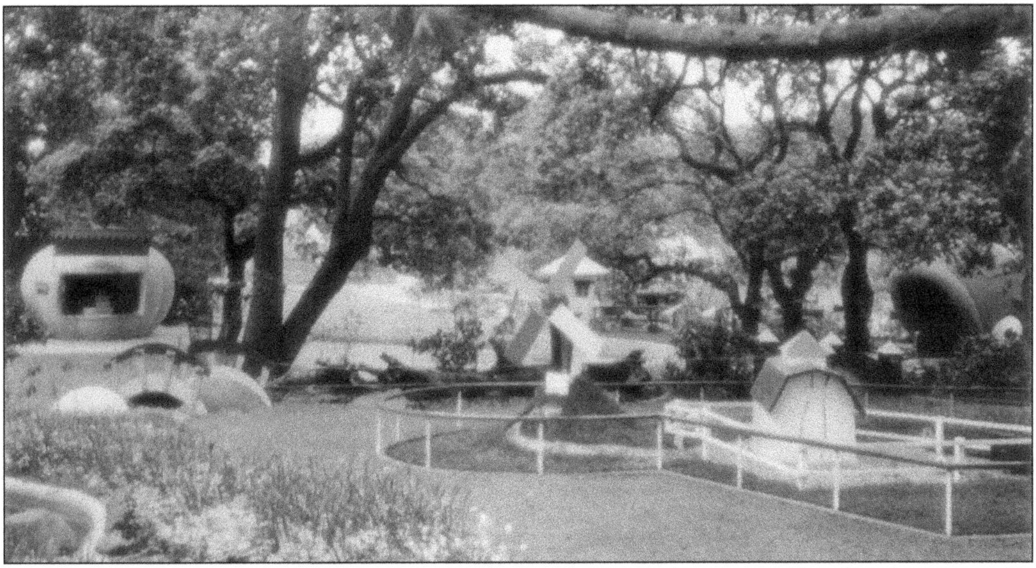

Little Red Hen Postcard, 1951. This children's tale about the virtue of hard work is a popular attraction in the center of Fairyland. The Little Red Hen pleads with her animal neighbors to help her plant, harvest, and mill her wheat and to bake it into bread, but none of them is willing. Yet when it is time to eat the bread, the animals eagerly volunteer. In the background are Willie the Whale and the Peter, Peter Pumpkin Eater Gift and Animal Feed Kiosk.

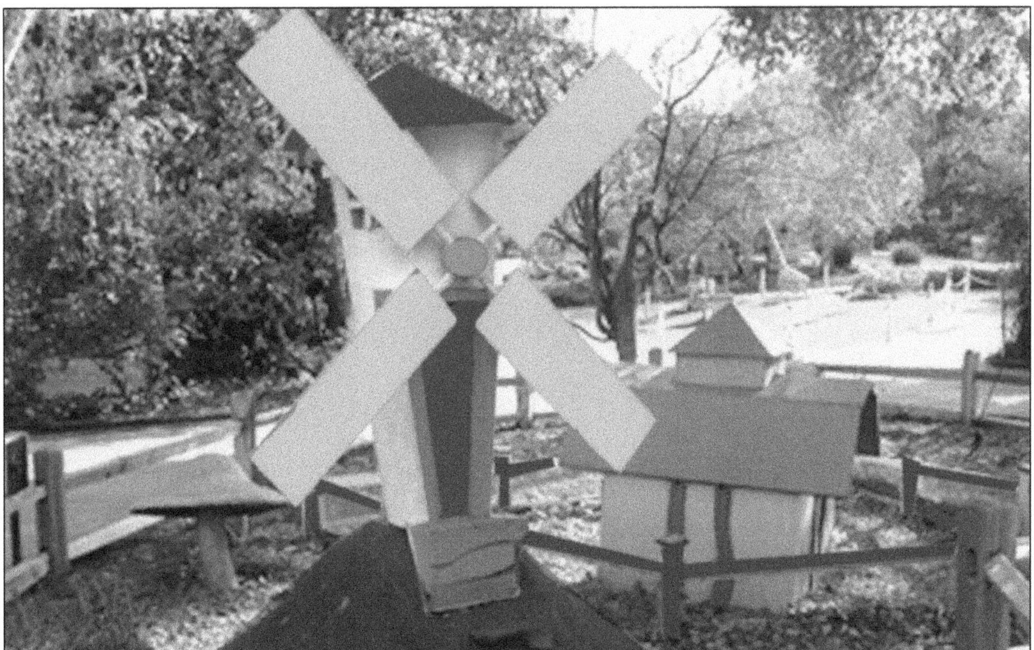

Little Red Hen Barn, 2011. This little barn by the windmill is where the chickens were housed; when not in their coops, they roamed freely throughout Fairyland. In spring, young farmers in the 4-H organization brought in baby chicks and gave lectures to the children on poultry farming. Fairyland's directors maintained from the beginning that storybook settings should be educational and functional as well as entertaining.

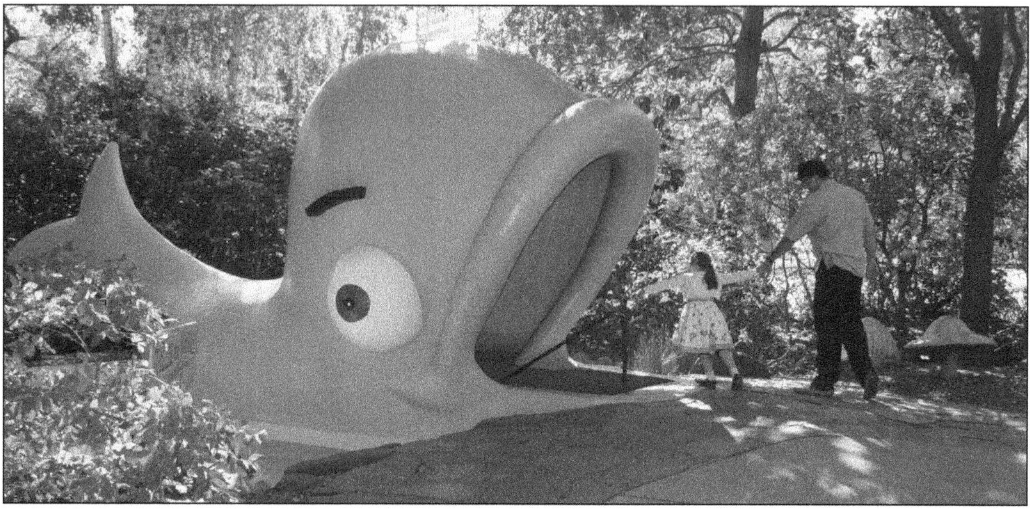

Willie the Whale, 1989. The little blue whale, Willie, is an unmistakable Fairyland icon. Inspired by a popular children's song from the 1950s, Willie invites youngsters to climb into his mouth and then out again. Wait and watch carefully, he spouts water every few minutes. Along with the Old Woman's Shoe and Goosey Gander's Castle, this attraction has been the one most frequently copied by other storybook parks.

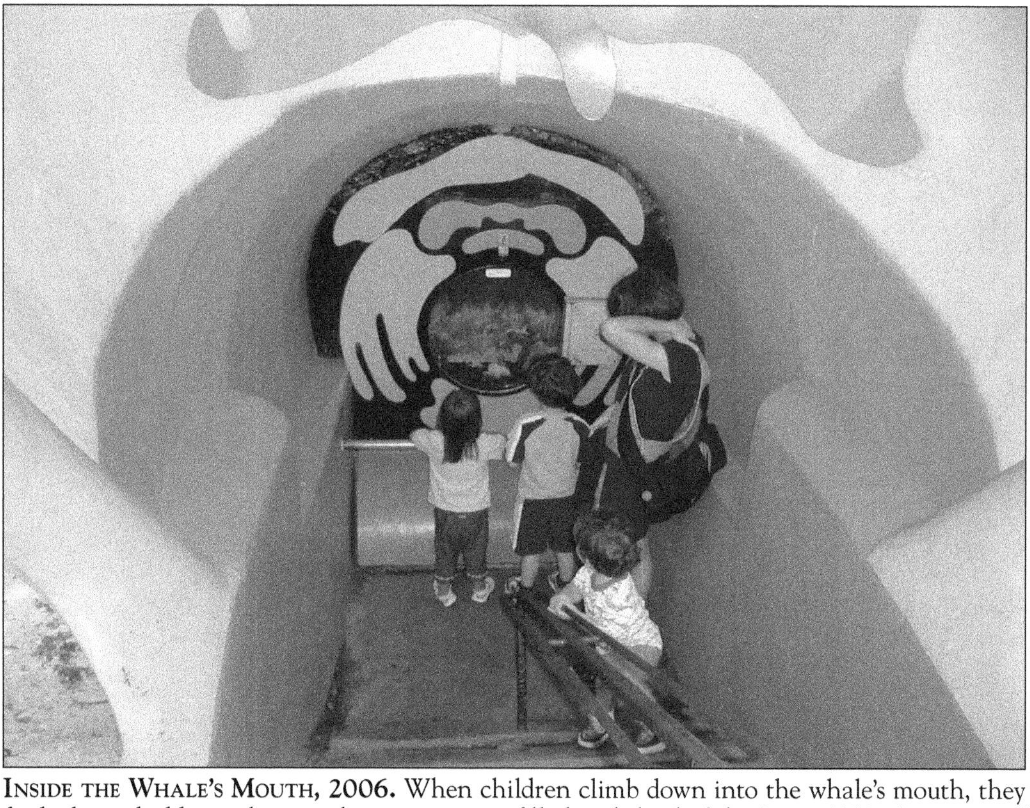

Inside the Whale's Mouth, 2006. When children climb down into the whale's mouth, they find what is hidden in his tonsils: an aquarium filled with lively fish! Since 1950, the image of Willie's open mouth has been emblazoned on piggy banks, stickers, and charm bracelets—all early souvenirs of Children's Fairyland.

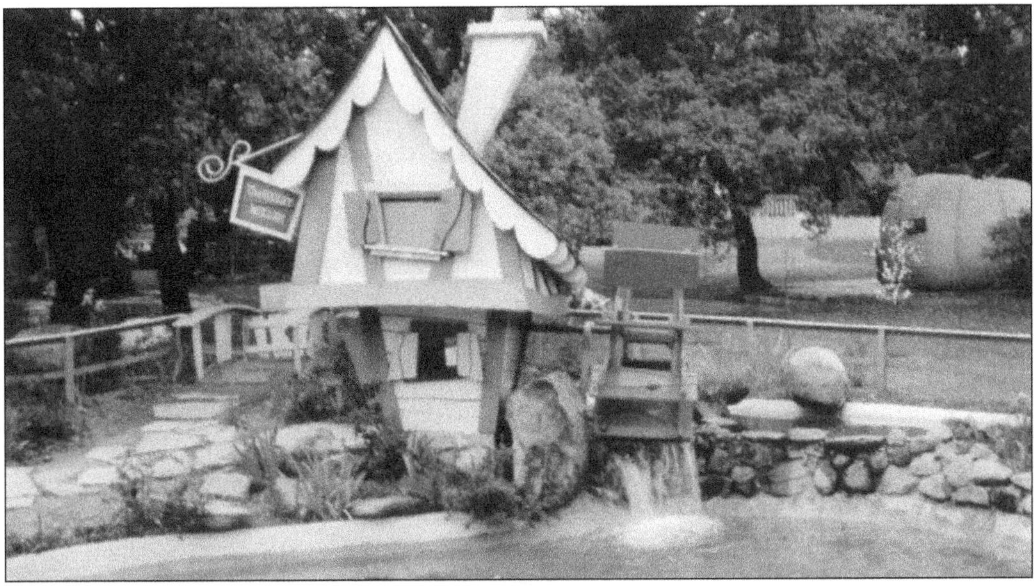

Merry Miller Pond, 1951 and 1980. This is the first set designed by William Everritt. Note the absence of right angles on the objects in this postcard? The story goes that Everritt's first concept looked like a charming English mill. When he presented the model to William Mott for approval, Mott was impressed with the artistry but said it looked too "real." Everritt did not take the criticism well: He grabbed a nearby bat and smashed the model to pieces on Mott's desk, then stormed out. Mott thought he would never see him again, but three days later Everritt returned with a model of the mill that was to become the template for all future Fairyland designs: oddly twisted and painted in vibrant colors. "That's it!" Mott cried. Thereafter, all the sets made up in whimsy and flair what they lacked in right angles.

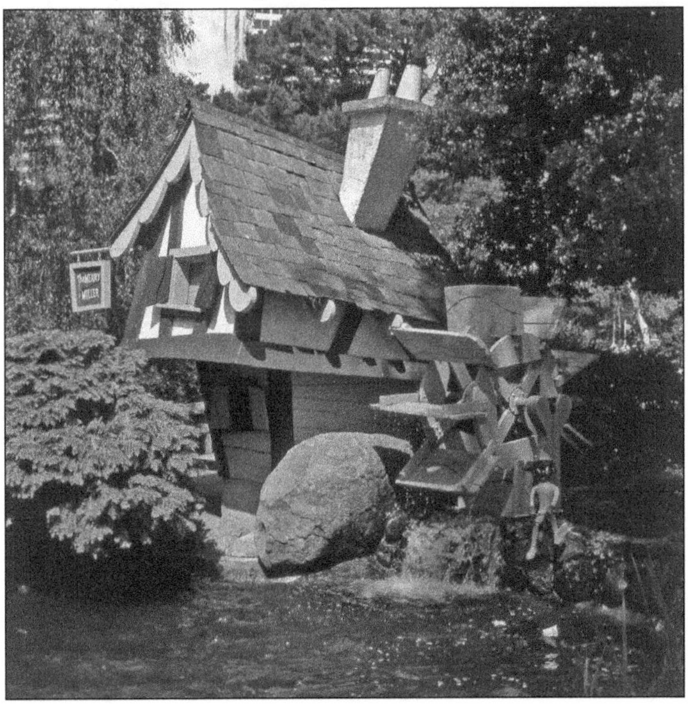

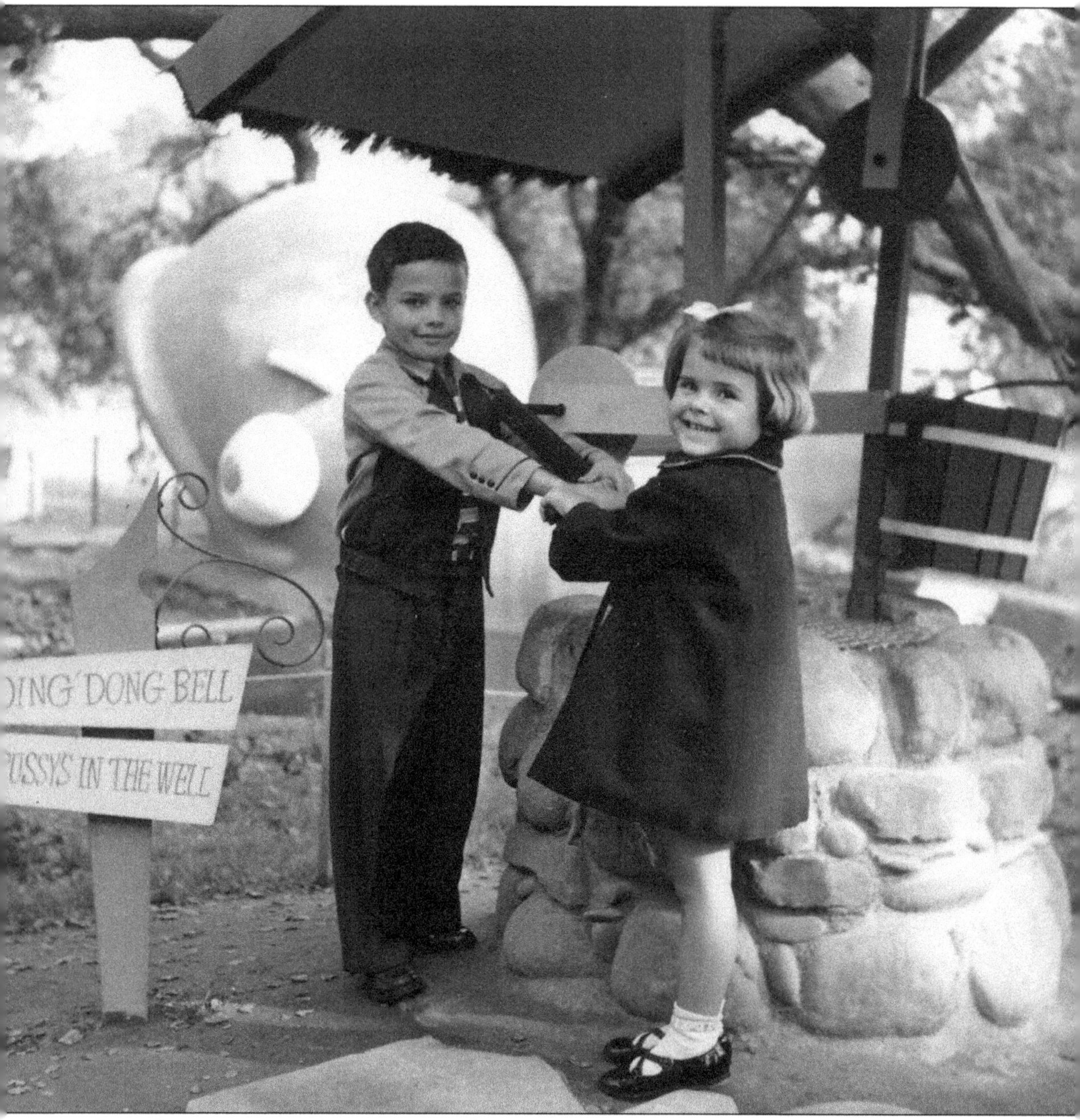

Ding Dong Bell, 1951. Ding Dong Bell, pussy's in the well! In the 1950s, this original set served as a holding pen for kittens until excited youngsters became too "hands on" with them. When the set was transformed into a wishing well, a mirror was installed so that children peering inside could see their own reflections. In Fairyland's earliest days, baby animals were a huge part of the park's charm, and instruction about their care and feeding was part of the Fairyland mission. William Mott briefly considered adding a pet lending library to the park that would allow children to take home Fairyland animals. A child would start with a small creature and exchange it after two weeks for a larger pet; Fairyland would supply food, a cage, and an instruction manual. The program never caught on and today would not even be considered for a host of good reasons.

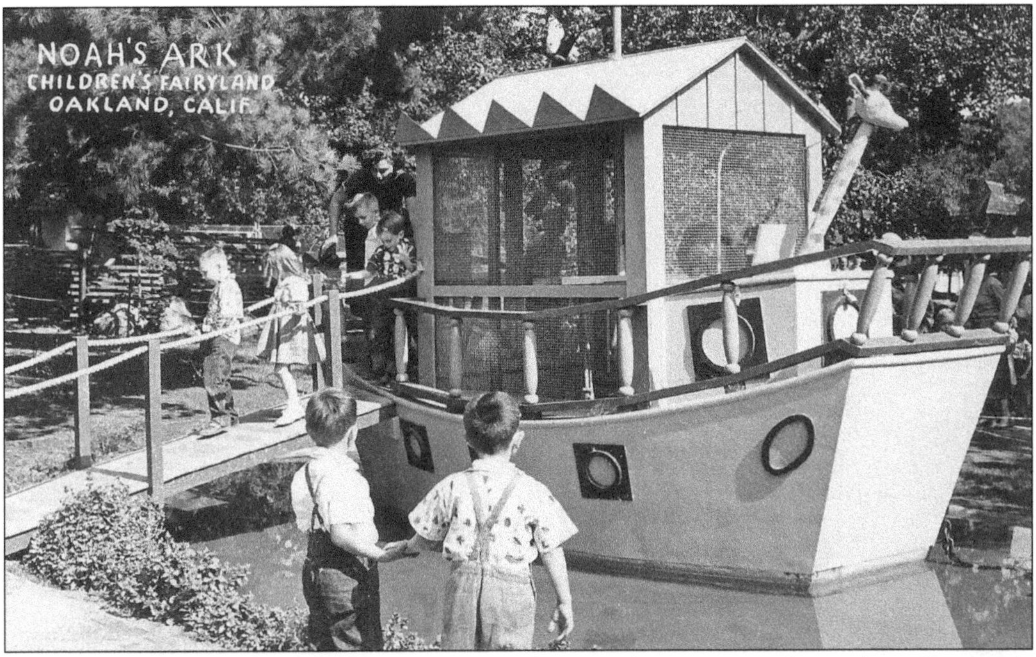

Noah's Ark Postcard, 1954. For 50 years, this popular attraction housed small animals and birds. How did a Bible story end up in a storybook park? In the 1950s, it would have been considered unexceptional: many children played with toy arks filled with pairs of plastic animals. They also memorized a poem: "My Noah's Ark is a pretty house, all painted red and blue / With many funny animals, just like those at the zoo. And when the door is open wide, I'll tell you what they do / The animals all get in line, and march out two by two." The card is one of a set of 13 black-and-white postcards produced by the Eastman Kodak Company under the series title "Real-Photo Postcards."

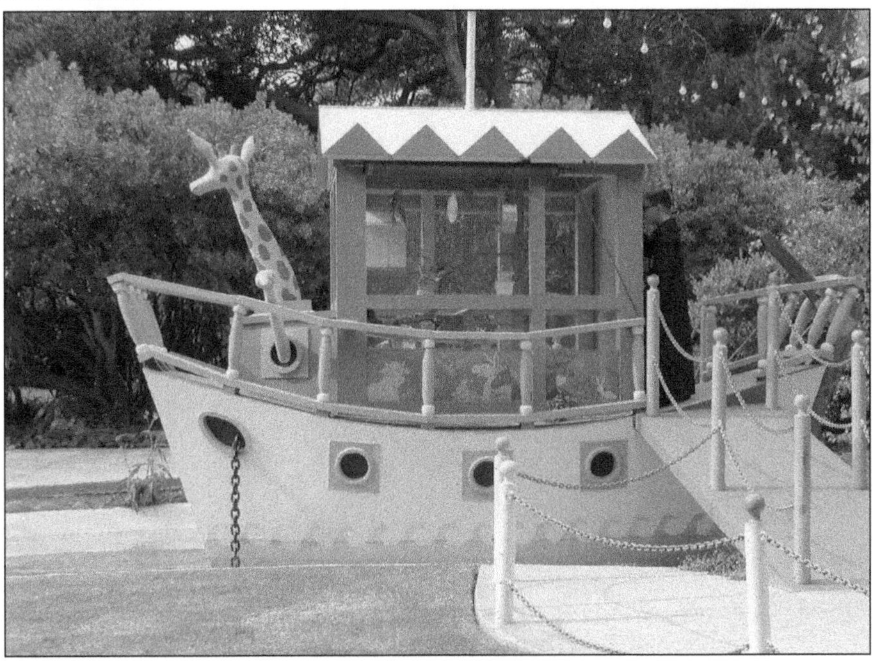

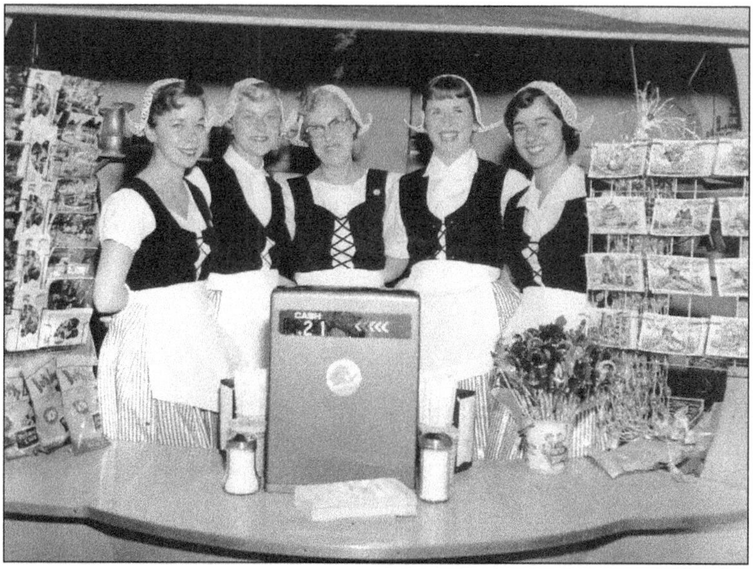

PETER PUMPKIN EATER'S GIFT SHOP, 1955. This small pumpkin-shaped building in the center of the park served as a souvenir stand, as well as housing the executive director's first office. In the photograph are costumed Fairyland staff members waiting to sell postcards, animal feed, and souvenirs.

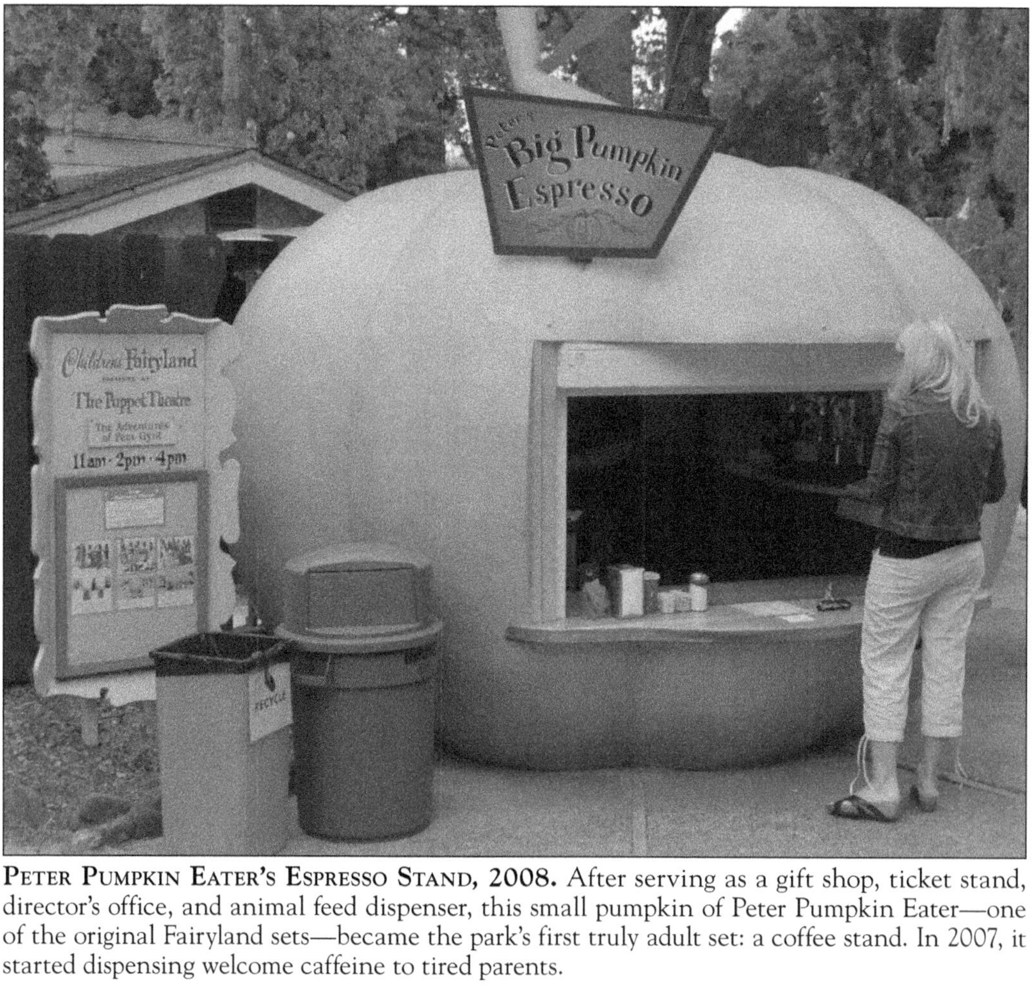

PETER PUMPKIN EATER'S ESPRESSO STAND, 2008. After serving as a gift shop, ticket stand, director's office, and animal feed dispenser, this small pumpkin of Peter Pumpkin Eater—one of the original Fairyland sets—became the park's first truly adult set: a coffee stand. In 2007, it started dispensing welcome caffeine to tired parents.

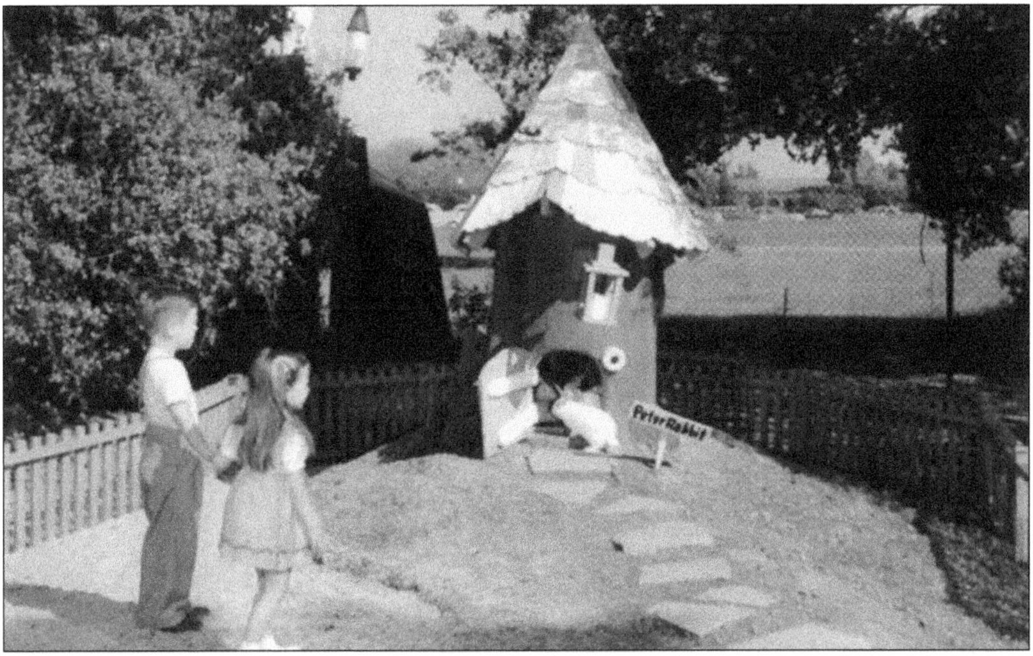

Peter Rabbit Postcard, 1951. This miniature house was home to one of Fairyland's most mischievous residents, Peter Rabbit. In the beginning, there were just two real rabbits, which soon produced an entire colony. The hill on which Peter's tree-log home stands had to be reinforced with heavy wire under the sod because his family kept burrowing to freedom.

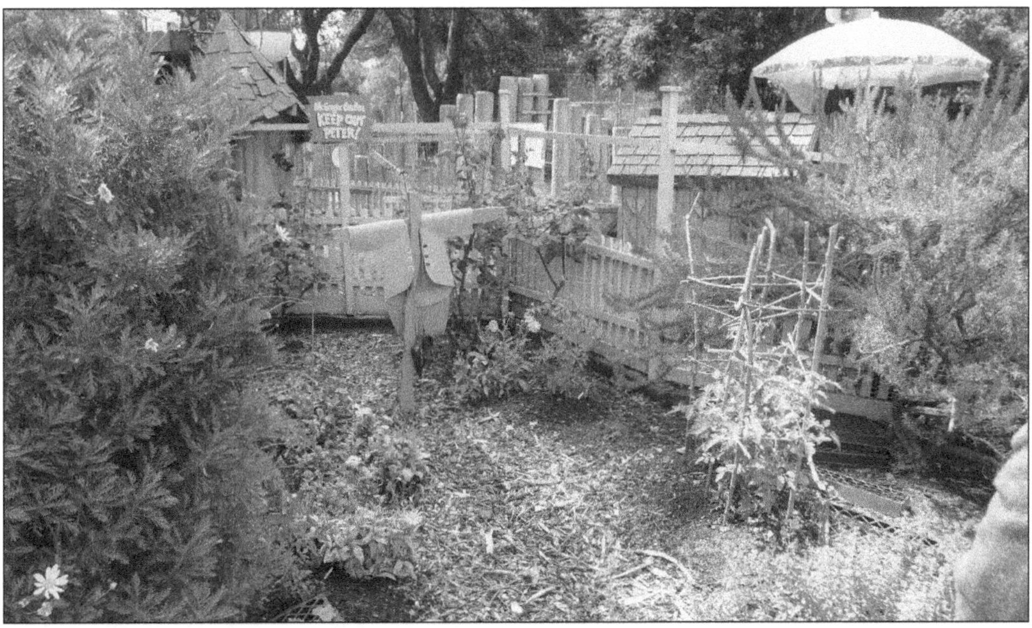

Mr. McGregor's Garden, 1994. Here is the garden that Peter kept escaping to. In the early 1990s, it became the first garden in Fairyland to use completely organic cultivation methods. Today, most of the food grown in the garden is fed to the park's resident animals, all of them vegetarian. They include miniature horses, donkeys, sheep, goats, chickens, and—in keeping with historical tradition—rabbits.

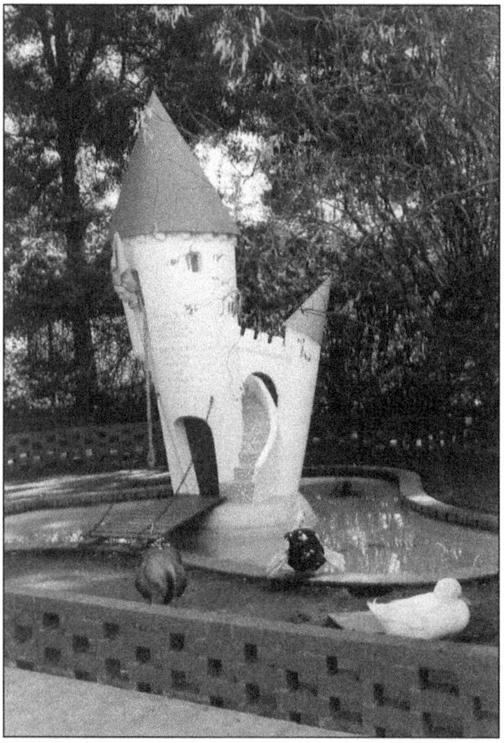

Goosey, Goosey Gander Castle, 1999. This lovely castle set was often copied by other storybook parks. It incidentally serves as a home for lost ducks and geese that fly over the avian skyways of Lakeside Park. During the 1950s, the castle became the home of local television star King Fuddle, a ventriloquist's dummy. By popular request, the princess overlooking the pond was later transformed into Rapunzel.

Hey! It's Feeding Time!, 1960s. Children were always eager to feed the Fairyland ducks, and Fairyland was always happy to provide hands-on activities. After the feeding, King Fuddle and his friend Bruce Sedley, from Oakland's Channel 2 television station, appeared and told stories. King Fuddle is supposedly 104 in Fairyland years. See chapter 5 for more about King Fuddle and Sir Sedley.

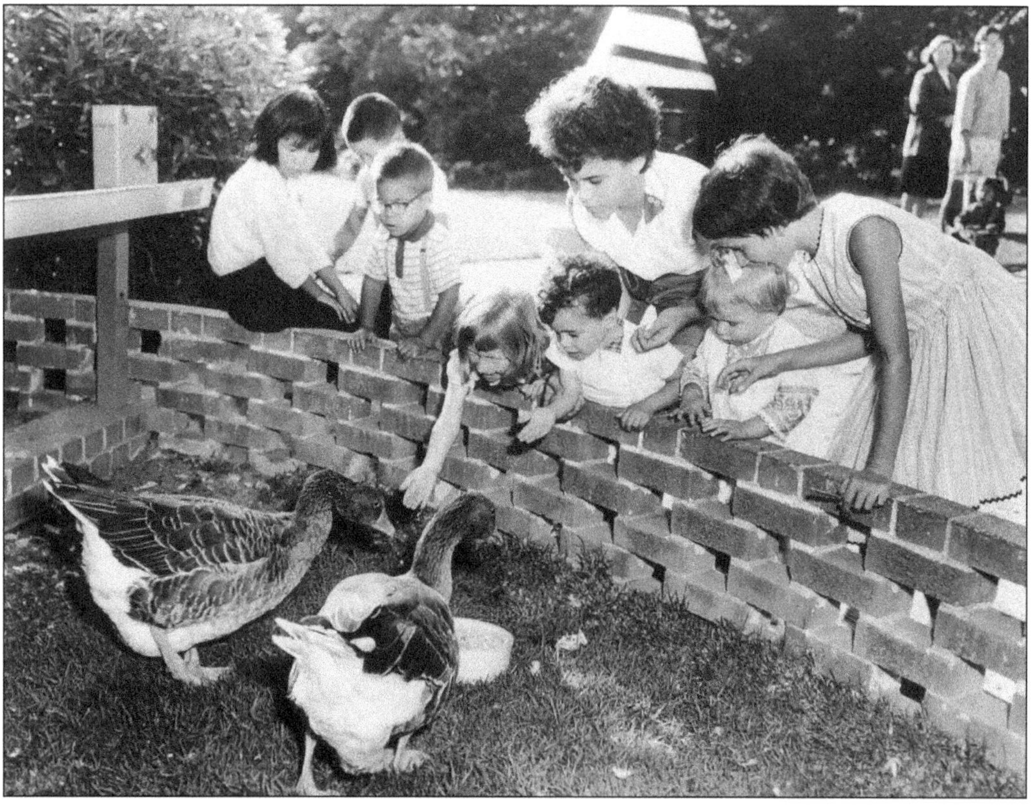

Mary Had a Little Lamb, 1955. This delightful set featured baby lambs and livestock. A "Mary" doll—a gift from the United Federation of Doll Clubs—was always seen looking out of the window. The last time the school was cleaned, staff members learned that the antique doll was valuable. The ornate fencing around the set was recycled from demolished Oakland Victorian houses.

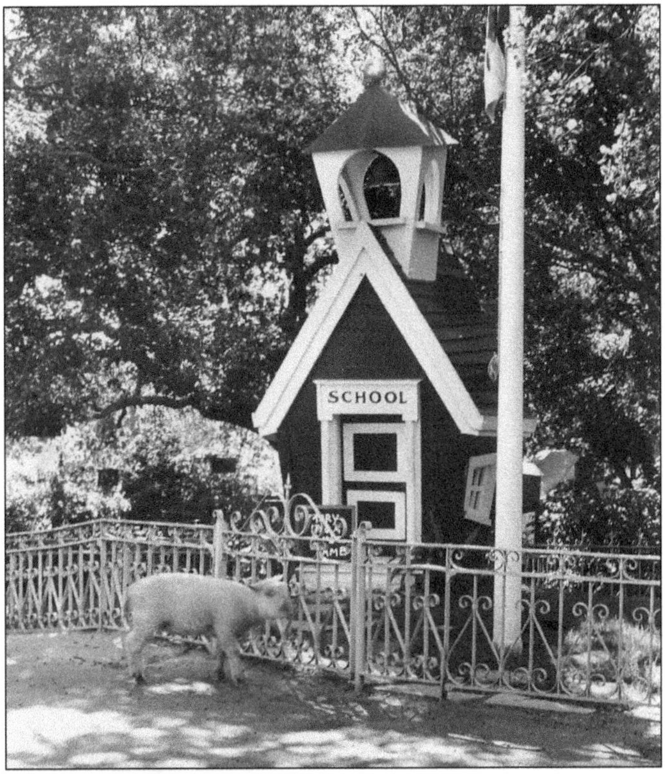

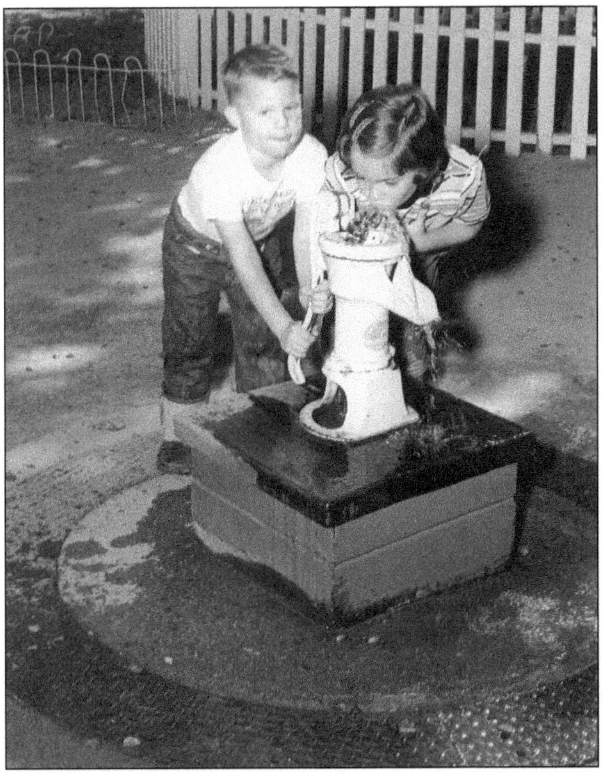

The Fountain of Youth, 1952. Even the drinking faucets have storybook themes at Fairyland. This fountain's powers may be purely mythical, but its presence still keeps visitors—even grandparents—feeling youthful. Pictured are Johnny Stover and Marsha Koperski; the photograph is part of the *Life* magazine article that announced Fairyland to the world.

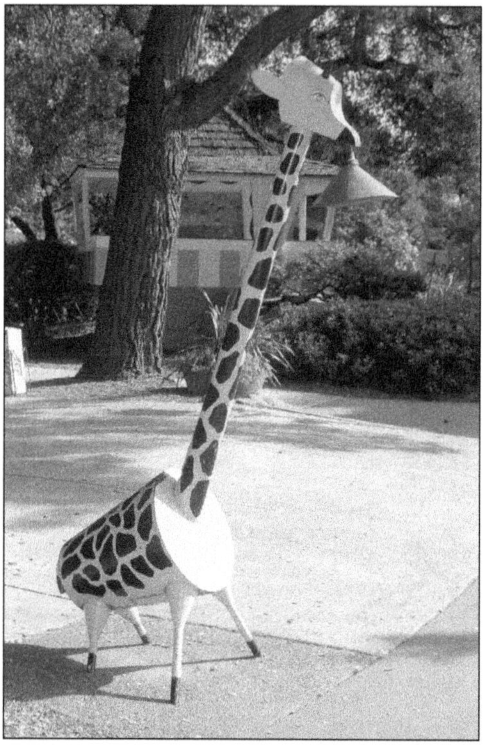

Fairyland Night Lighting, 2008. What better way to light a children's park than with tall giraffes holding lamps in their mouths? Six of these elongated light fixtures were stationed throughout the park when it opened. Over the years, they have been moved around. Although nonfunctioning today, they still act as handy climbing objects for young visitors.

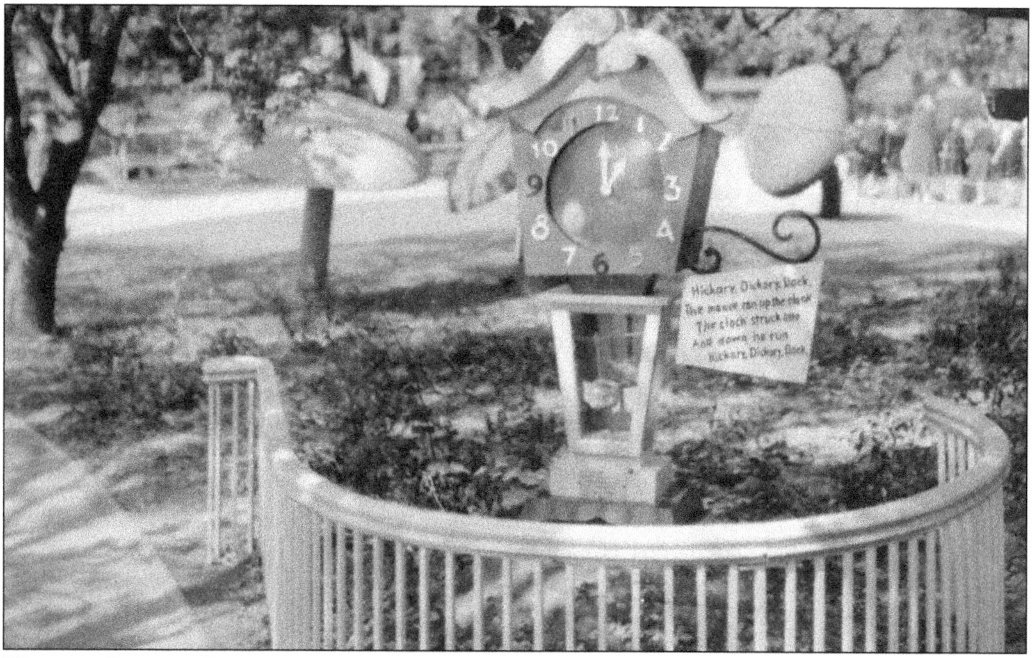

Hickory, Dickory Dock Postcard, 1951. Not only did this clock's hands move to teach children to tell time, it also housed a family of live mice that scampered around on a wheel inside the face of the clock. Many of Fairyland's original sets were built to be animal enclosures, as well as attractions. This philosophy began to change in the 1970s as Fairyland's managers accepted that animals needed more room and amenities.

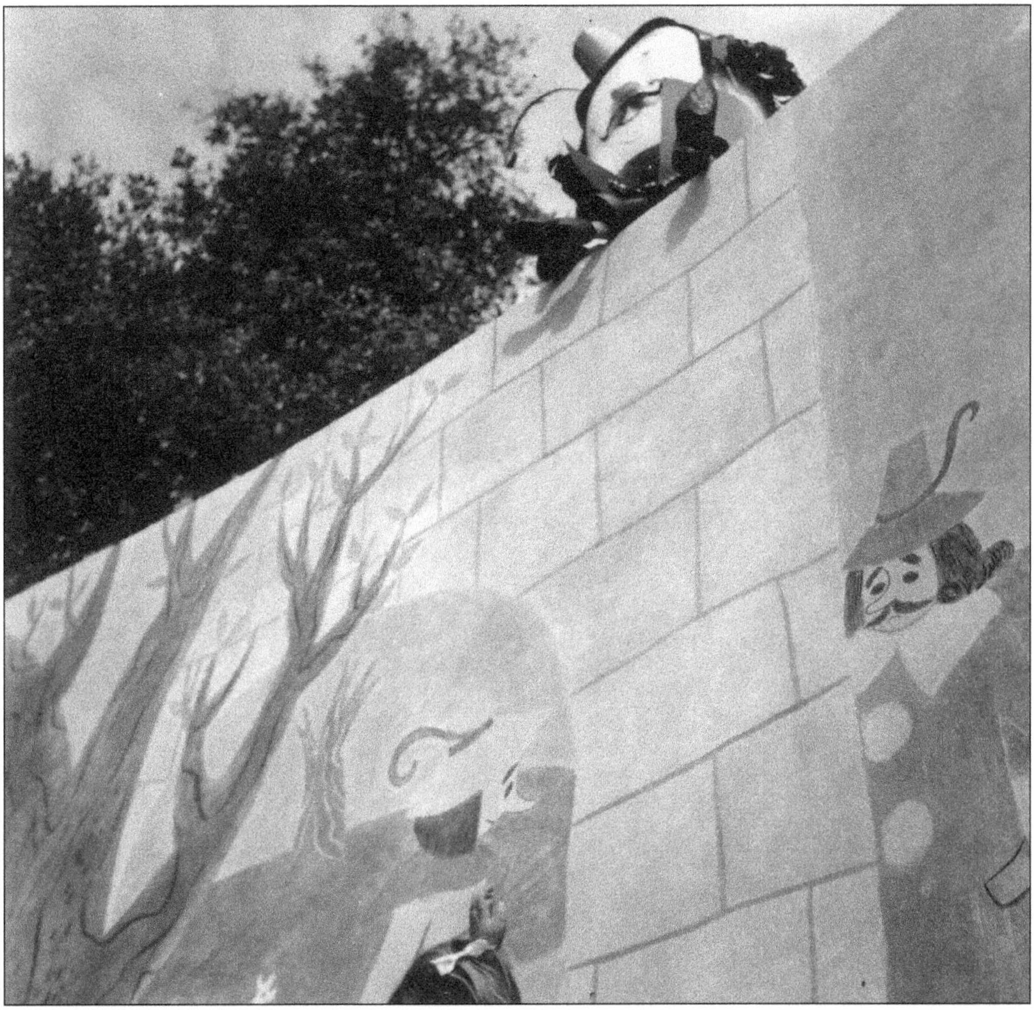

Humpty Dumpty Nursery Rhyme Wall, 1951 and 2008. Another popular park character is Humpty Dumpty, who perches atop a long, curving wall that depicts more Mother Goose rhymes. The original mural was a fresco designed by G. Frederick Peters, Lilian Kodani, and Robert Sterling, art students at the University of California, Berkeley. Behind the wall, on both sides, are family restrooms. Before the new entrance plaza was completed in 2000, Humpty was the last figure guests saw as they left Fairyland. In 1983, artist-in-residence Marilyn O'Hare and her son Kevin repainted the wall; the new mural, pictured below, incorporates numerous nursery rhymes to encourage early-childhood literacy.

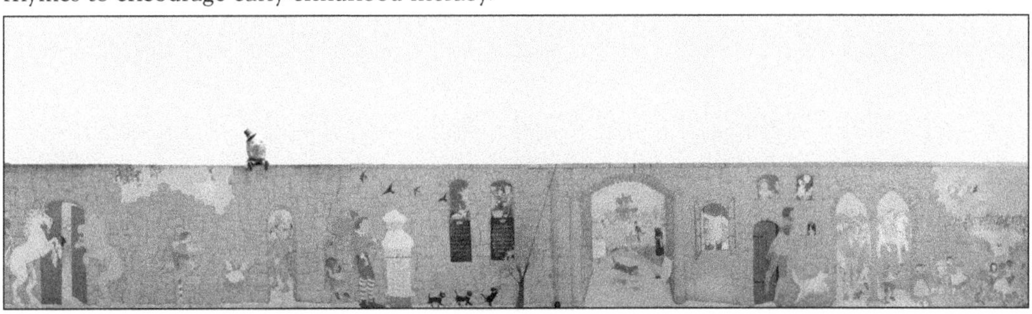

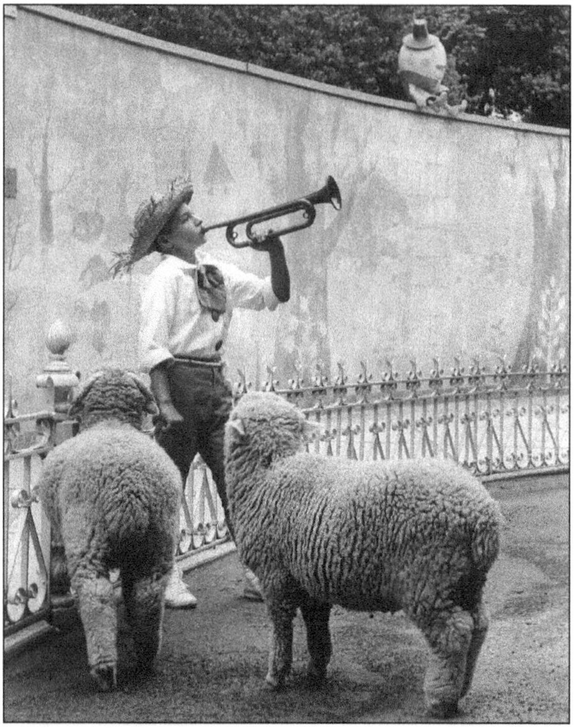

Calling the Sheep, 1961. Gregg Owens, Little Boy Blue, uses his horn to gather sheep from Mary's Schoolhouse. Since its opening, the park has invited young actors to portray nursery rhyme characters. Visiting children get a big thrill out of seeing other youngsters playacting for their benefit. Owens went on to become the zoo director of a sister park, San Jose's Happy Hollow Park and Zoo.

Froggy Went A Courtin', 1959. Fairyland's queen, Diane Duarte, greets her froggy friend as he travels the Merry Miller stream to court Missy Mouse. For 30 years, the park chose a young girl to reign as queen of Fairyland. She held court for one year and then passed her crown to another lucky child.

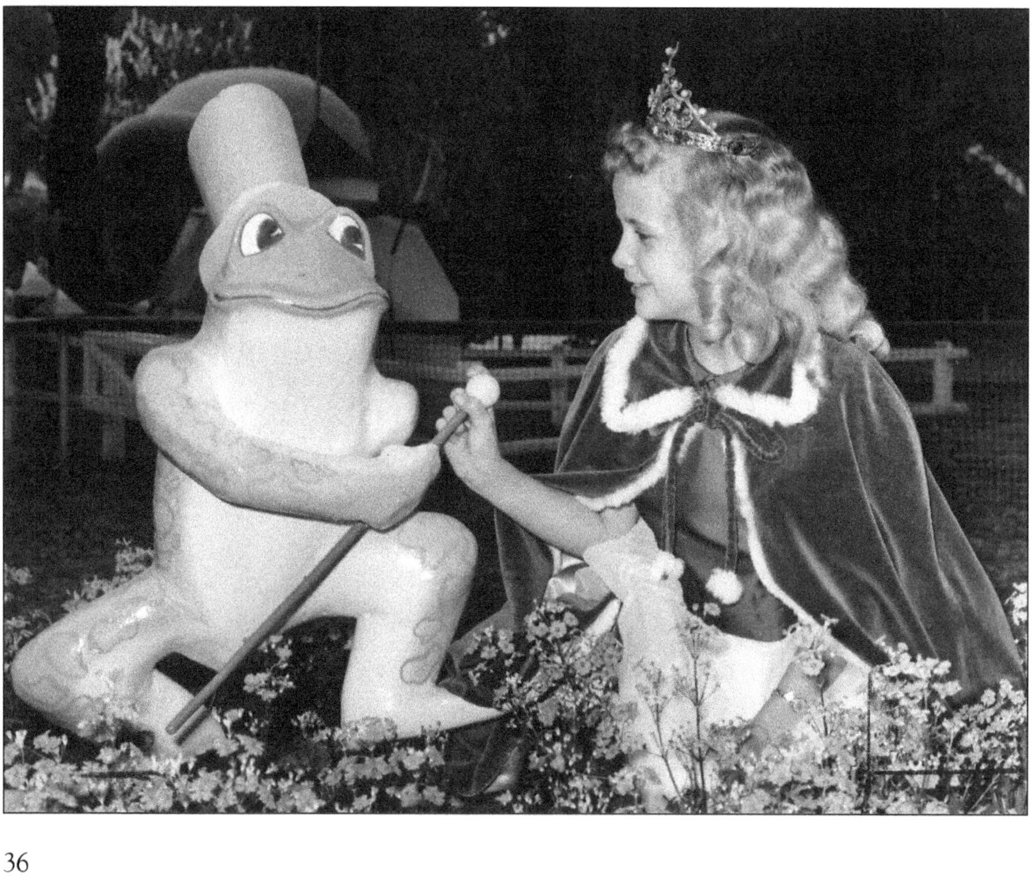

Three

Fairy-Tale Flora and Fauna

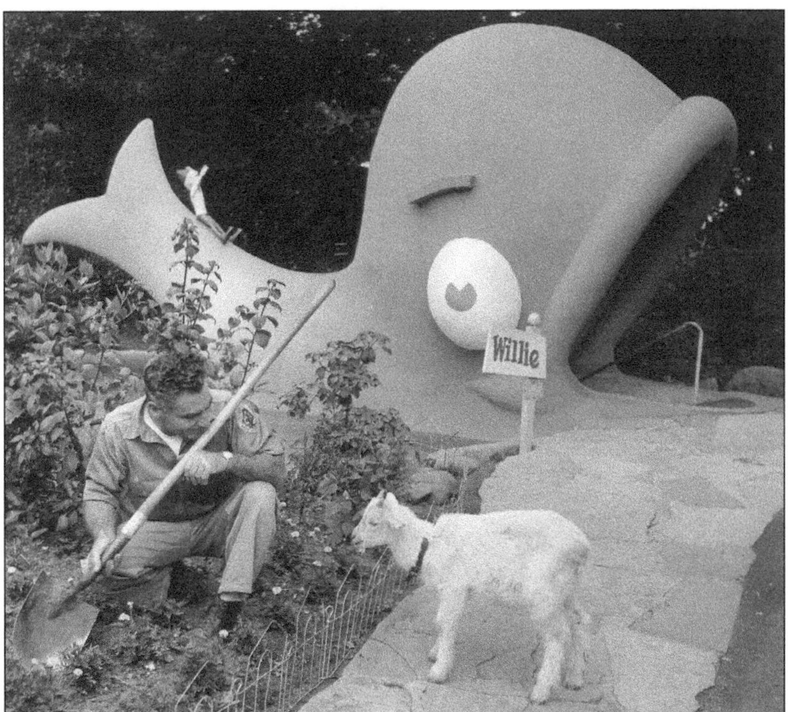

Let's Have a Talk, 1959. Manuel Marino, the park's first gardener, suggests that Marshmallow the goat stop kidding around and look elsewhere for a meal. Each storybook set in the park is surrounded by plantings that are carefully researched and indigenous to the region in which the story originated.

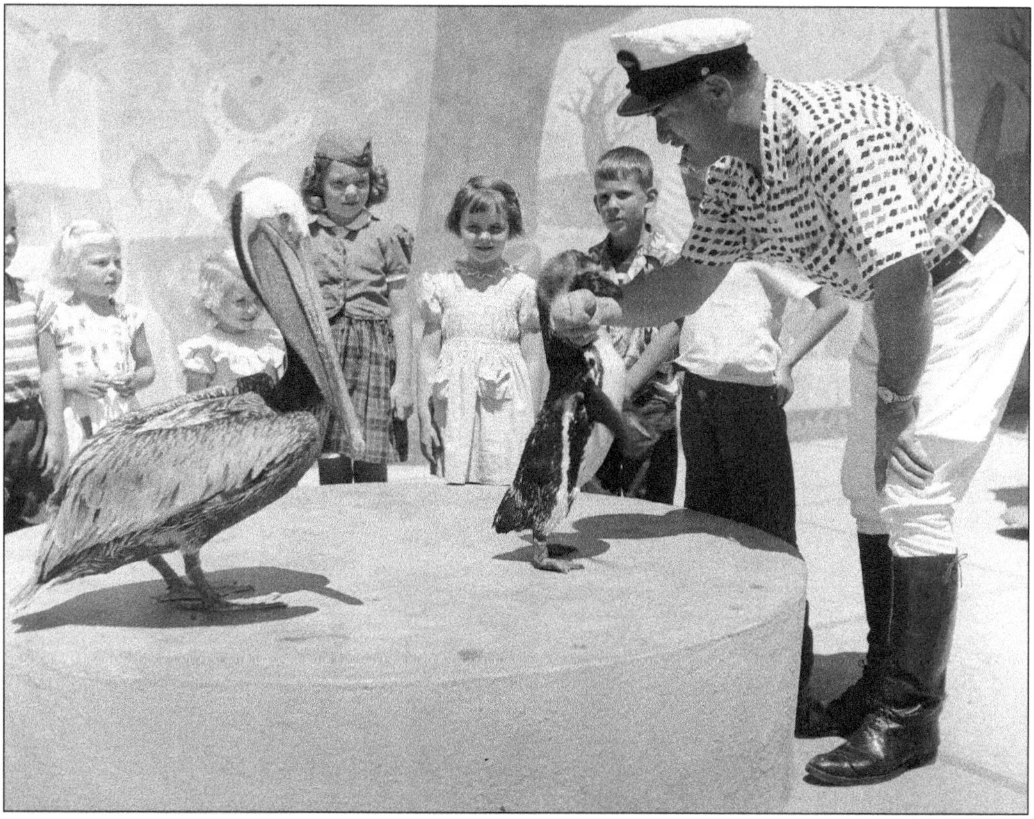

THE PERRI AND PENNI SHOW, 1953. For a single season, animal keeper Homer Snow hosted an aquatic show featuring Perri the Pelican and Penni the Penguin. Although popular, the show was discontinued because of lack of city funding.

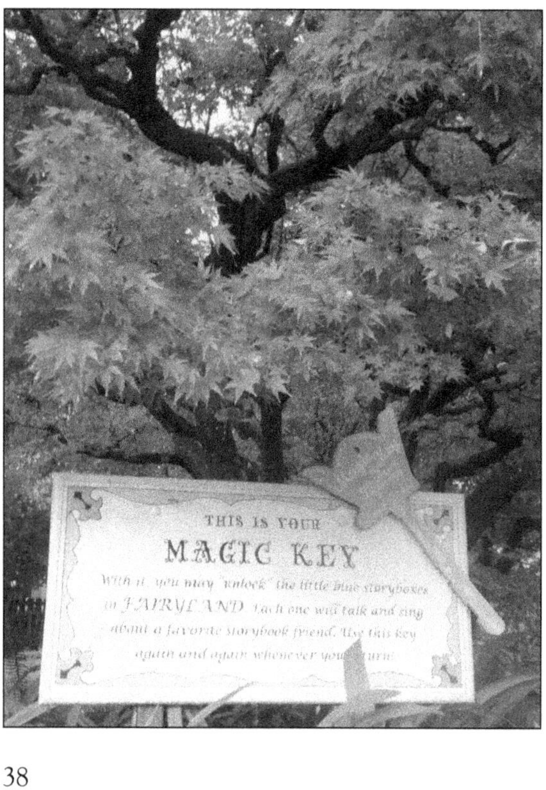

FAIRYLAND IN BLOOM, 2010. Many types of trees grow in Fairyland's 10-acre park. The original gardeners planted whatever looked good; pines, redwoods, tulip trees, ginkgos, and Japanese maples surrounded the aging native oaks. It takes great skill to keep all of the trees healthy because their roots have different requirements.

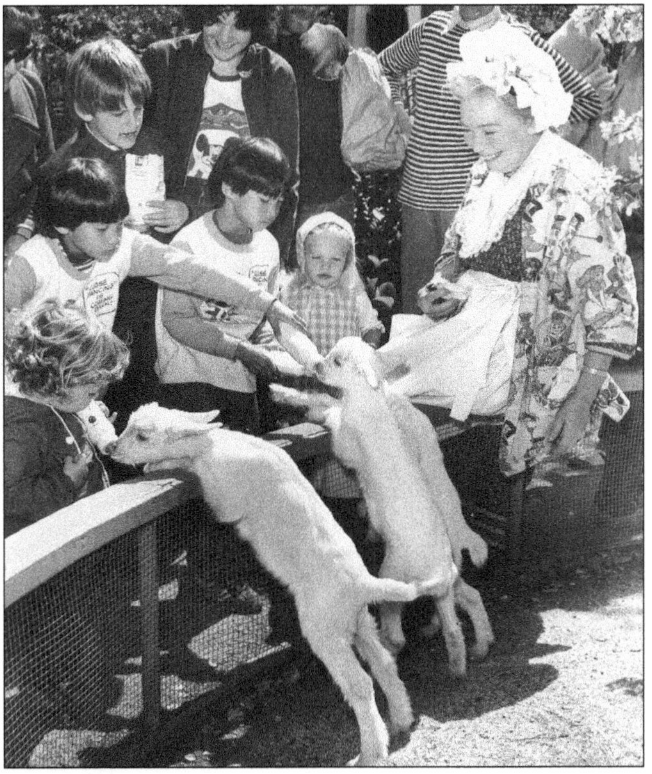

The Old Woman's Many Kids, 1970s. Adonna Houston, Fairyland's Old Woman in the Shoe ticket taker and animal keeper, allows children to bottle-feed the park's baby goats. Houston was a park mainstay who greeted visitors as they passed through the Shoe. Whenever PoPo the Clown was away on a "goodwill" tour, she would become LoLo in his place. The pair shared a circus background.

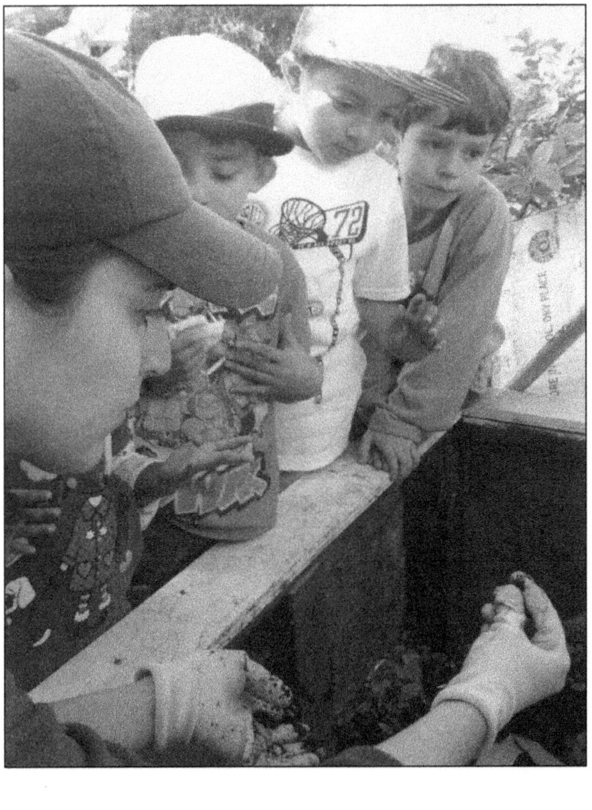

Planting Seeds in Young Minds, 2012. Jacqueline Salas, Fairyland's landscape supervisor (foreground), teaches children about the proper care of soil at a park Garden Day. She makes sure that the grounds are organically managed: No harsh chemicals or fertilizers find their way to these plants. Thanks to her efforts, Fairyland is now a certified wildlife habitat recognized by the National Wildlife Federation.

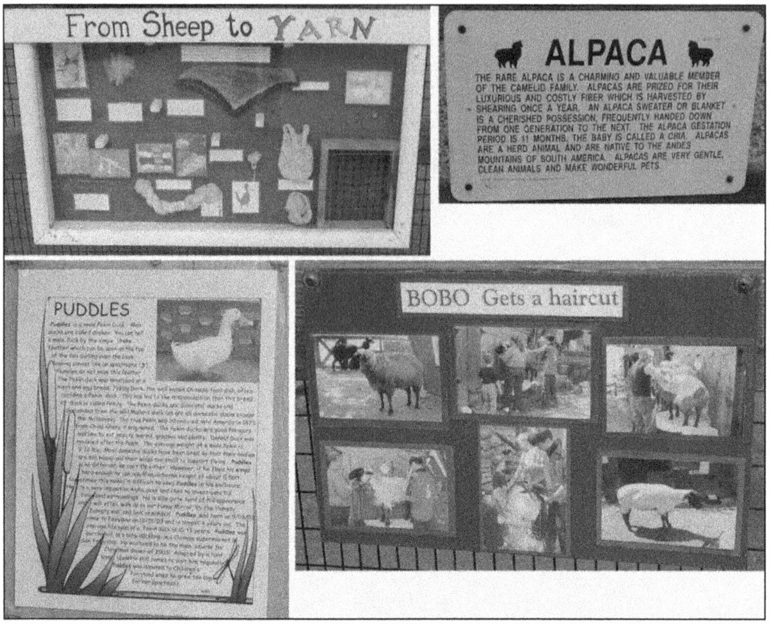

ANIMAL EDUCATION AT FAIRYLAND, 2005. Education and literacy are important duties of Fairyland's animal keeper, who continually comes up with new signage and displays like these to inform children about the animals they see. Many Oakland children come to Fairyland having never petted a tame animal; the interactive displays make the experience a friendly one.

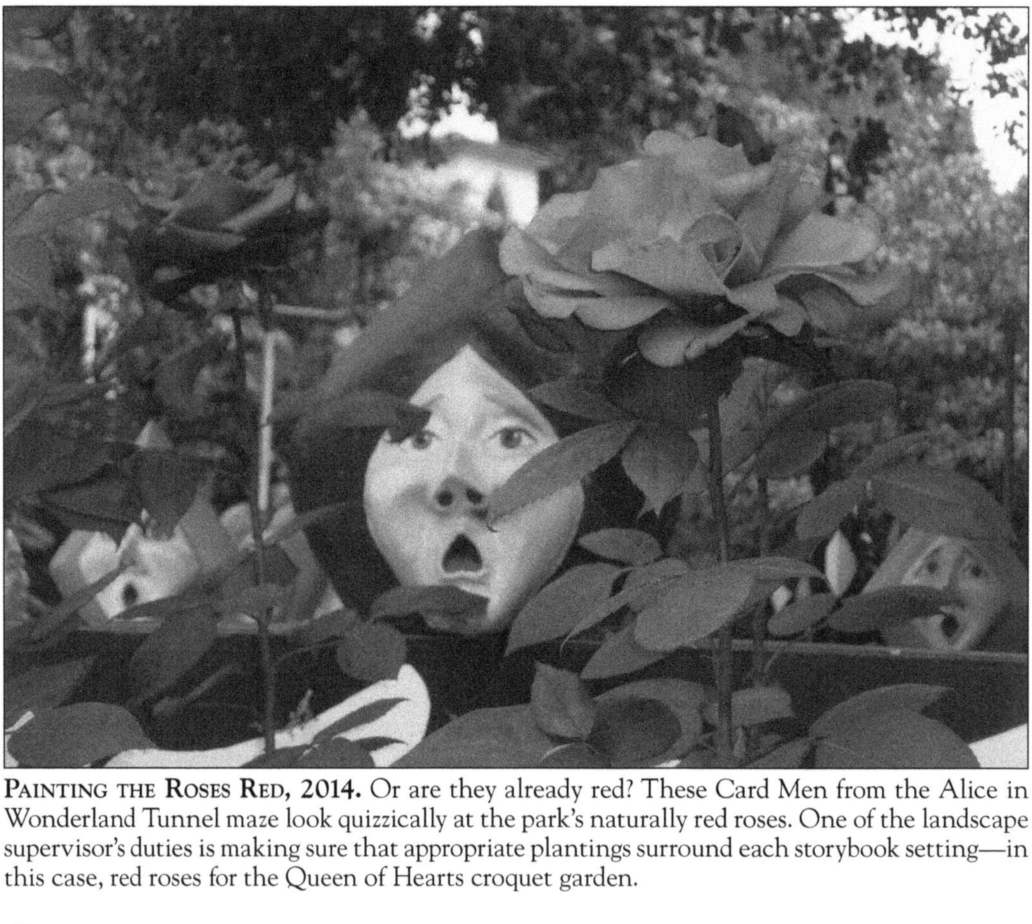

PAINTING THE ROSES RED, 2014. Or are they already red? These Card Men from the Alice in Wonderland Tunnel maze look quizzically at the park's naturally red roses. One of the landscape supervisor's duties is making sure that appropriate plantings surround each storybook setting—in this case, red roses for the Queen of Hearts croquet garden.

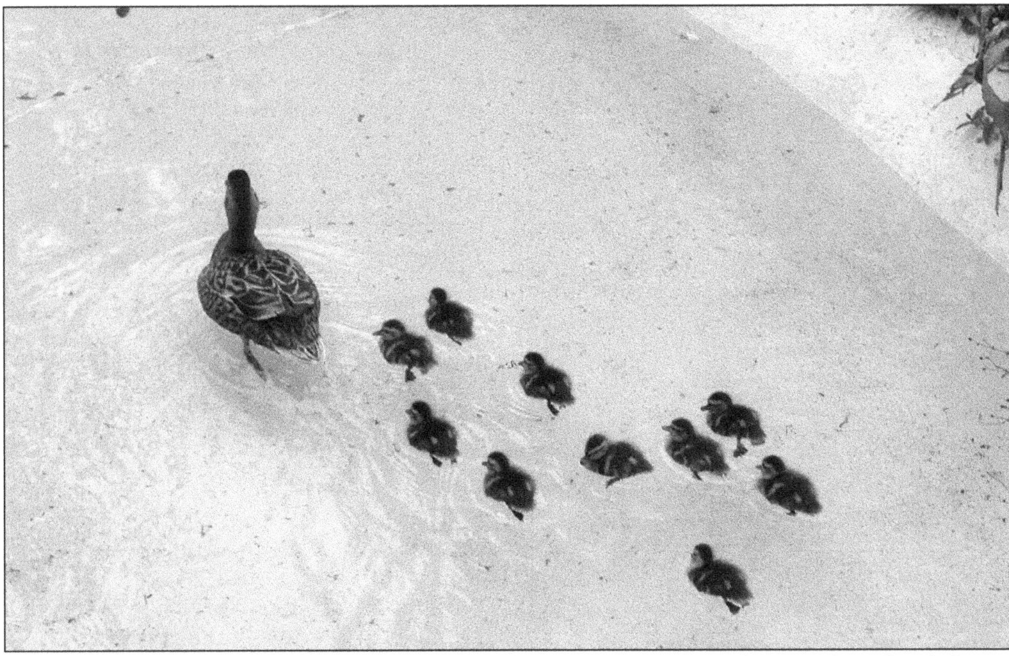

Swimming Is for Ducks Only!, 1990. It must be spring: Mama Duck is teaching her babies to swim in the Goosey Gander pond. Lakeside Park, a stopover for many types of birds, was declared a National Wildlife Refuge in 1869—three years before Yellowstone became a national park. It was the first such refuge in the United States.

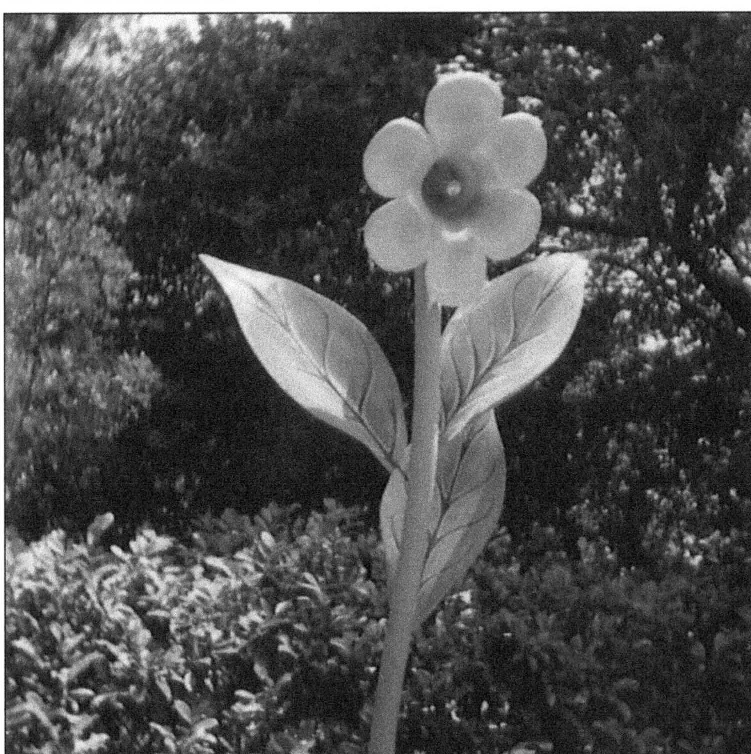

Growing 'Em Big in Fairyland!, 1999. Fairyland flowers come in all sizes, colors, and materials. This bloom is one of many that were part of the park's early sound system; hidden speakers broadcast music and public announcements. Now they are just a colorful part of their natural surroundings.

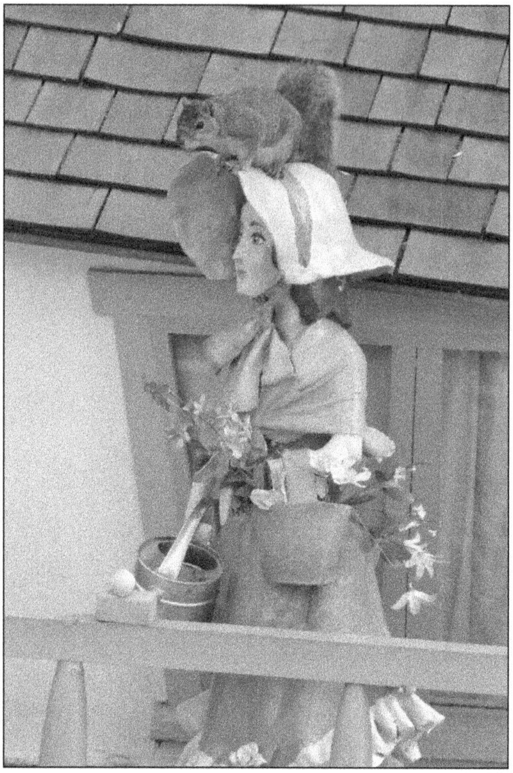

THAT IS NOT A HAT DECORATION, 2010. Fairyland's most common predators are squirrels, like this one perched on Mary, Mary, Quite Contrary's hat. Children love the squirrels, which do help the natural environment by collecting nuts—but they also beg for food (even from unguarded baby strollers) and pose an ongoing challenge to park gardeners.

OLD WEST JUNCTION, 2014. Flowers and brush native to arid California paint the landscape surrounding Old West Junction, a play area that celebrates tall tales and the lore of the West. Cactus and succulents landscape the train tracks of the Jolly Trolly, the child-size train that passes through Old West Junction.

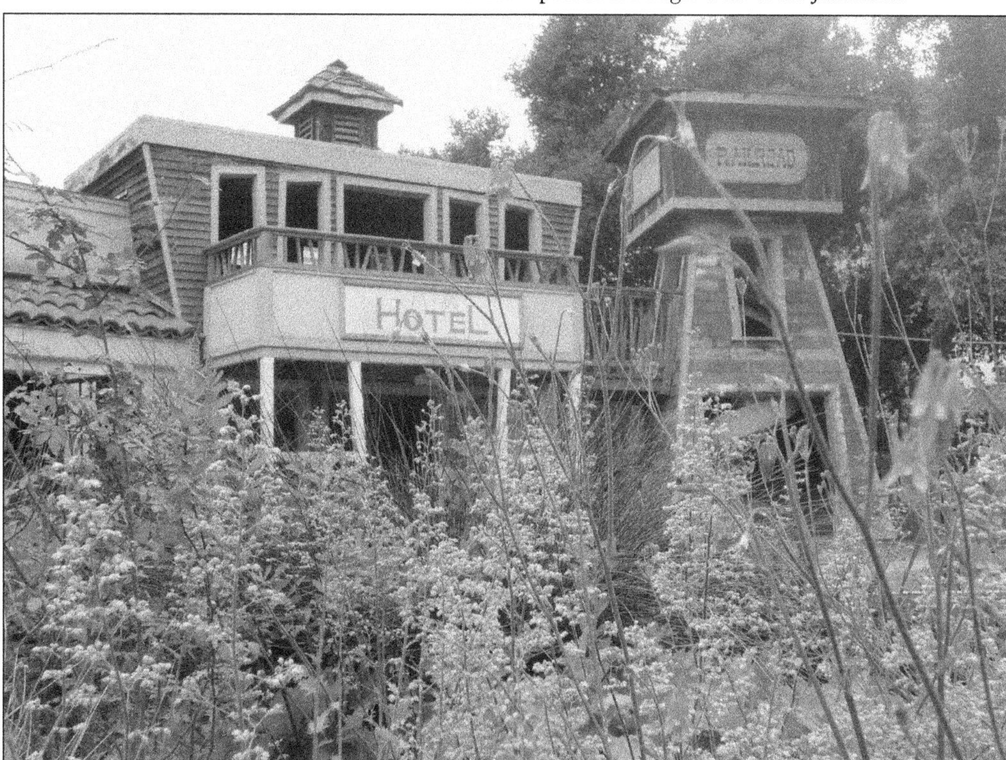

New Life in Fairyland, 1978. Many of the park's four-legged residents come to the park as newborns. After they arrive, the park invites children to help name them. The name of this miniature horse has been forgotten, but it is clear he or she is looking forward to the next bottle-feeding.

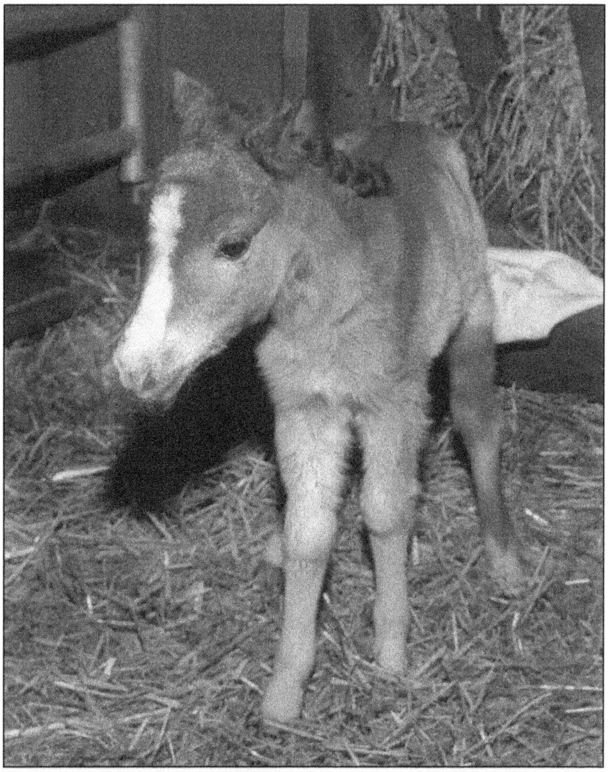

Helping Hands, 2013. The children of Fairyland's summer camp work together to form a big seed ball encased in earth. When they finish, natural pollinators will disperse the seeds. It is one example of organic gardening in Lakeside Park and a way of teaching city children about their natural surroundings.

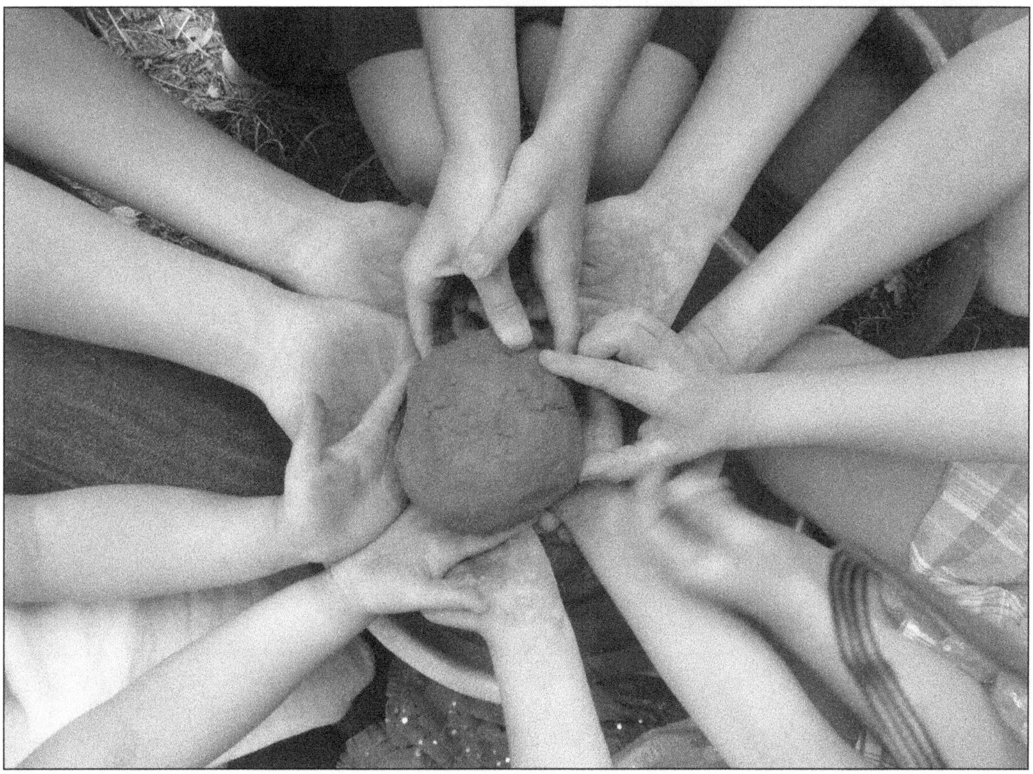

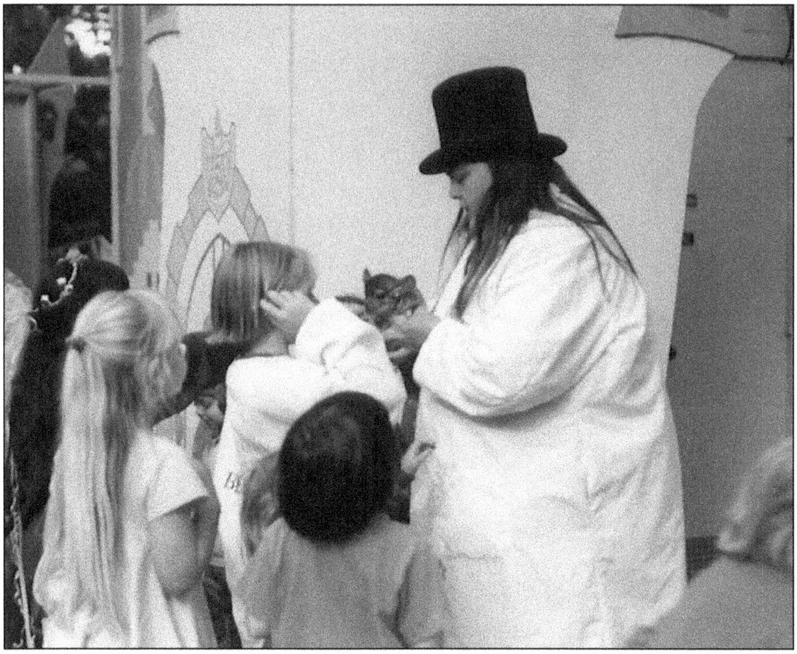

Doctor Dolittle Is In, 1995. One of the programs available for schoolchildren touring Fairyland is a visit with Dr. Dolittle, a program created by former animal keeper Linda Burt and based on the classic children's stories by Hugh Lofting. Burt would don a top hat and lab coat to teach the kids about animal behavior. Here, she is teaching about chinchillas.

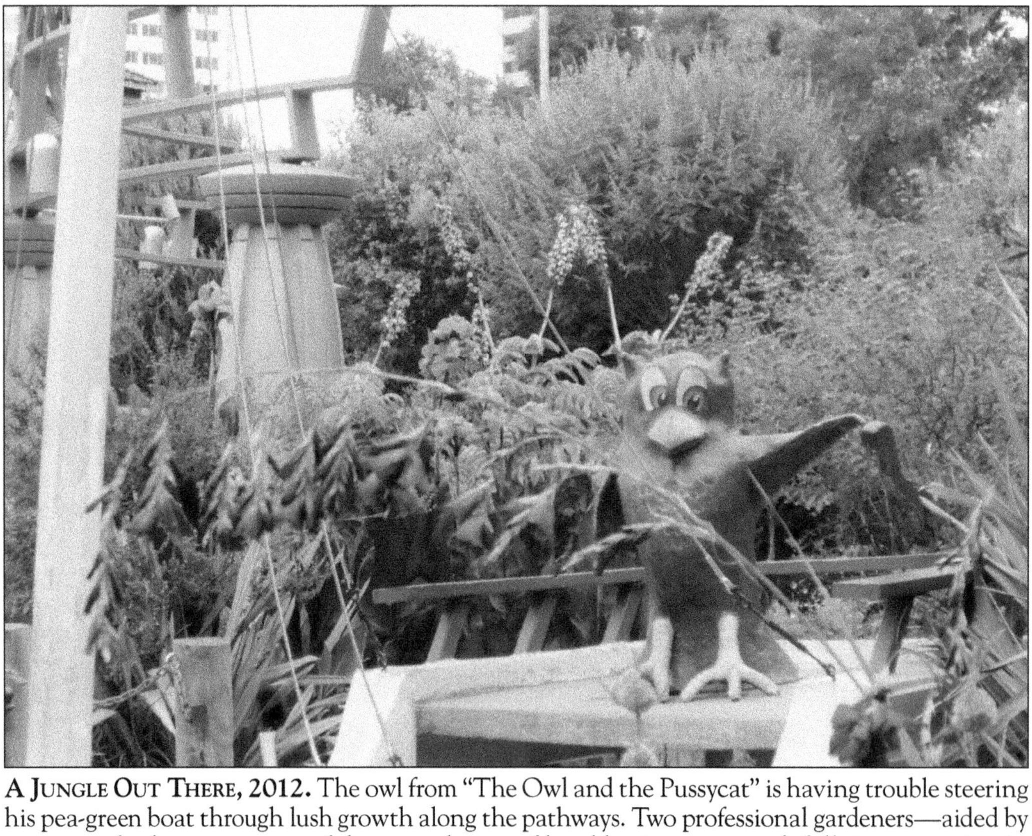

A Jungle Out There, 2012. The owl from "The Owl and the Pussycat" is having trouble steering his pea-green boat through lush growth along the pathways. Two professional gardeners—aided by an army of volunteers, some of them employees of local businesses—work full-time to maintain Fairyland's 10 acres of plantings.

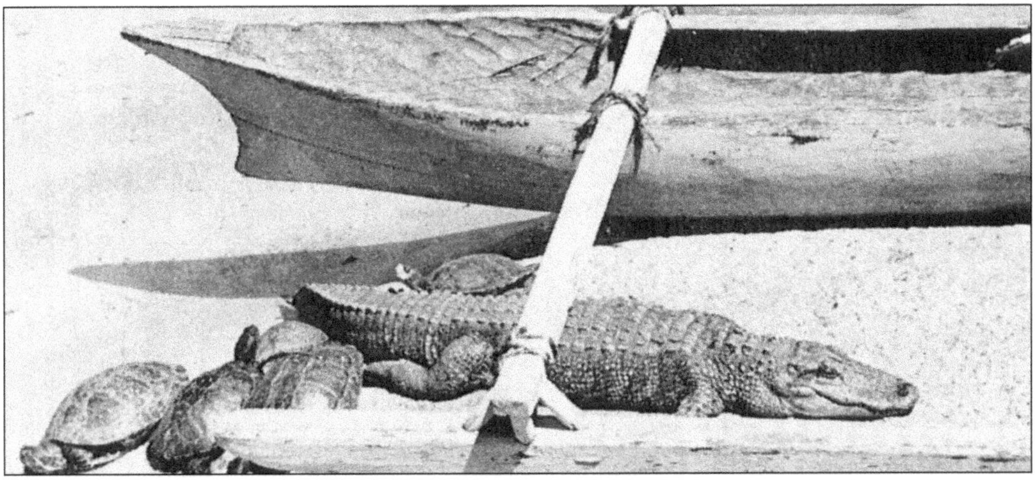

Warming in the Sun, 1955. Mr. Crocodile and a few of his tortoise friends relax in the sun on the beach of the Robinson Crusoe Island set. While this set and others were once home to many exotic animals; today only domesticated creatures—chickens, ducks, and sheep among them—live at Fairyland.

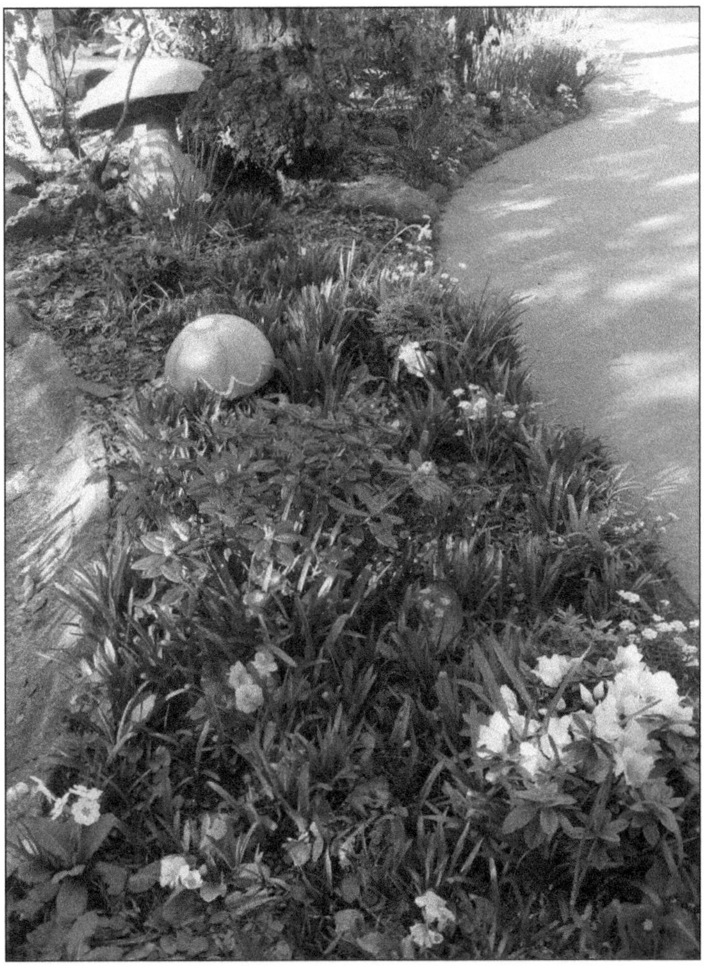

Colorful Pathways Abound, 2000. In 2014, the park became an official monarch butterfly way station. Fairyland's gardeners grow milkweed—the only plants this species will eat—to attract caterpillars, then harvest and protect them as they form chrysalises. Within 10 to 14 days, the butterflies emerge and swarm the park, providing a colorful display for visitors and ensuring that insects and other animals thrive in Lakeside Park.

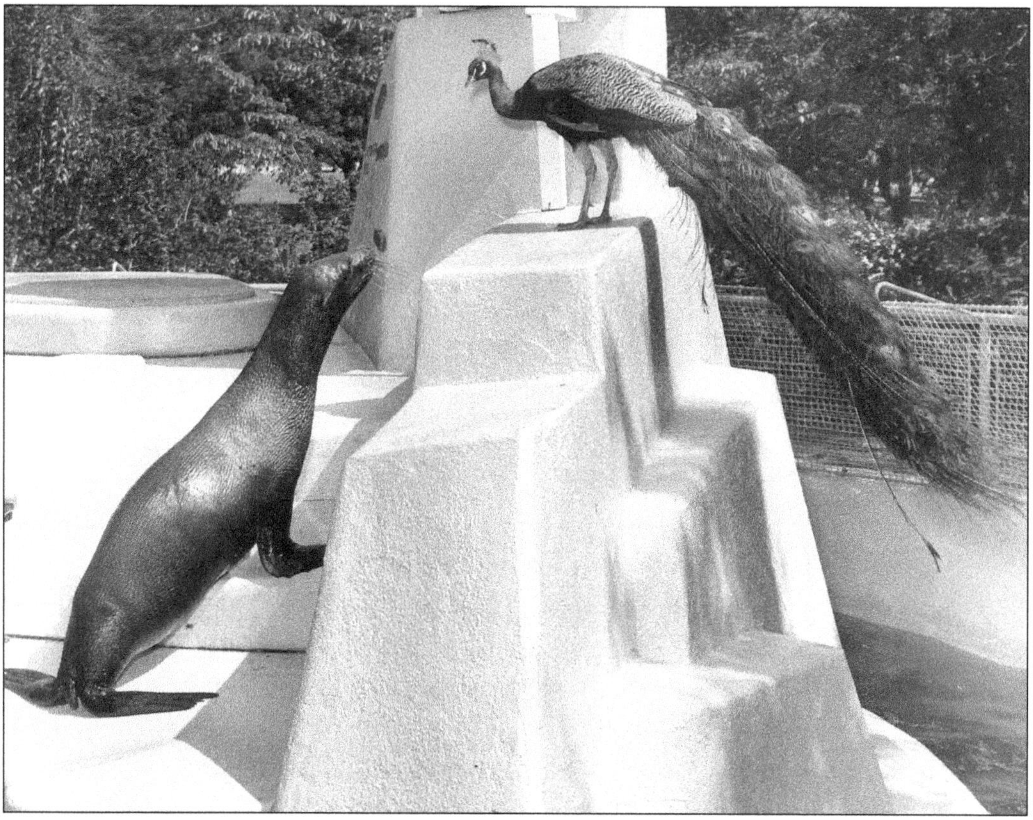

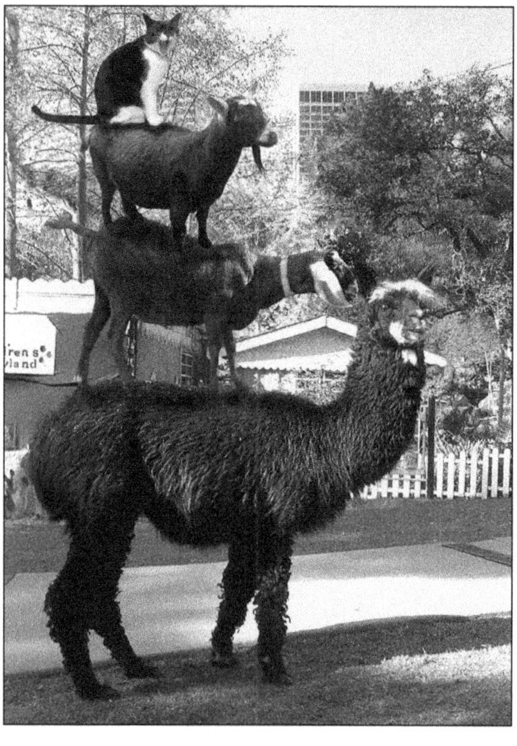

THAT IS NOT A SEAL!, 1964. Sammy the seal is displeased that the peacock, Caliph of Baghdad, has decided to roost on his slide. At one time, many animals were allowed to freely wander the paths of Fairyland—chickens, rabbits, peacocks, and even monkeys. Today, they are housed in safe, comfortable dwellings.

ANIMAL SINGERS OF BREMEN, 2009. This promotional photograph depicts Jewel the cat, Tina and Anton the goats, and Juan the alpaca auditioning for animal singing roles in the Berkeley Symphony's recording of "The Butterfly Tree," a musical retelling of the Grimm brothers' tale "The Bremen Town Musicians." Selected animal voices accompany the symphony and singer Joan Baez on the piece, which was released on CD.

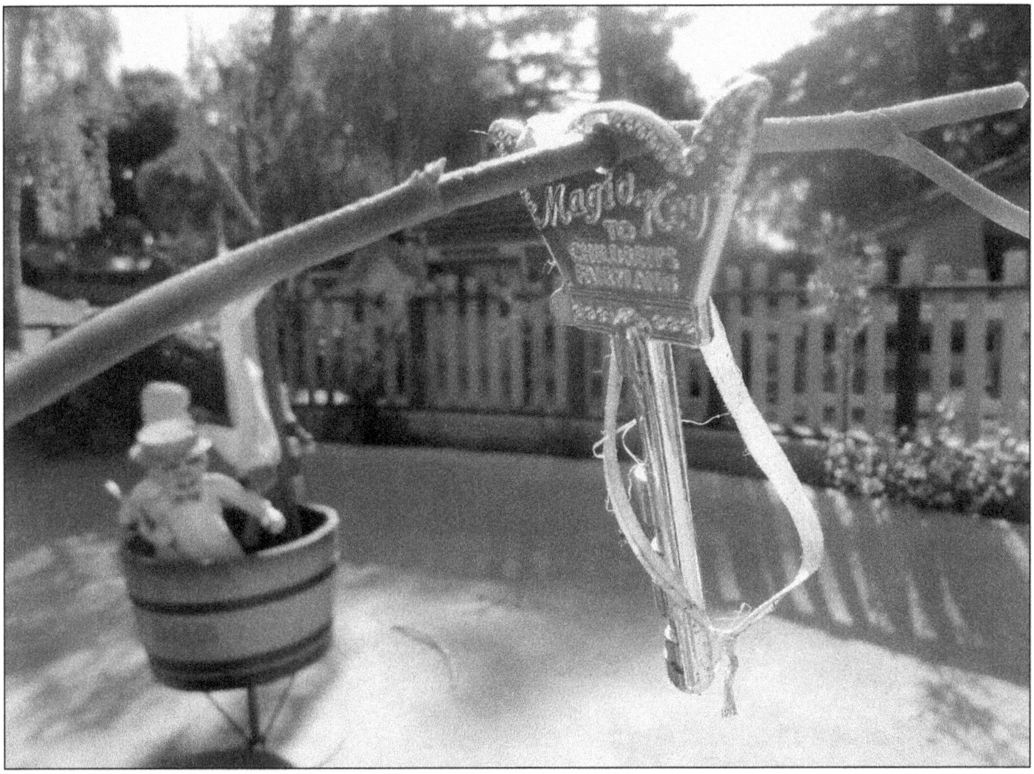

Nature Finds a Way, 2015. The Three Men in a Tub are confused: With no water in the pond, they cannot figure out how to sail over and rescue the silver Magic Key that operates Fairyland's talking Storybook Boxes. Some unlucky child dropped it in the bushes, and a creeping vine has snagged it and carried it into the sky.

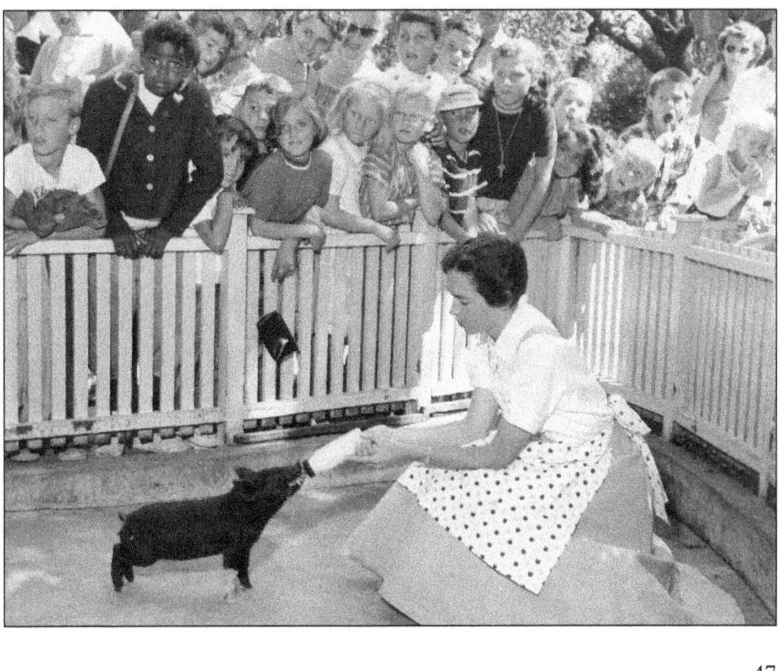

Feeding Time!, 1957. Adjacent to the Three Pigs' houses was housing for live piglets, which each day were bottle-fed by children. Here, Porky gets a bottle from the animal keeper. For its first 25 years, the park was home to baby animals only. As animals grew larger, they would be transferred to local zoos, farms, and care centers.

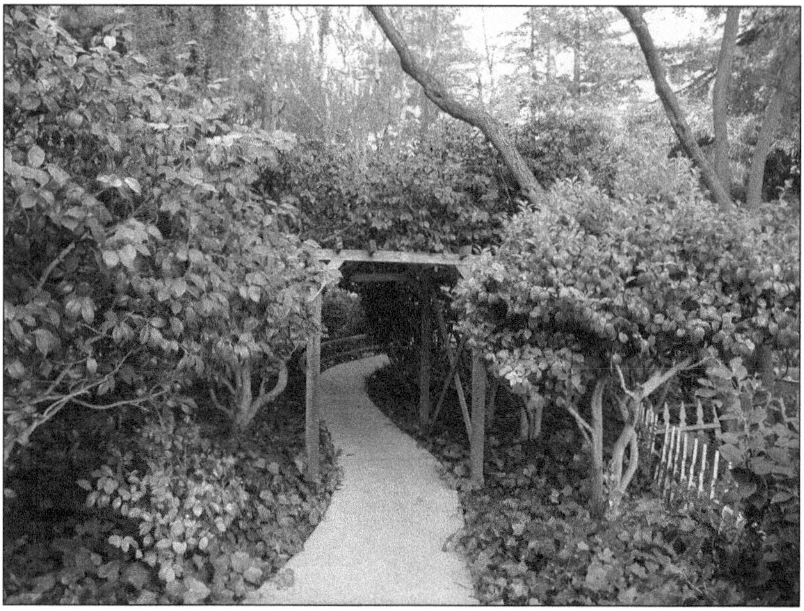

Finding a Secret Garden, 2011. Many Fairyland paths wind playfully around themselves; lush, colorful plantings may hide a secret entrance to another adventure. Why not find a circle of mushrooms and bravely step into the center? According to legend, that is another secret way into the fairy world.

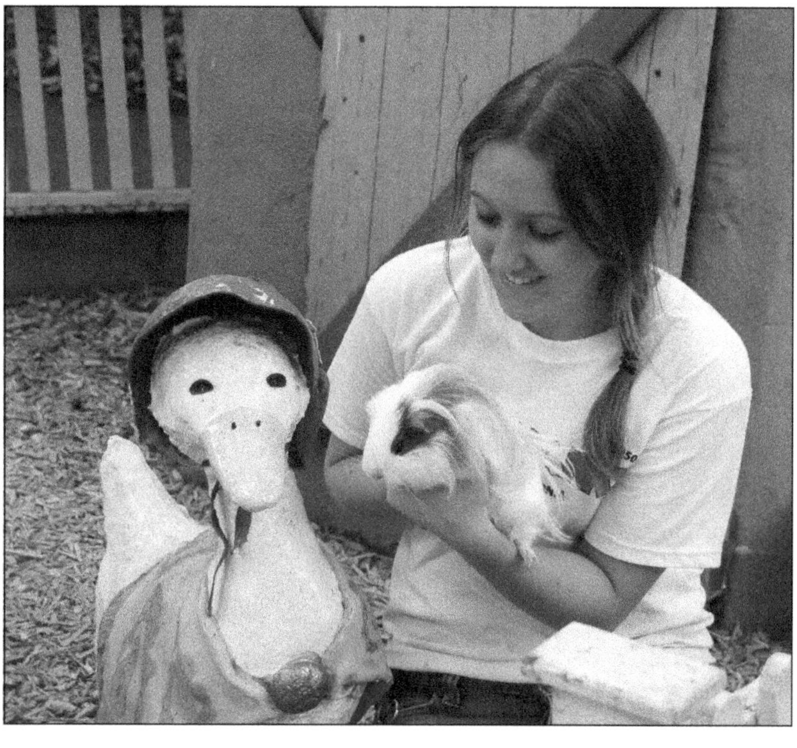

She Just Wants a Kiss, 2008. Animal volunteer Micah McKechnie holds her favorite animal friend, Emowyn the guinea pig, as Jemima Puddle Duck looks on warily. Peter Rabbit Village is home to Jemima Puddle Duck's Guinea Pig Farm, inspired by one of several Beatrix Potter stories honored at Fairyland.

A Woodland Elf Throne, 2014. This elfin throne was once a mighty redwood in the picnic area. On Arbor Day, arborists gather at Fairyland to help trim the canopies of the park's gigantic trees. Some branches and cuttings are transformed into benches and natural settings for the park. After this log was cut, an artist shaped the wood; a coat of varnish later, it was fit for a king.

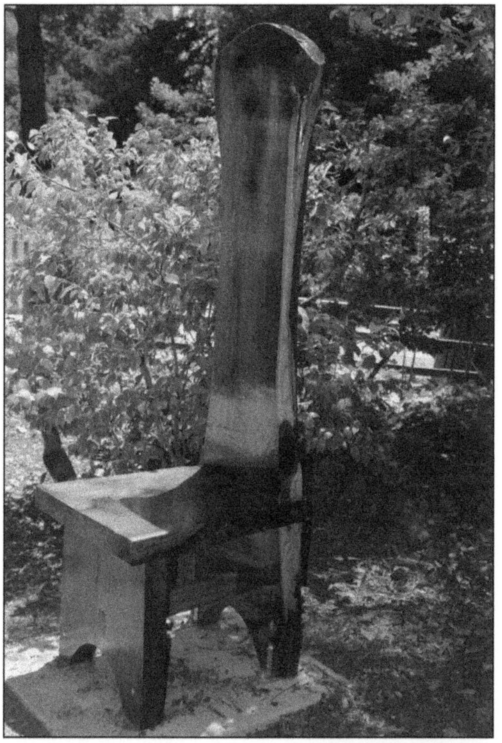

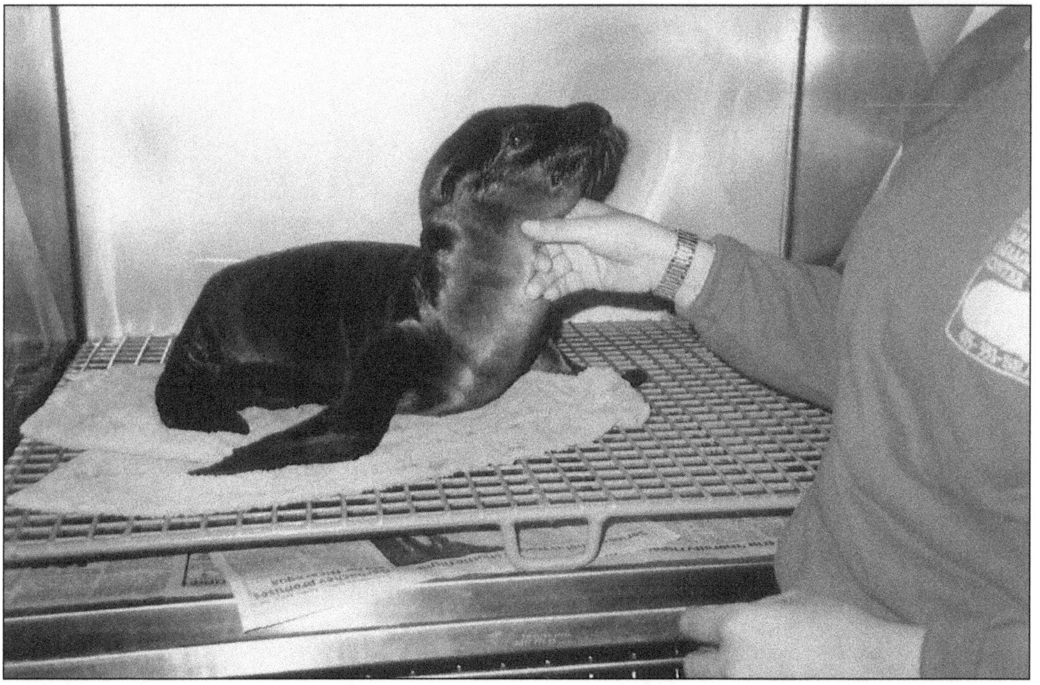

A Seal of Approval, 1980. When Fairyland had a seal set, staff members helped the Marine Mammal Center in Marin County rescue injured seals. Li'l Tommy was born at Fairyland to a blind mother who abandoned the pup. Marine Mammal Center volunteers came to the park and cared for it.

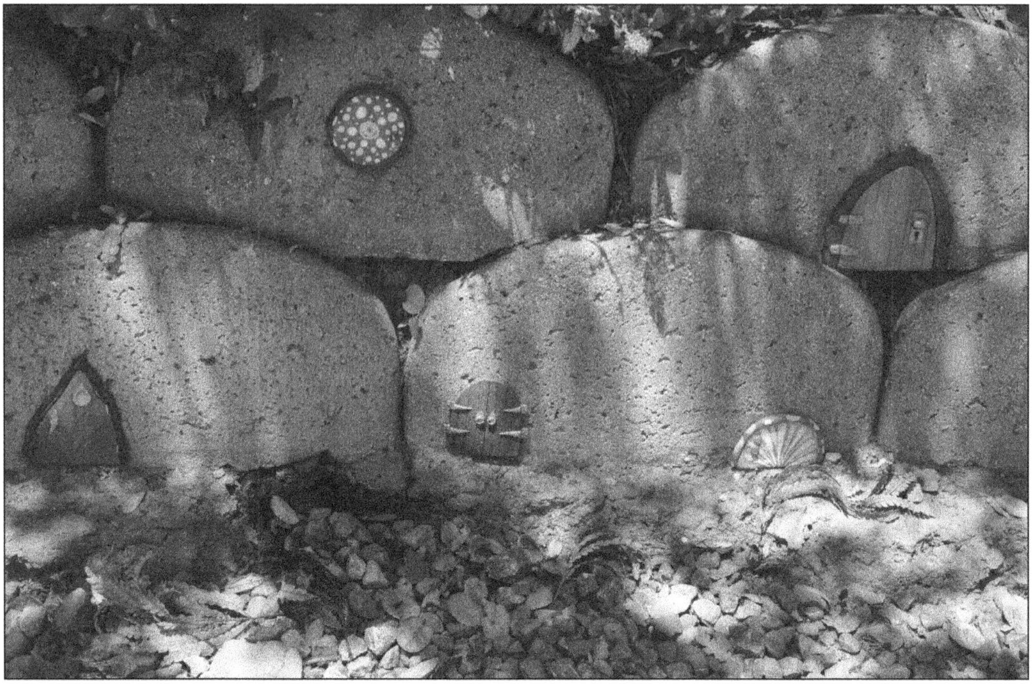

Fairy Real Estate, 2014. Amid the gardens of Fairyland are tiny fairy doors that, according to legend, are openings to the fairy world. In fact, the doors are the creations of Shannon Taylor, Fairyland's art and restoration director. Only Taylor knows how many doors are hidden in the park; one way to know that one has been discovered is to listen for the excited squeals of children. This fairy condominium is located by the train tracks.

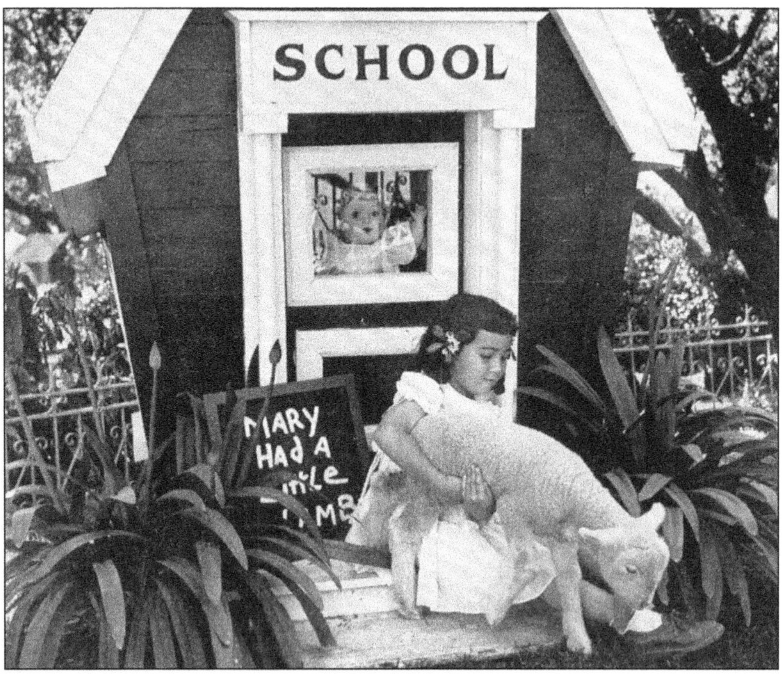

Late for School, 1956. Heather Burgos, who portrayed Mary of "Mary Had a Little Lamb," is trying to convince this little lamb to return home and not follow her. A Mary doll—a gift from the United Federation of Doll Clubs—peeks out of the schoolhouse window.

Four

The Park Expands

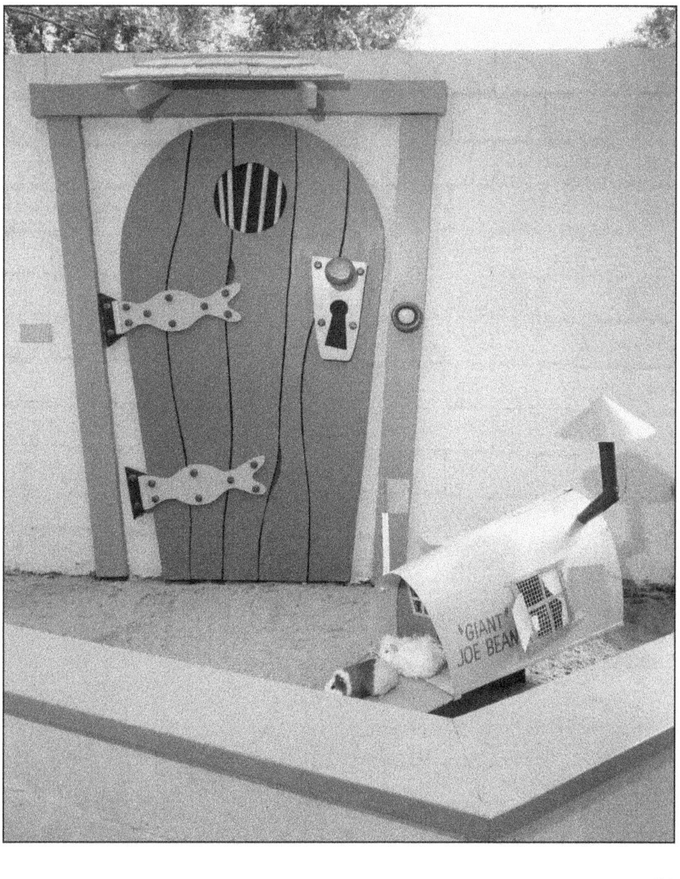

Giant Joe Bean, 1951. This set served a dual purpose: On the backside, behind the door, is the outer wall that held opening day dedication plaques. Inside, the wall served as a children's petting zoo. "The Giant Joe Bean" is a children's poem about a giant who uses a telephone pole for a cane and a cloud for a pillow; it was written anonymously for a magazine.

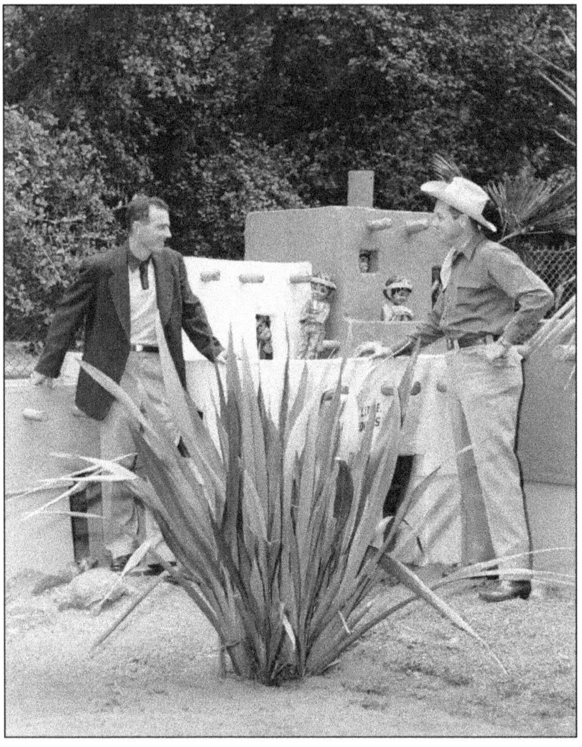

Ten Little Indians, 1953. This Indian pueblo, located next to Giant Joe Bean, was home to tortoises, rabbits, guinea pigs, armadillos, and snakes. "Ten Little Indians" was once a popular counting rhyme, but in 1984, it was deemed culturally insensitive. Fairyland staff worked with local tribal representatives to transform the theme into the tale of "How Coyote Brought Fire to the People." It was removed in 1999 to make way for a larger entrance plaza.

Sugar Plum Party Area, 1951. The park's first area for children's catered birthday parties—there are now three party areas—featured a revolving lollipop tree. The parties were notable enough to be listed in the *Oakland Tribune*'s society pages. Park host Edna Wetter, in costume, is seen serving the children their goodies.

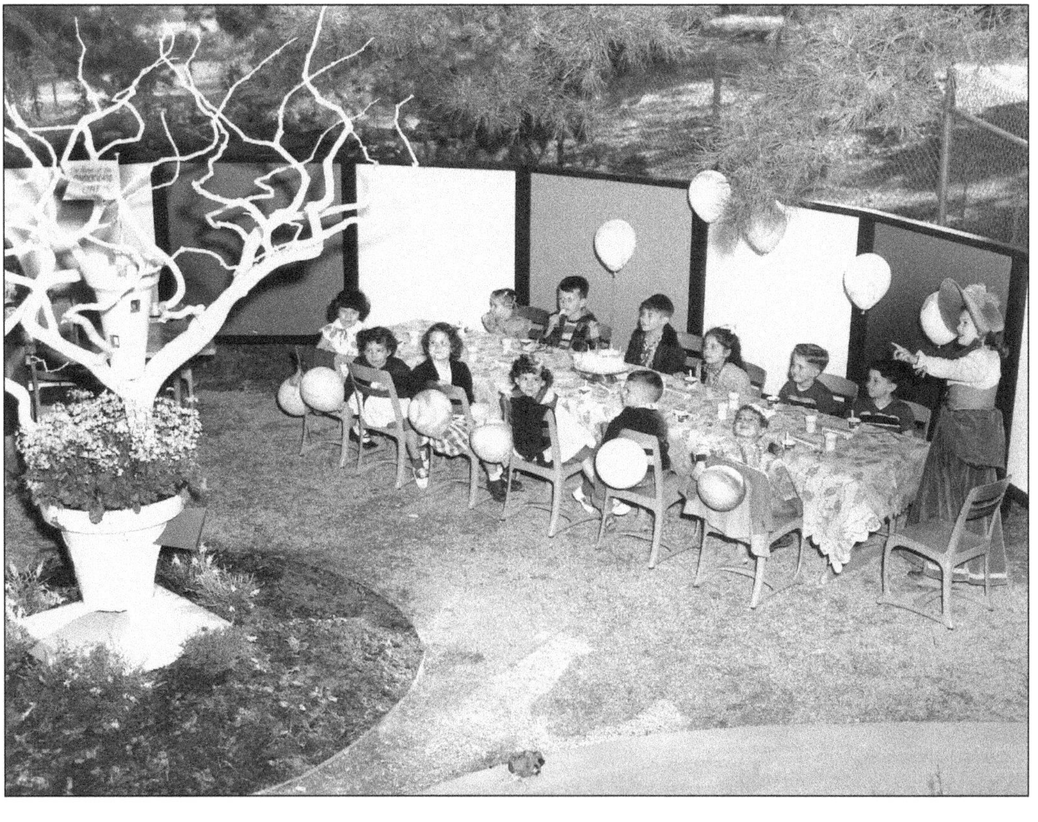

The Walrus and the Carpenter Set, 1971 and 1951. This pool for seals was inspired by the poem in Lewis Carroll's *Through the Looking Glass*, the sequel to *Alice's Adventures in Wonderland*. The seals would climb the rocky ledges to sleep in the sun, or slide down the chute to frolic in the pond. What patrons did not know was that the set featured rescued seals. The Marine Mammal Center (MMC) in Marin County rescued injured animals from the ocean and brought them to Fairyland, where MMC staff members cared for them. Visitors could purchase fish from a vending machine located nearby to feed the seals. The set closed in 1990 after neighbors complained about the animals' loud barking. At right, Zonkers the seal is seen enjoying his home, which closely resembles William Russell Everritt's 1951 model, seen below.

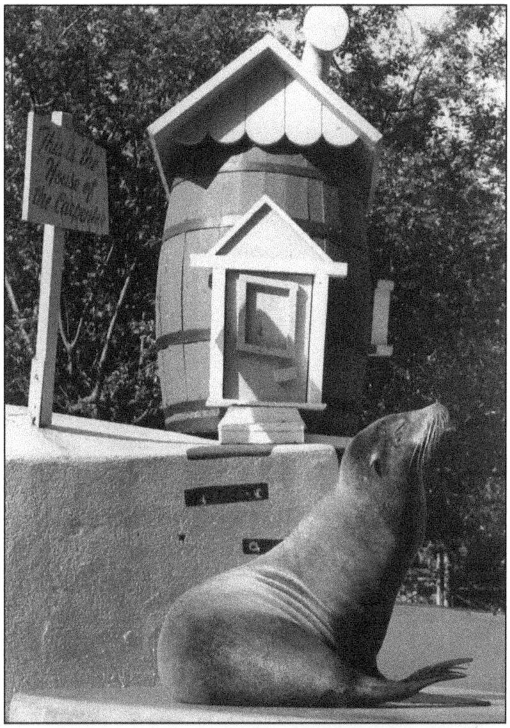

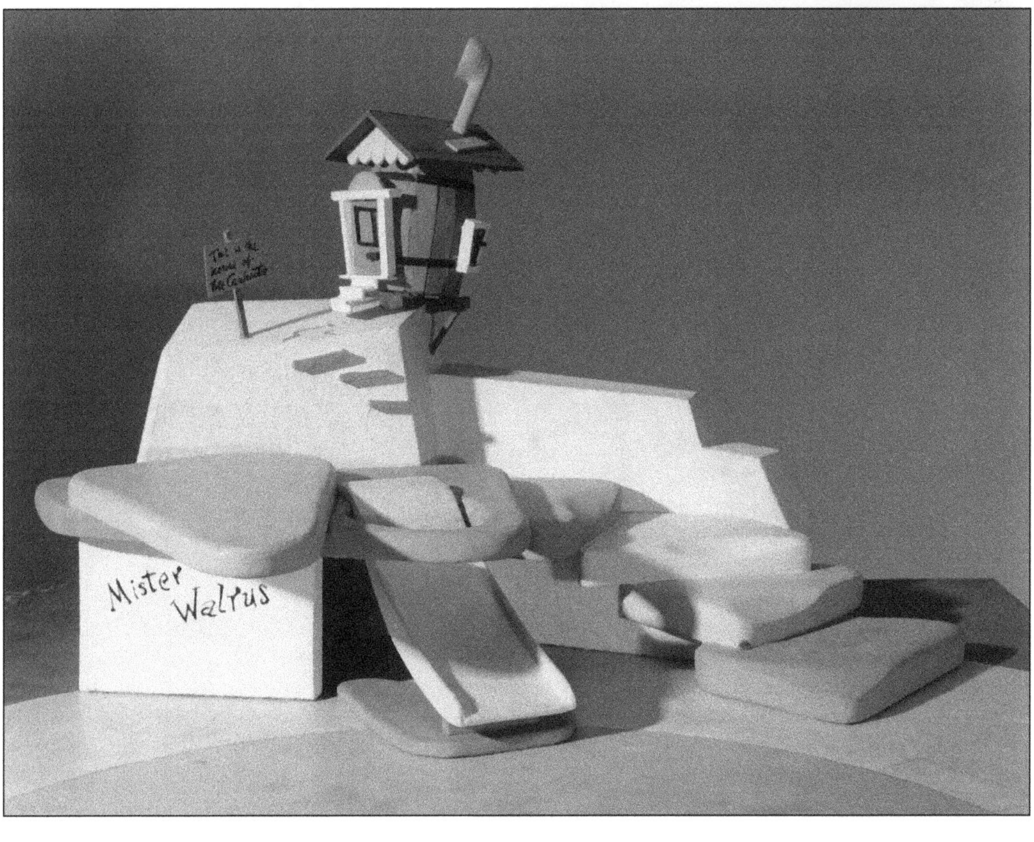

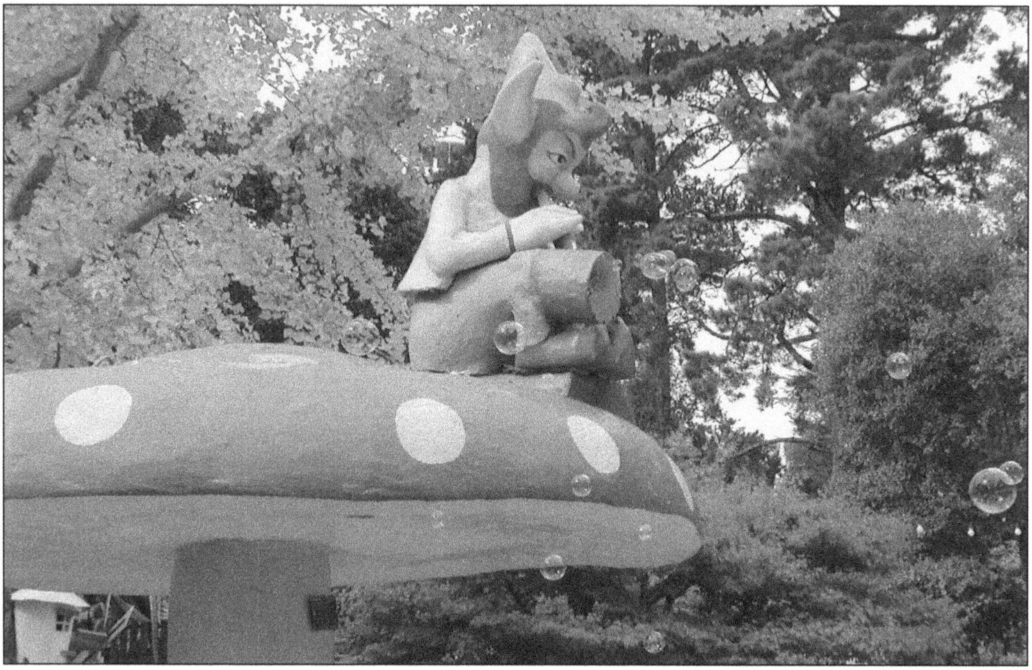

Oswald the Bubble Elf, 1975. One of the most popular attractions in the park is this jolly fellow, who sits on his mushroom and blows bubbles for children. Oswald was donated to the park by two brothers, Tom and Frank Winston, before they went off to fight in Korea in 1952. The dedication plaque bears a quote from Oscar Wilde: "The best way to make children good is to make them happy."

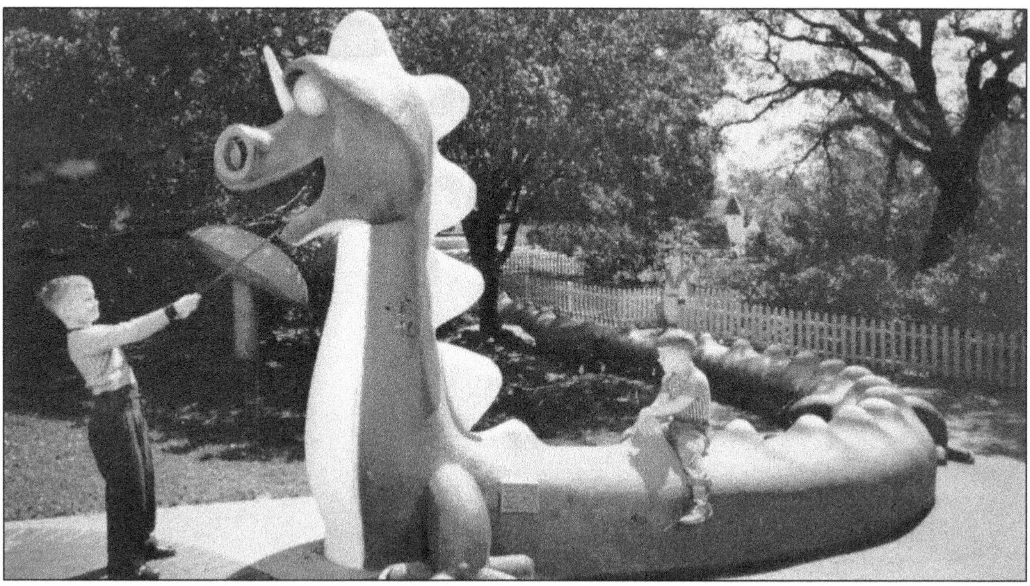

Happy Dragon Postcard, 1957. The dragon's long tail can seat many tired adults; when its long tongue is pulled, the dragon speaks, telling tales about the park. The popular set was a gift from Helen O'Neil and Oakland Advertising and Marketing Club. Although the dragon is painted green in this photograph, in 2000 someone finally translated the Chinese characters on its plaque. They read "Golden Dragon."

Cuckoo Clock Tower Slide, 2000. This building is not only a slide, it is also a timepiece. Large clocks adorn three sides of the tilted rooftops; cuckoo birds nest above them. The slide was built specifically for the smallest visitors: it is a gentle spiral that delivers a toddler into a waiting grown-up's arms.

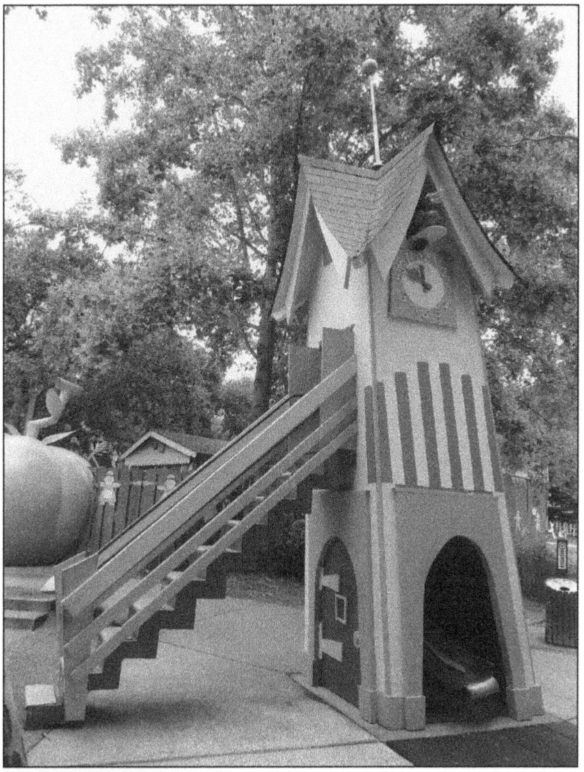

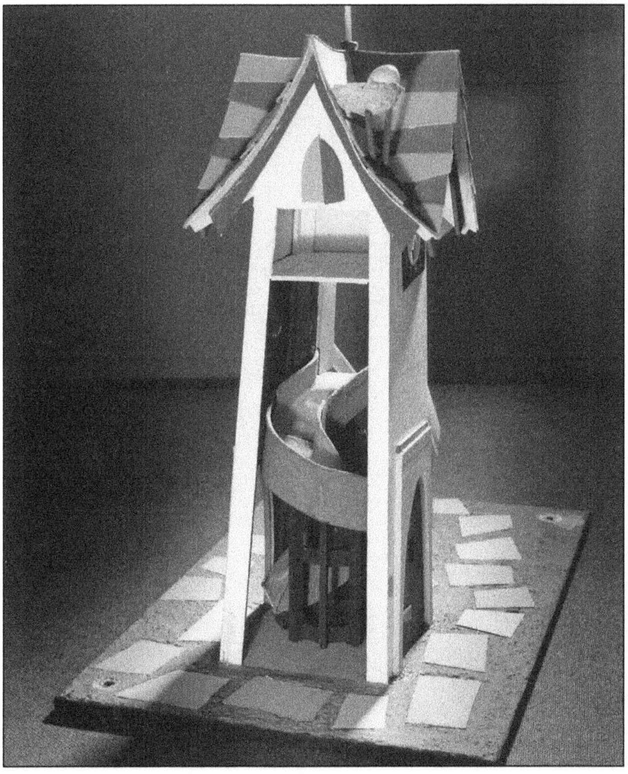

Cuckoo Clock Slide Model, 1952. The cross-section of architect William Russell Everritt's maquette reveals the twisty slide; built in 1953, it was one of the first of its kind. Early Fairyland models like this one provided aesthetic, as well as structural, guidelines: each one supplied an intricate color scheme for artists to follow.

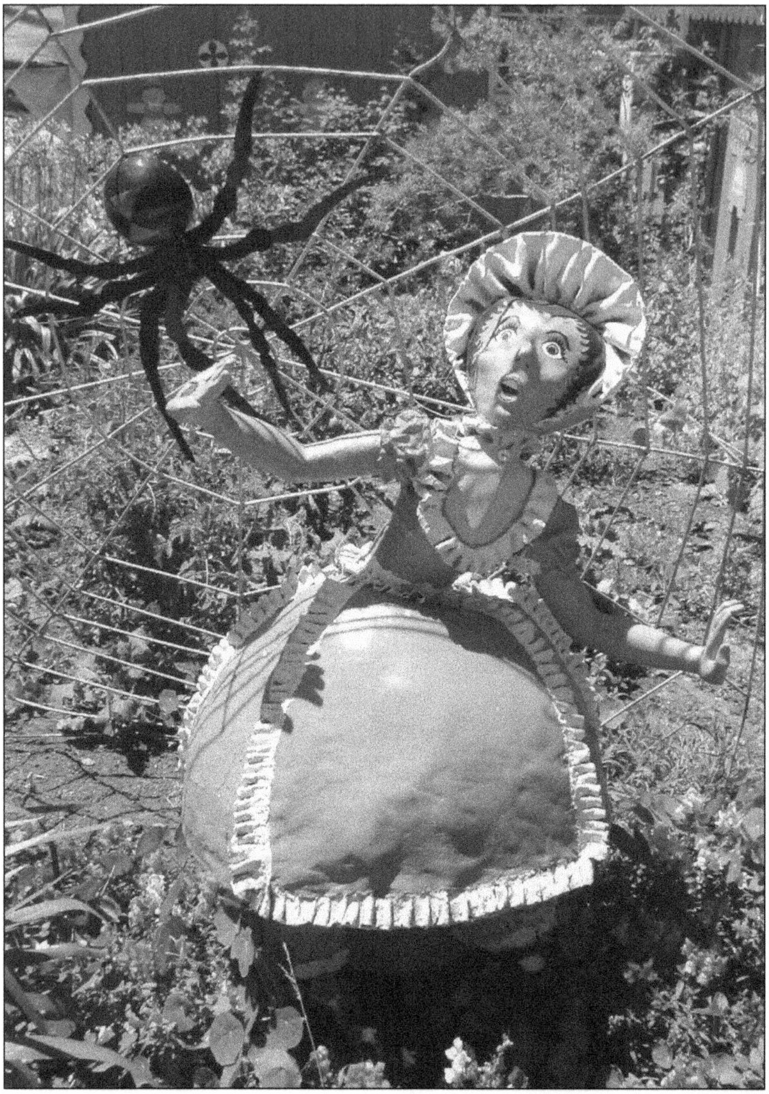

LITTLE MISS MUFFET, 2005. This nursery rhyme set has been popular since its introduction in 1953. Over the years, Miss Muffet has had many different spiders, from comical to menacing. The one pictured here was a gift from a Bay Area exterminating company that affixed the insects to the tops of its vans. The photograph below shows how Miss Muffet's garden was expanded in 2008 and turned into an organic display garden. On days when Fairyland is open to the public, families can enter the garden, help with planting, and harvest ripe fruits and vegetables. Fairyland's two full-time gardeners make sure the garden changes with the seasons.

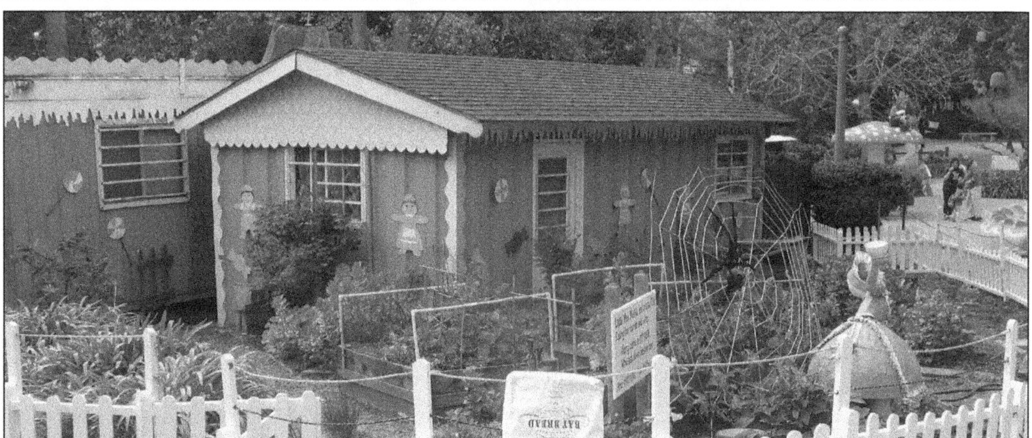

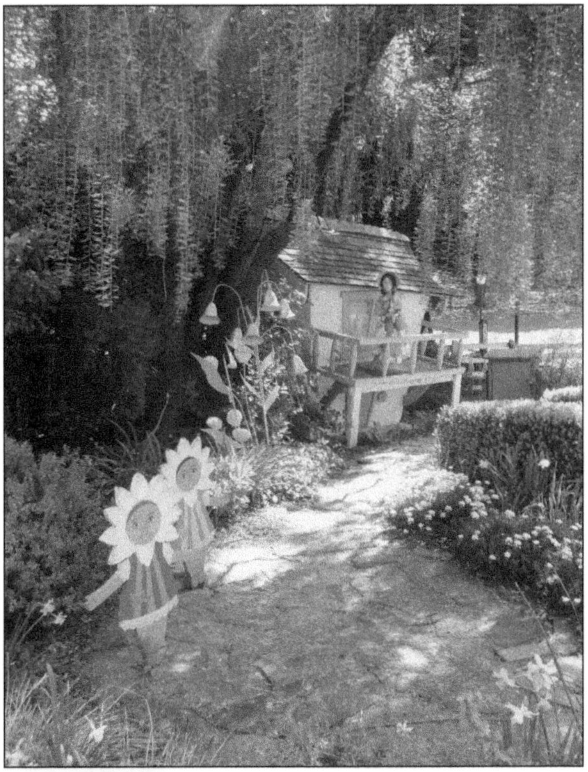

MARY, MARY, QUITE CONTRARY, 2000. How does her garden grow? Very well, thank you. This tranquil setting is home to the park's fabled gardener, Mistress Mary, who is accompanied by cockle shells and pretty maids "all in a row." The flower gardens were designed to teach young children about gardening and caring for nature.

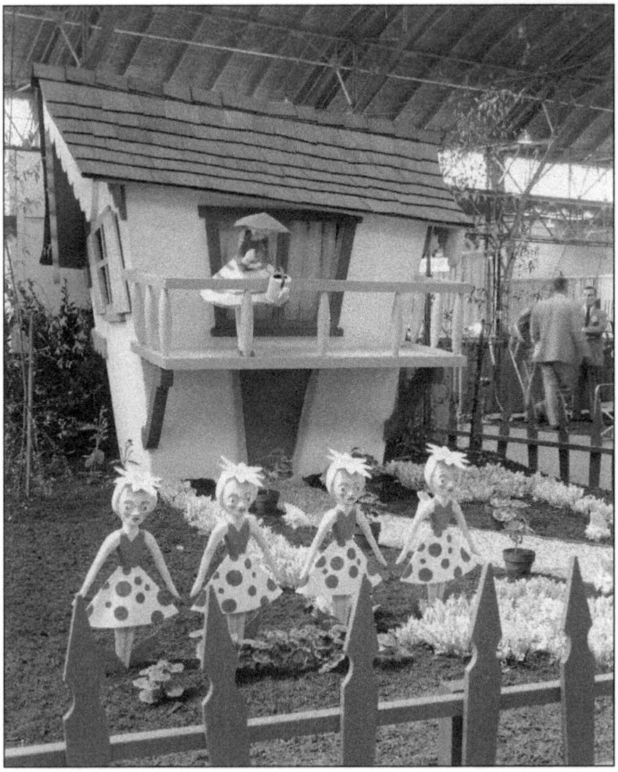

SAN FRANCISCO FLOWER SHOW, 1954. Many of Fairyland's sets began life as exhibits in local garden expositions such as the flower show—a clever scheme dreamed up by park founder Art Navlet that helped defray the cost of a set. After an exhibit closed, the set was rebuilt at the park. Garden expositions consisted of elaborate set pieces surrounded by the latest in floral design. Pictured is the Mary, Mary set in its original splendor.

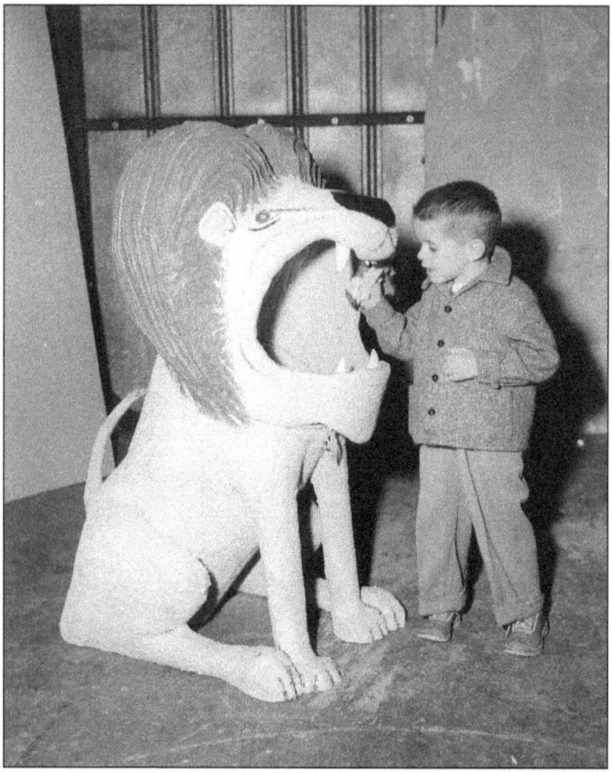

Louie the Lion Wastebasket, 1957. Even the trash bins in the park are distinctive and unusual. Besides Louie here, the park also had garbage cans that were shaped like kangaroos and pelicans. In the early 1970s, Louie was converted to a water fountain; now, fascinated children brave putting their heads into his mouth to get a drink.

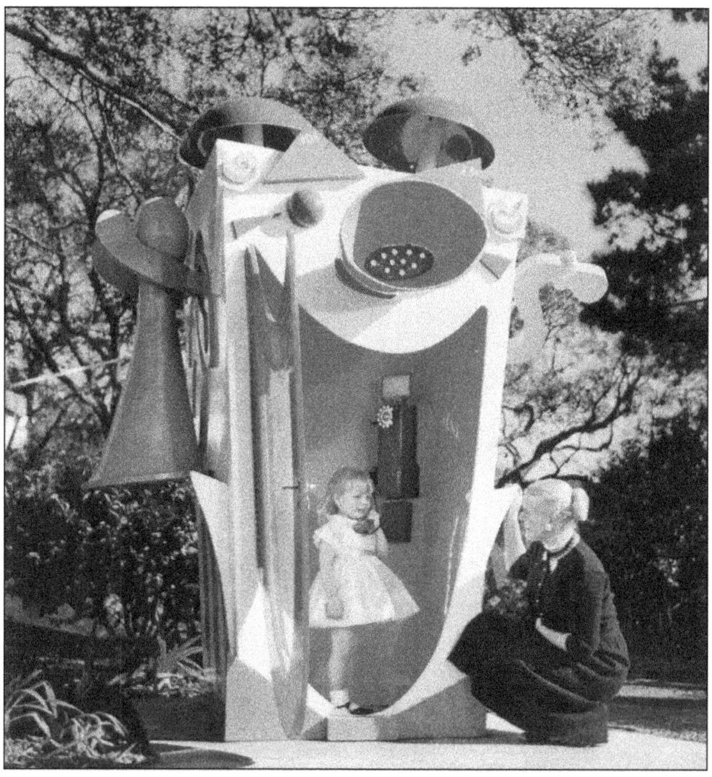

Clown Telephone Booth, 1956. Katherine Pederson helps her daughter Nelsine make a phone call. This one-of-a-kind phone booth, a gift from the Pacific Telephone and Telegraph Company, resembled a giant clown's face; the smile-shaped door could be closed for privacy. The phone company had an educational goal: to teach small children how to use a phone to call family members. The fixture was removed in 1975.

Fairyland Post Office, 1954. An attraction that particularly thrilled Walt Disney when he visited Fairyland was this tiny building, the smallest official post office in the nation. A postmistress was always on duty, and children could mail Fairyland postcards with a cancellation that read, "Fairyland Station Oakland, Calif." Here, queen Connie Quakenbush mails the first letter. The office was decommissioned in 1976 because of federal budget cuts.

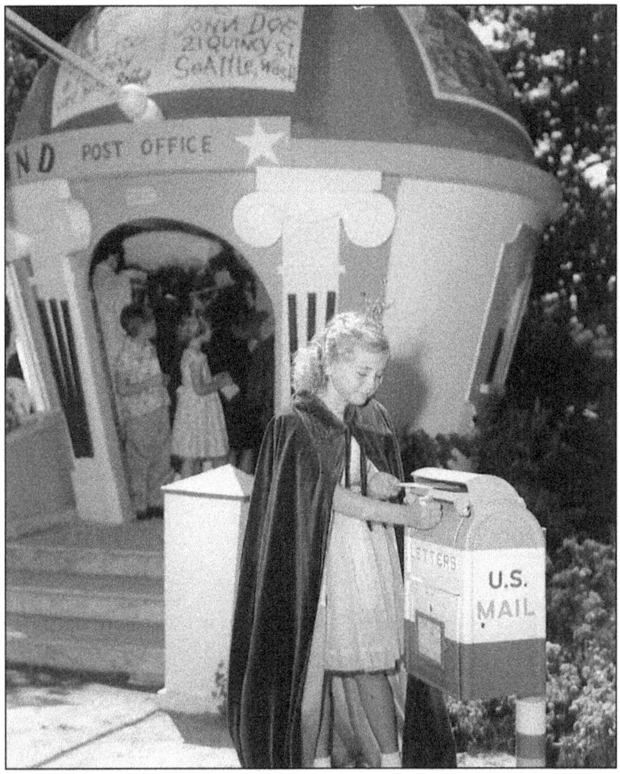

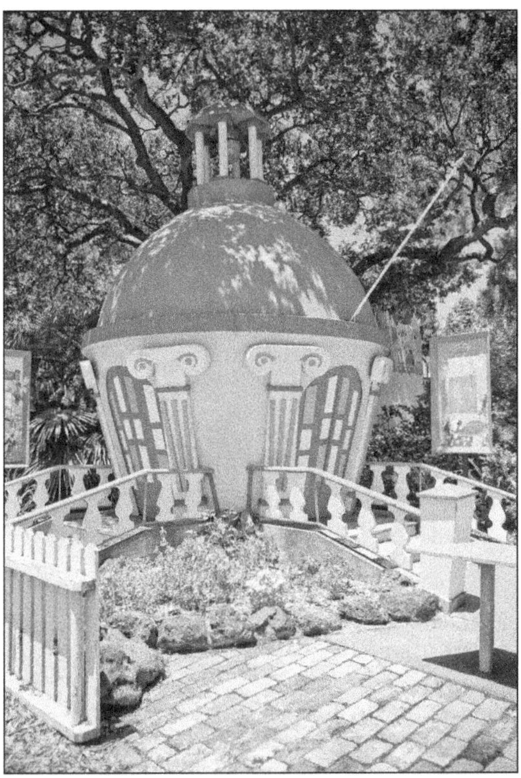

Fairyland Art Gallery, 2004. In 1976, the post office reopened as a children's arts and crafts gallery dedicated to Michael Richardson Kern, a talented child artist who was killed in an automobile accident. A second dedication was added in 2000, to Marilyn O'Hare, who had been the park's resident artist for 37 years. Each weekend, children take part in free arts activities led by local art teachers.

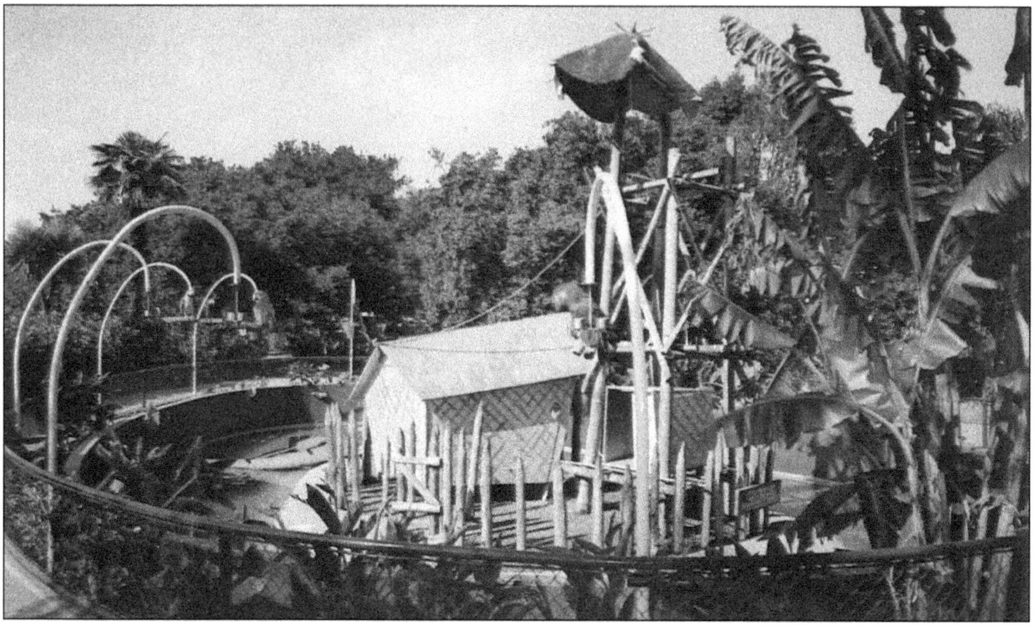

Robinson Crusoe Island, 1957. The Robinson Crusoe set was sponsored by Victor Bergeron, owner of the Bay Area's legendary Trader Vic restaurants. The island featured tropical parrots, crocodiles, and spider monkeys. The monkeys were infamous for escaping their island and visiting buildings in nearby downtown Oakland. This image is one of a set of 13 postcards photographed and released by William G. Murray.

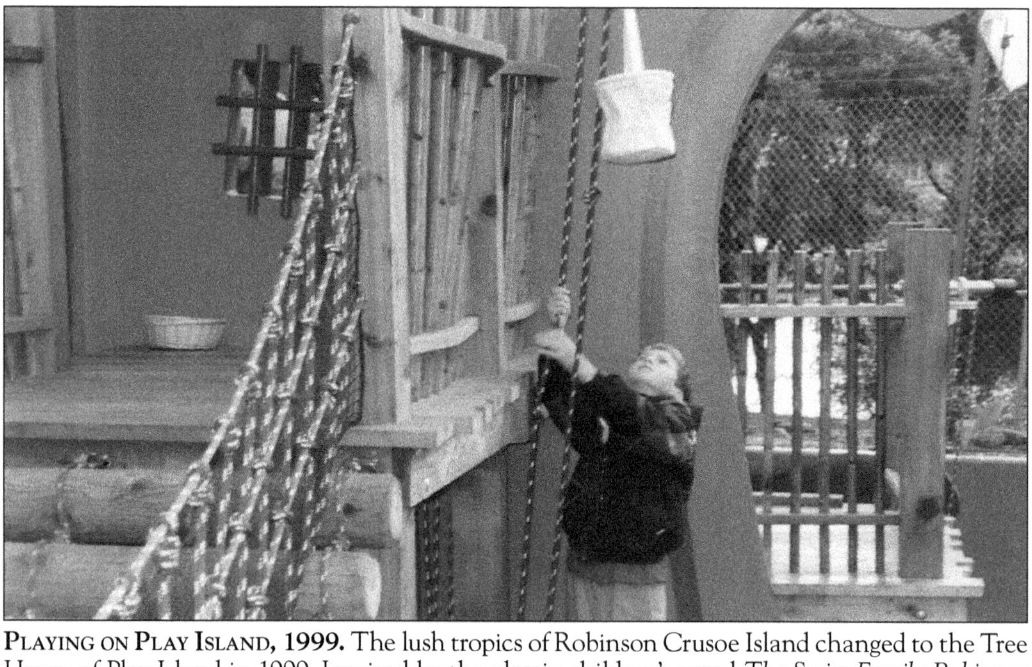

Playing on Play Island, 1999. The lush tropics of Robinson Crusoe Island changed to the Tree House of Play Island in 1999. Inspired by the classic children's novel *The Swiss Family Robinson* and conceived by Donald Sibbett, a noted contemporary designer of children's exhibits, the island features interactive exhibits that encourage imaginative play. The attraction is equipped with a treehouse, shipwreck, swinging rope bridges, musical instruments, and a sandy beach play area.

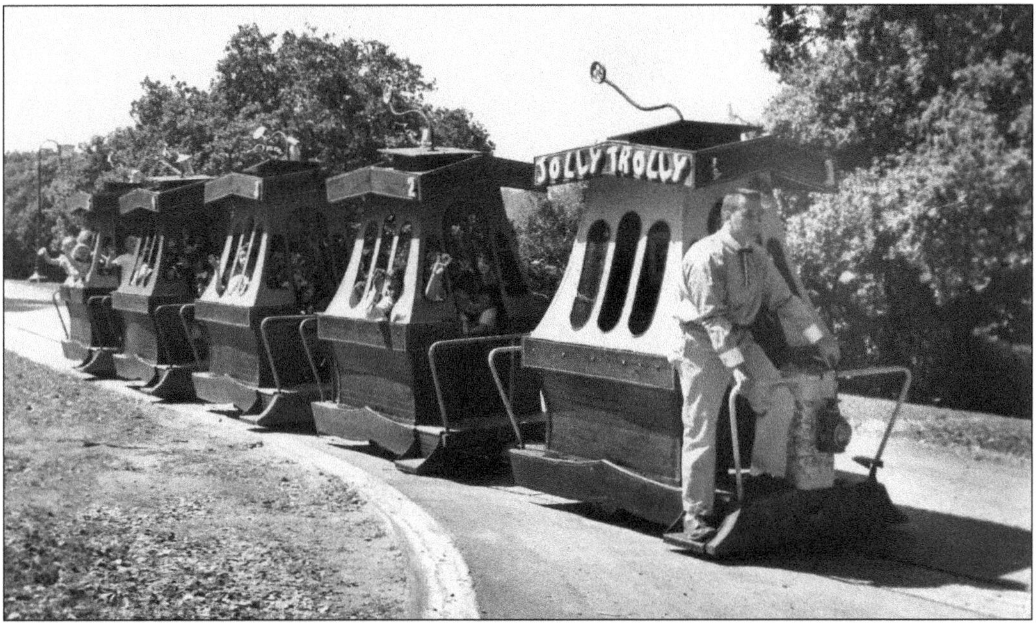

Jolly Trolly Train, 1956. Jack Francis, a retired Oakland motorcycle officer, and his partner Sam Dougherty built this unique little train that runs through Fairyland. The design is based on *Toonerville Folks*, a 1950 cartoon strip by Fontaine Fox. Billed as "a scenic ride for families under the oaks," the train traveled in Fairyland, as well as around and through Lakeside Park. Jack Francis is seen here traveling through Lakeside Park.

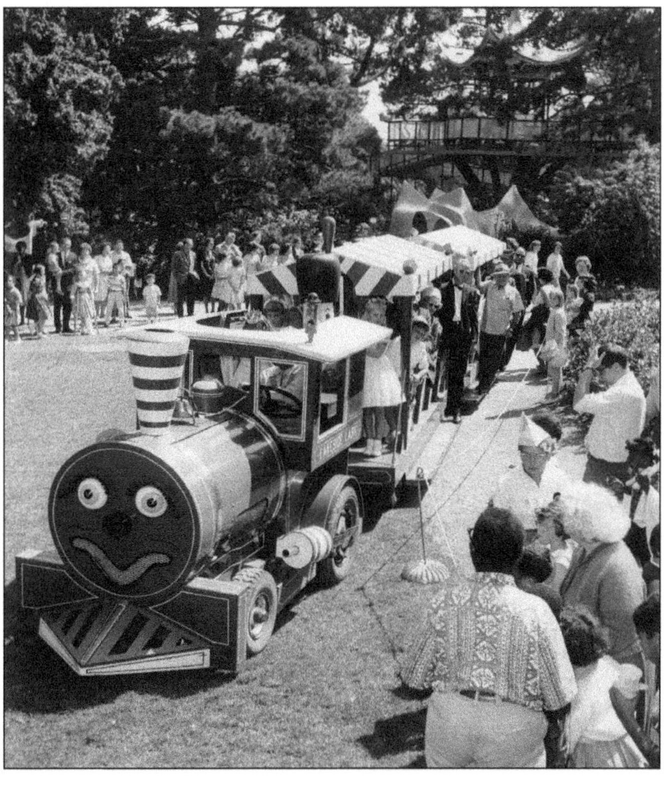

Lakeside Lark, 1974. In 1959, Jack Francis built the Lakeside Lark, a whimsical "toy" train with a smiling face and candy striping that traveled without a track. Built from a World War II plane-hauling tractor, the train had a large windup key and two passenger cars carrying up to 40 travelers. The train followed the pathways of Lakeside Park, taking visitors from Fairyland to their cars.

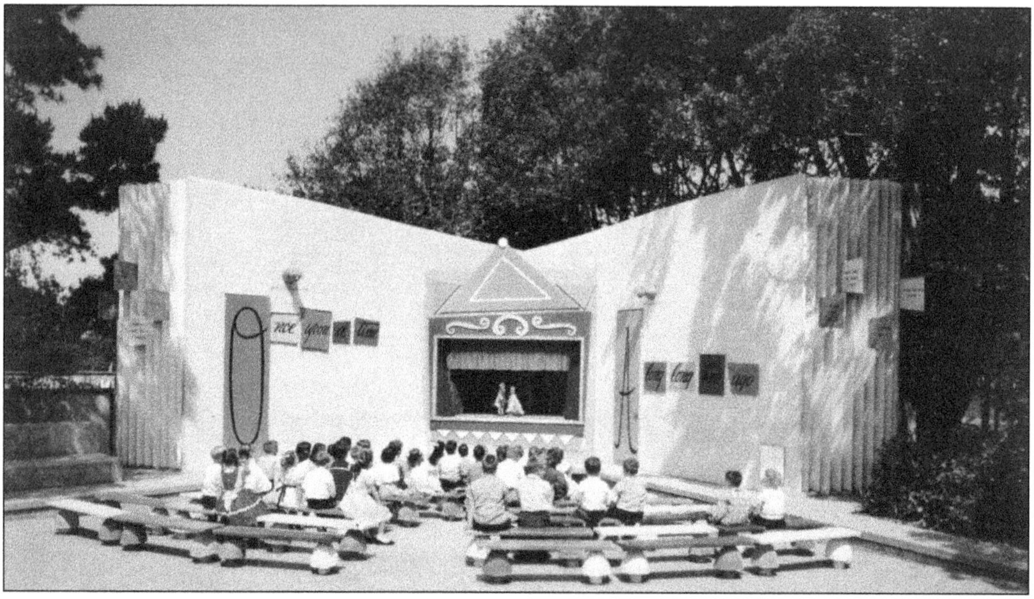

OPEN STORYBOOK PUPPET THEATER, 1957. One of the premier attractions in Children's Fairyland is the puppet theater. Opened in 1956, it is the oldest continuously operating professional puppet theater in the United States. A masterly design by William Russell Everritt allows puppeteers to perform with hand and rod puppets, as well as with marionettes. Fairyland has received an award from the Puppeteers of America for outstanding achievements in puppetry.

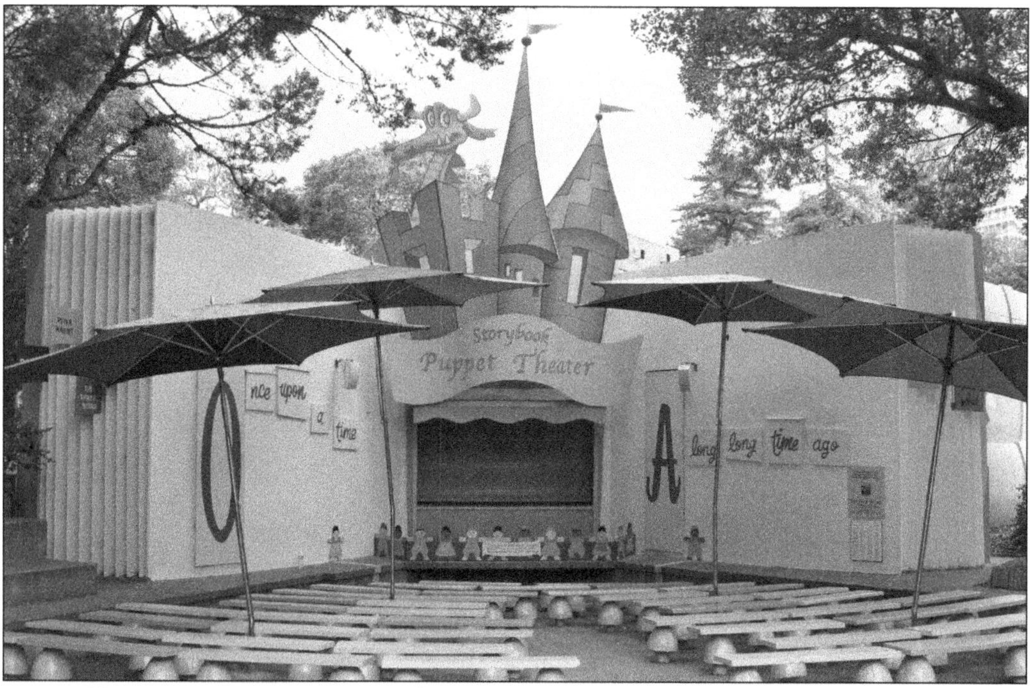

PUPPET THEATER REMODEL, 2006. For the puppet theater's 50th anniversary, Fairyland redesigned the original building. Additions include a storage area, a new workshop, and pop-up storybook cutouts that allow for a higher ceiling to create larger dramatic effects. Performances are still given three times a day—at 11:00 a.m., 2:00 p.m., and 4:00 p.m..

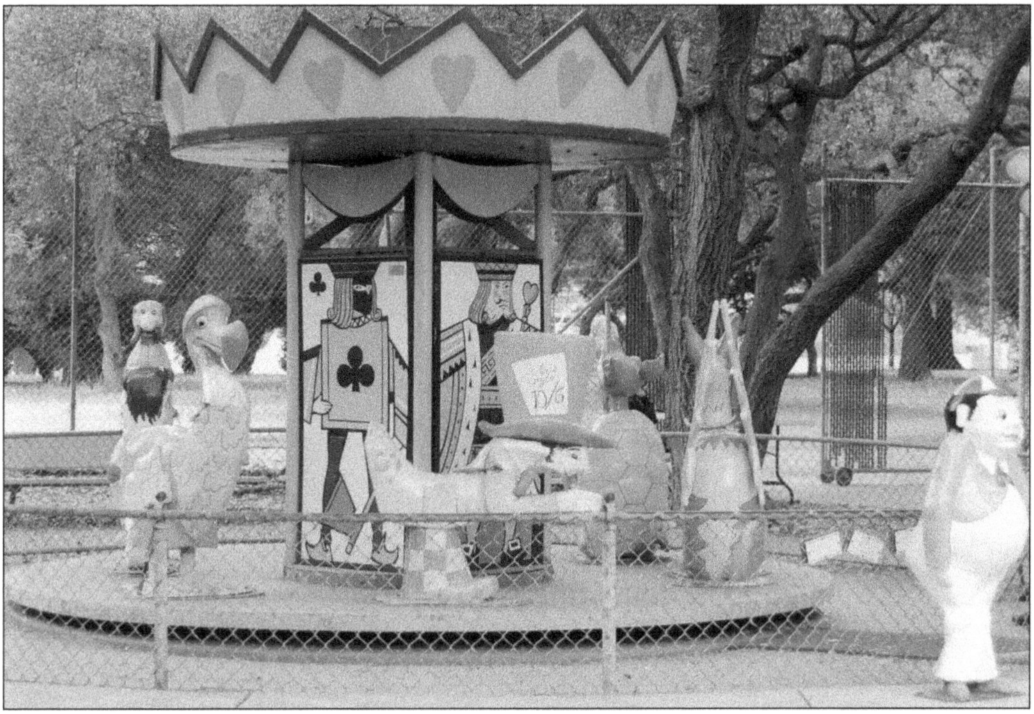

ALICE'S WONDER-GO-ROUND, 1999. This small merry-go-round came to Fairyland in 1956 after making an appearance, and a splash, at the San Francisco Spring Garden Show. The carousel features large "Alice in Wonderland" fiberglass figures built by Gordon Mortenson and painted porcelain panels of the Queen of Hearts and her cohorts. The set was designed by William Russell Everritt and brought to life by City of Oakland artists. To ride the carousel, children must weigh no more than 90 pounds; children under 36 inches tall must be accompanied by an adult.

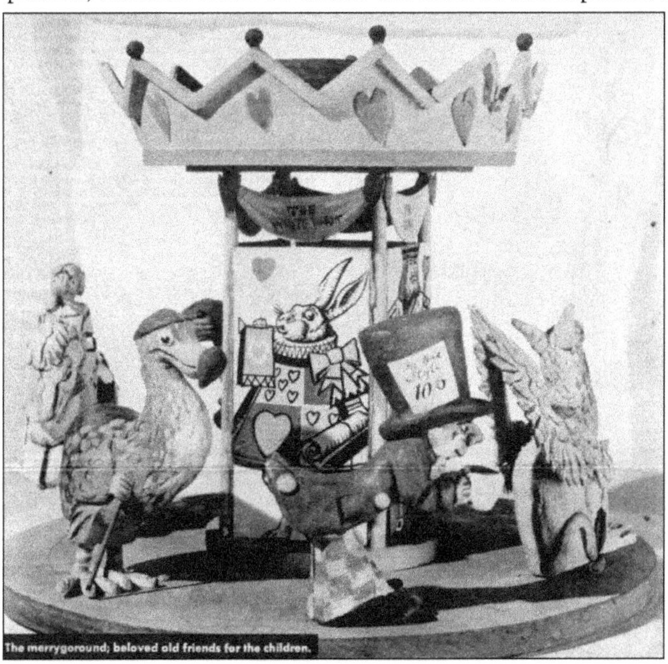

The merrygoround; beloved old friends for the children.

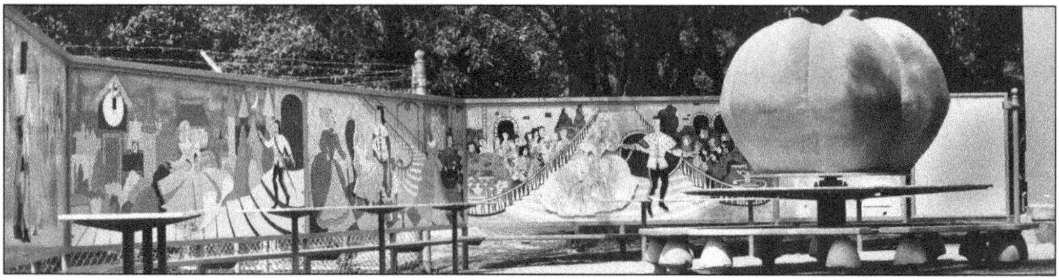

Cinderella Party Area, 1957. This regal setting for children's birthday parties originally featured a slide shaped like a glass slipper and a giant pumpkin serving table. When the fairy godmother host waved her magic cake server, the pumpkin was raised aloft and gifts were "magically" presented. Around the perimeter were murals depicting the Cinderella story painted by the advanced art class of Miramonte High School.

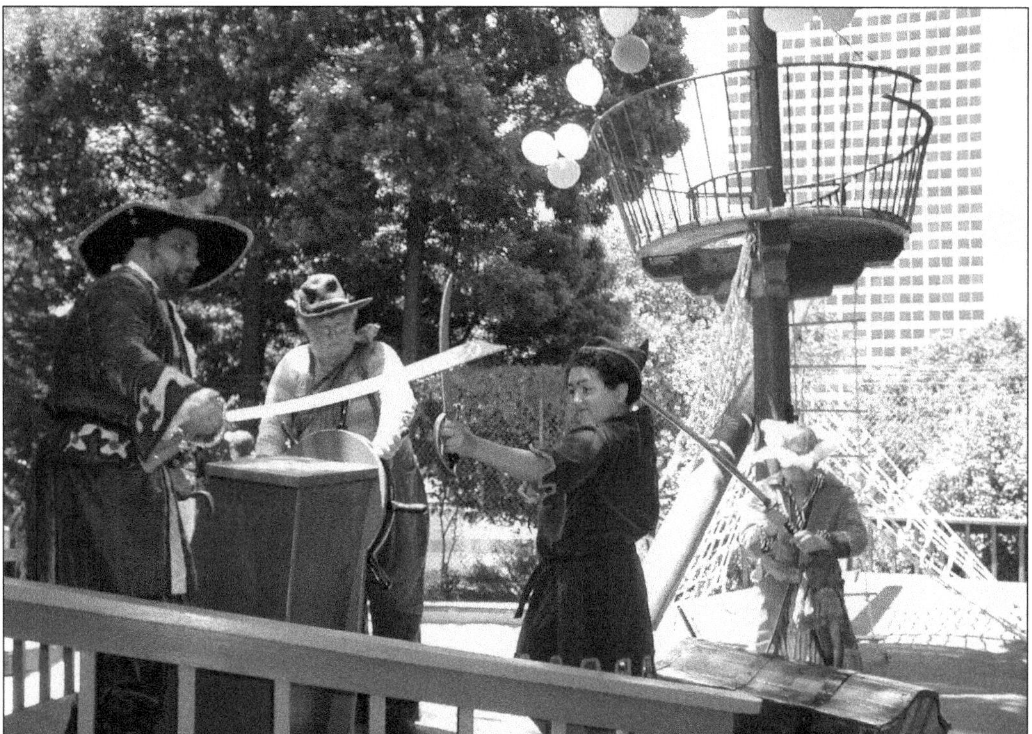

Peter Pan Pirate Ship, 2000. In 1969, Captain Hook sailed his ship, the *Jolly Roger*, to Oakland. The ship includes a steering wheel, ropes to climb on, and a crow's nest; it is set in sand for a soft landing after walking the plank. Here, Carl LaRue (Hook) and Jacob Basri (Pan) fight while Nate Shugars (Smee) navigates.

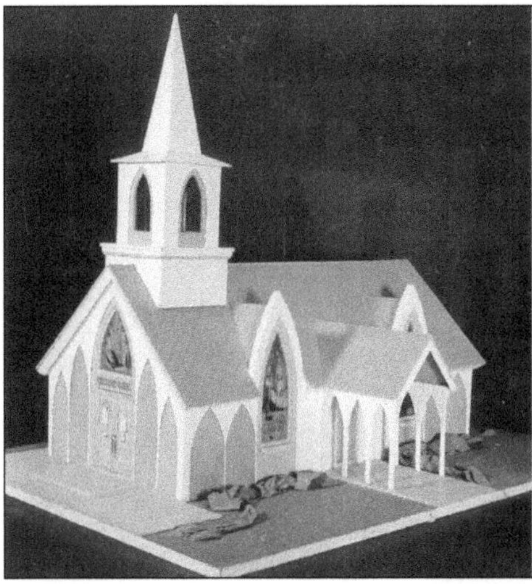

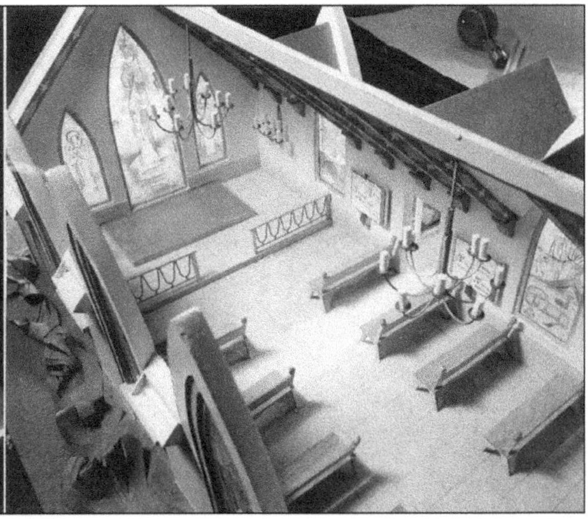

CHILDREN'S CHAPEL OF PEACE, 1970. This miniature chapel features stained-glass windows designed by children, as well as a pipe organ specially made to accommodate a child's fingers. Its construction was sponsored by many civic organizations; its design is one of William Russell Everritt's most spectacular. At its dedication in 1957, the chapel was blessed by a priest, a minister, and a rabbi. Today, it provides a quiet spot for rest and reflection. It has also been used for weddings and wedding vow renewals; during the December Fairy Winterland festivities, it is where Santa Claus welcomes children.

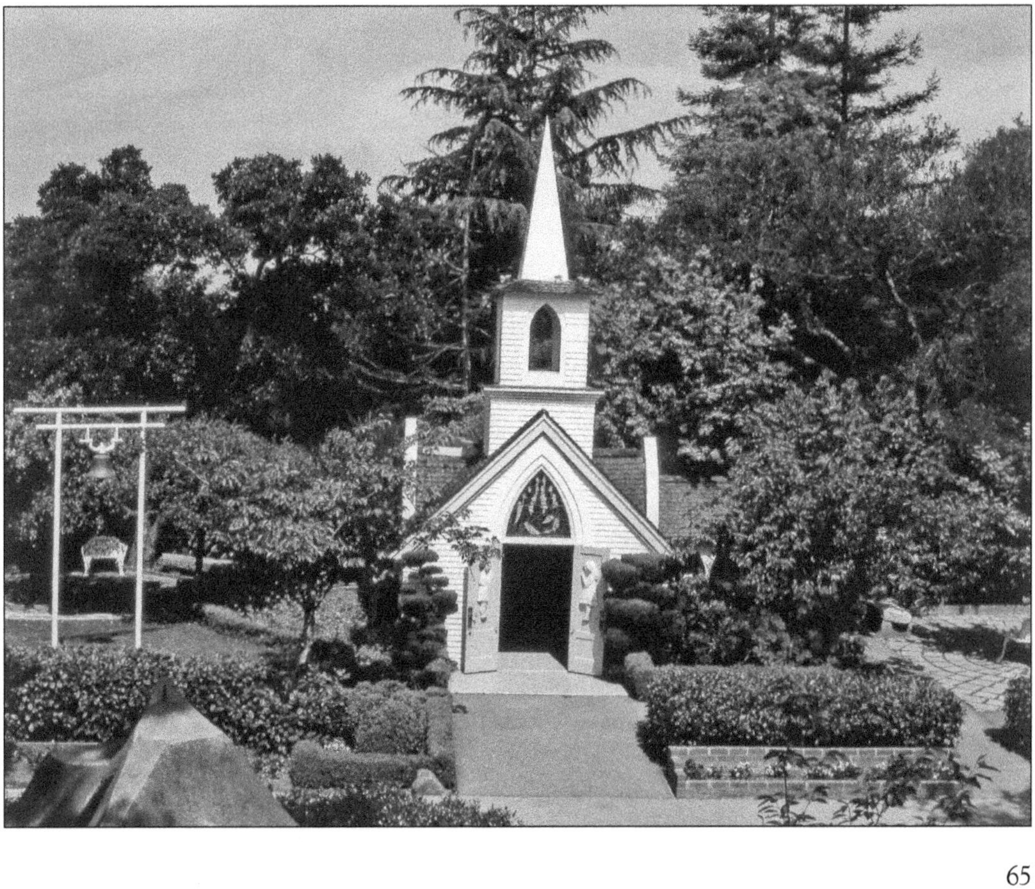

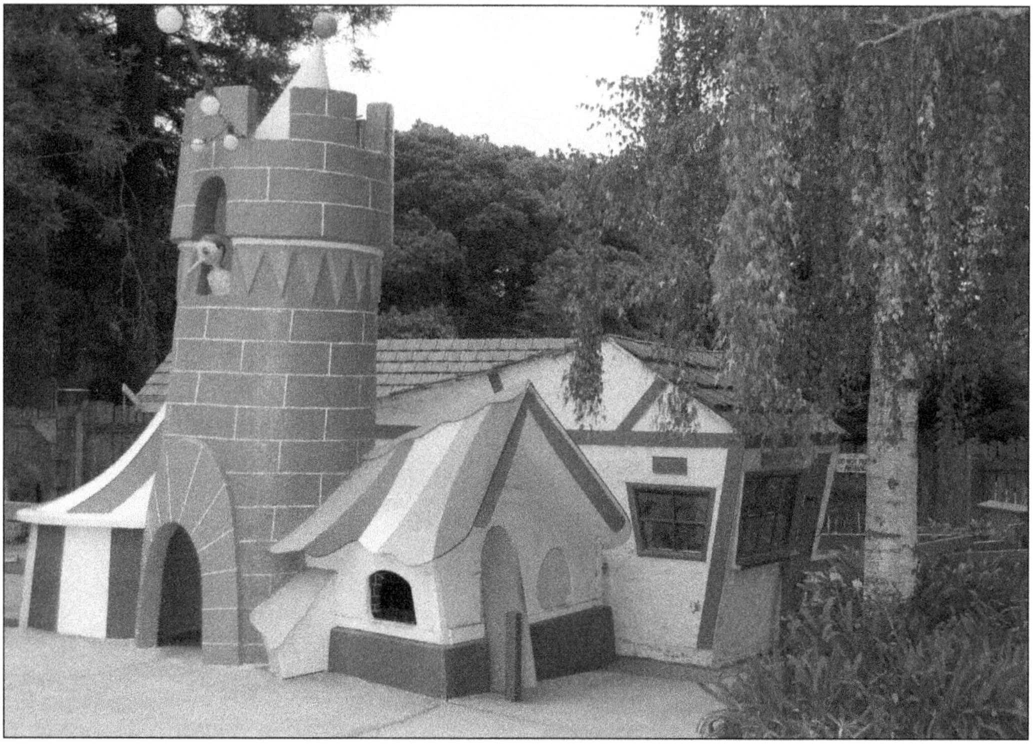

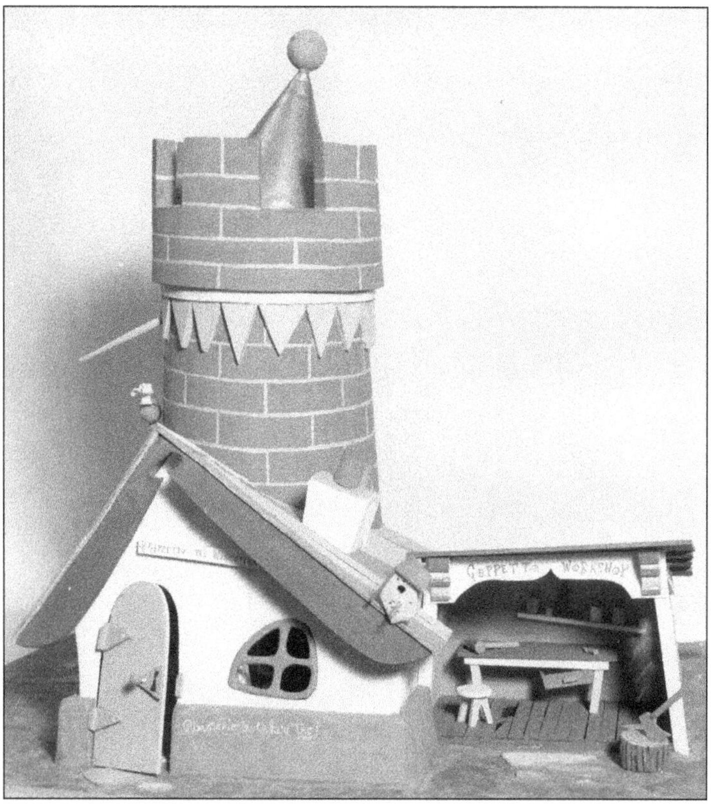

PINOCCHIO'S CASTLE, 2000. The East Bay Italian American Federation sponsored this depiction of the classic Pinocchio story. The buildings—one of Fairyland's original sets—feature a detailed workshop of Geppetto the woodcarver and the castle of the Blue Fairy (called the Fairy with the Turquoise Hair in *The Adventures of Pinocchio*, the original 1883 tale by Carlo Collodi). Behind the set was the circus tent home of two live burros representing the naughty boys of the tale who had been transformed into donkeys. William Russell Everritt's 1956 model is simple and charming, with Pinocchio's long nose prominent in the tower.

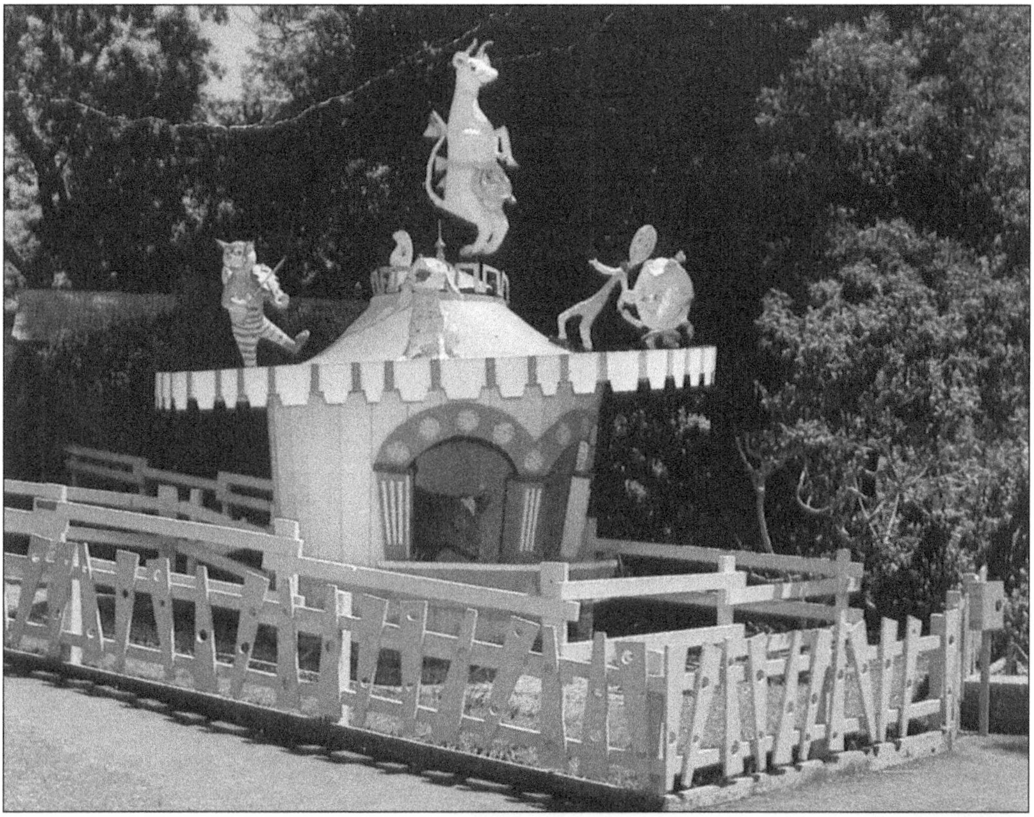

Hey Diddle, Diddle, 1972. Inspired by the nursery rhyme, this barn is where baby calves and other livestock lived. Daily bottle feedings with young heifers were crowd pleasers; the cow figure, which jumps over the revolving moon, was also a big hit. This is one of 13 very rare postcards, all of which were photographed by Mike Roberts of Berkeley.

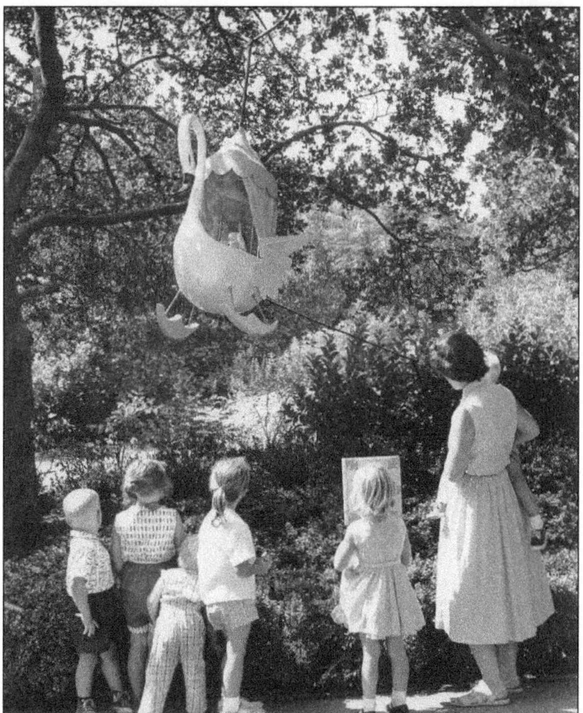

Rock-a-Bye Baby, 1959. The Gerber Products Company, maker of baby foods, presented the park with this creative lullaby set. Suspended in the treetops, a baby rocks back and forth in a swan cradle. Nursery rhymes sometimes do come true: In 2006, the wind did blow, the cradle did rock, and down came one of the trees—cradle and all.

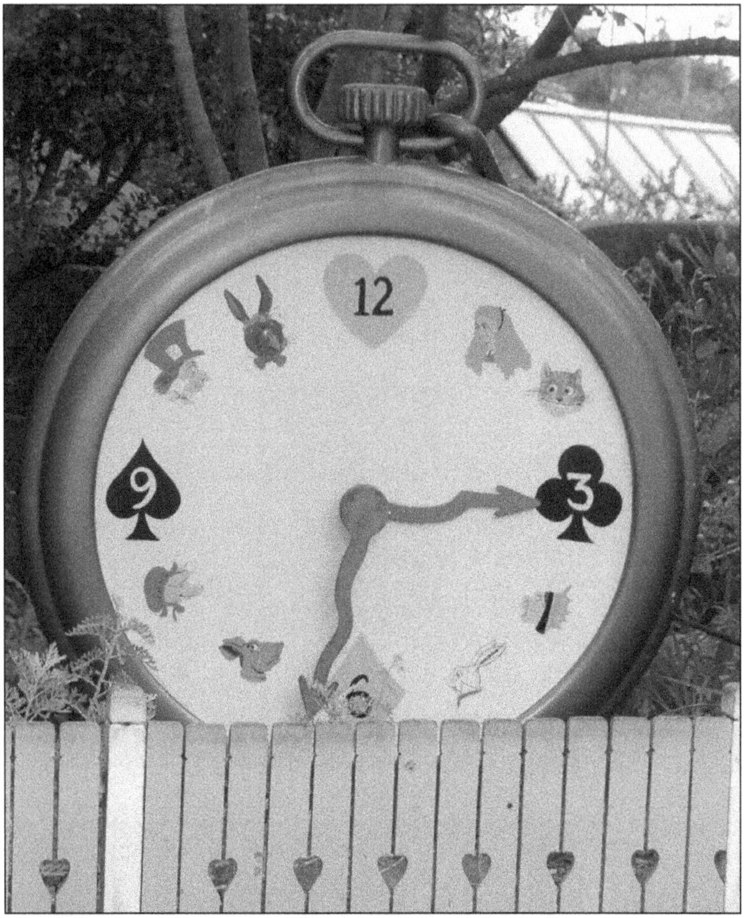

Alice in Wonderland Tunnel, 1989. Fairyland's first interactive play set, the Alice in Wonderland Tunnel, opened in 1962. The White Rabbit's giant pocket watch, which runs backward, stands by the entrance to his rabbit hole. Like Alice, children run down the tunnel and encounter fiberglass figures from many of Alice's adventures. At the end, they must find their way back through a card-man maze. One proposed feature that never made it into the final design was an array of cameras mounted inside the tunnel to allow parents to monitor their children from outside. The fiberglass figures were created by Gordon Mortenson.

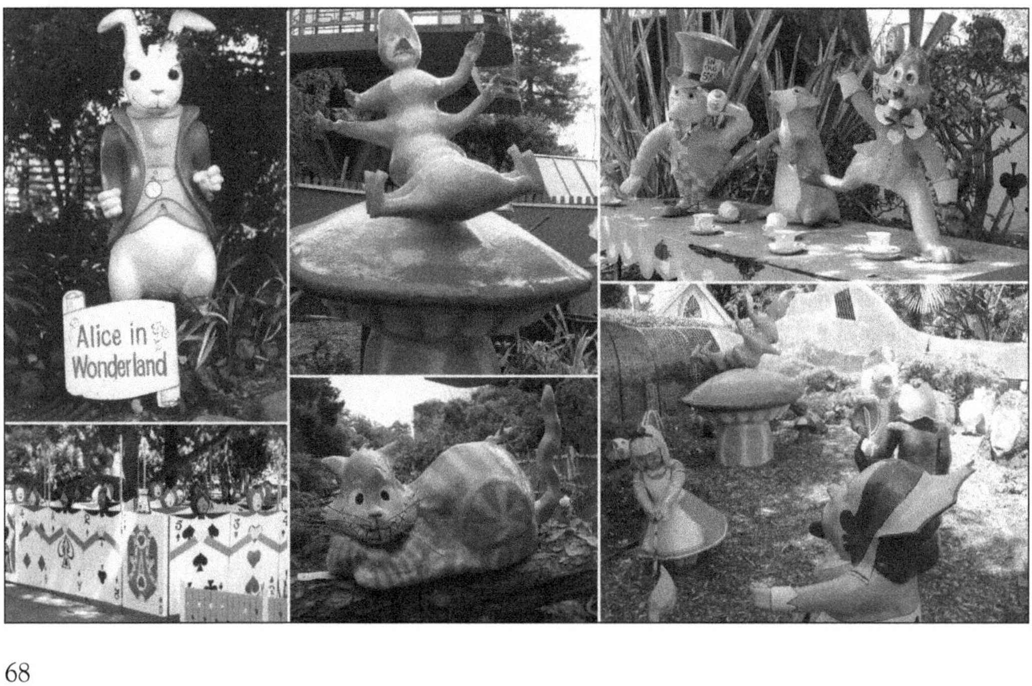

Five

Entertainment Everywhere

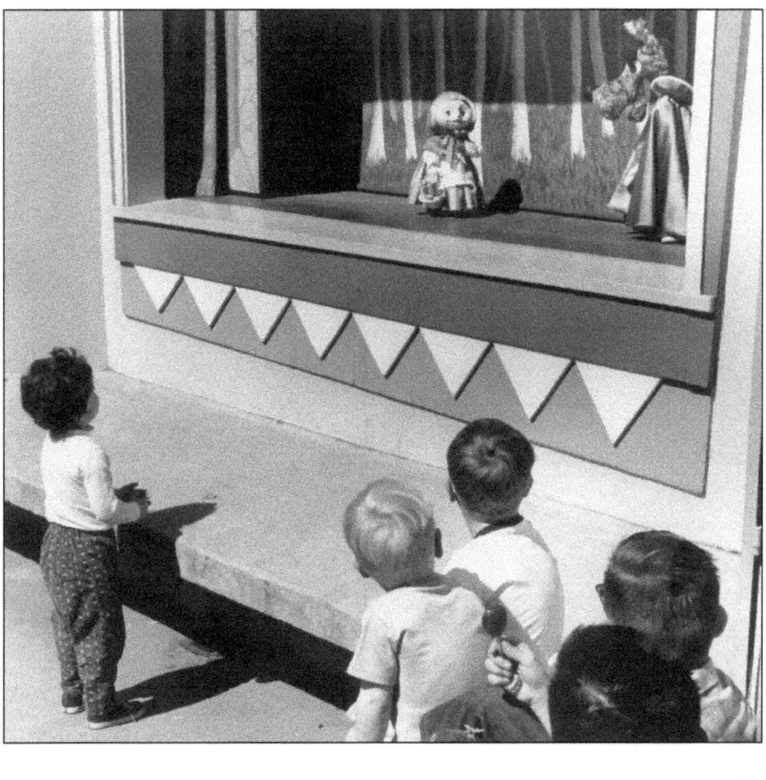

It Is Puppet Show Time!, 1958. From the beginning, Fairyland's creators insisted that puppetry was a good way to teach literacy. Fairyland's puppet theater excels at producing puppet shows based on fairy tales from around the world that respect the authenticity of each culture. In the photograph, toddlers are spellbound by the Hayward Marionettes' production of *Red Riding Hood*. The marionettes were created by Tony Urbano.

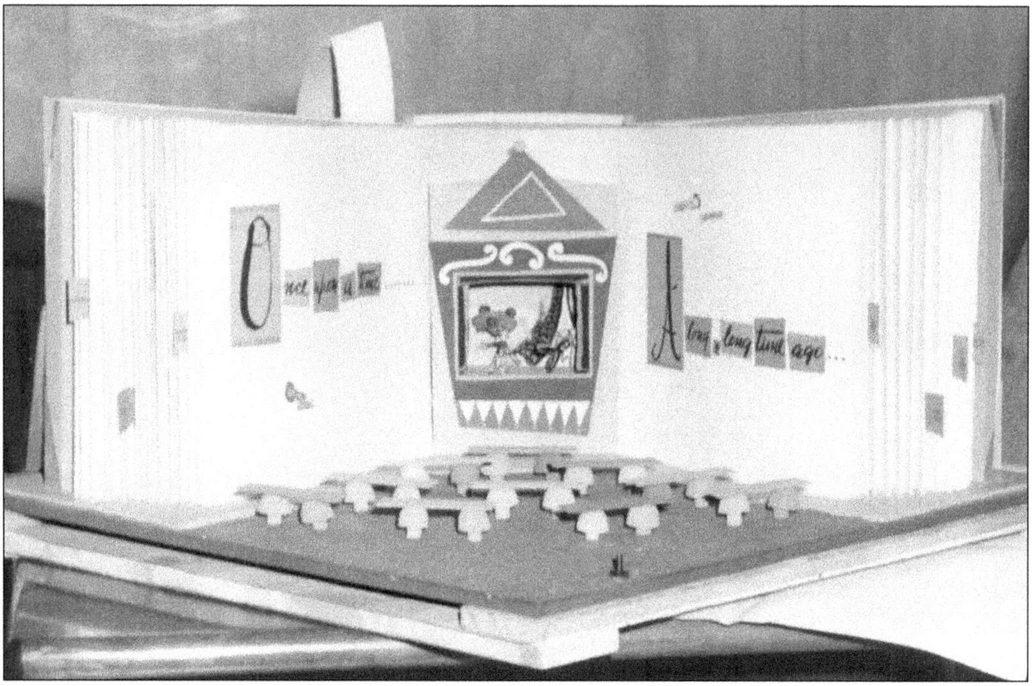

Model of Storybook Puppet Theater, 1954. William Everritt's original design for the Storybook Puppet Theater included signs on the sides of the building that opened like doors so that puppets could engage the audience from all sides. The theater was conceived with the help of professional Bay Area puppeteers, whom Everritt had asked to describe their dream theater. The theater can comfortably seat an audience of 200 children and adults.

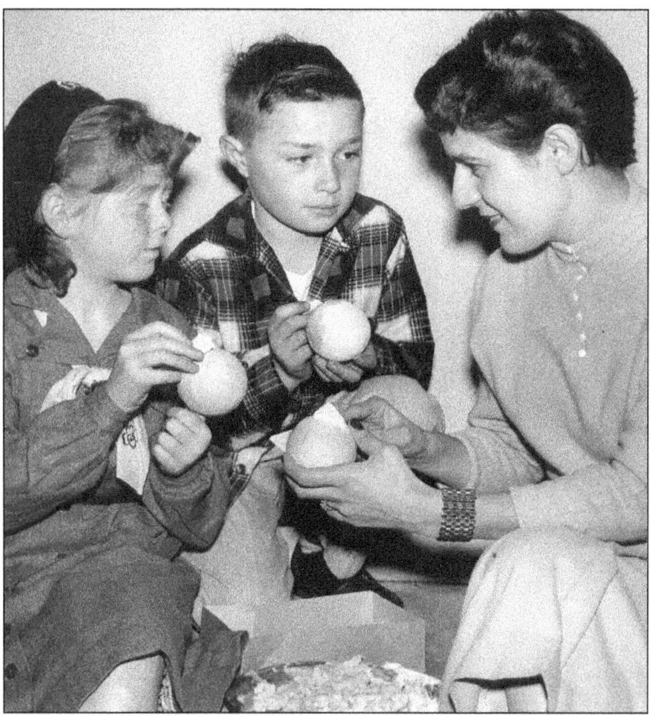

Dorothy Hayward Puppet Class, 1956. Besides performing and creating puppet shows from popular tales, the duties of the theater director included teaching. In this photograph, the park's first puppet director, Dorothy Hayward, teaches Katy Powers and Edgar Grant how to make simple hand puppets. It is the park's philosophy that if children are inspired by what they see, they should be able to touch it and become engaged with it.

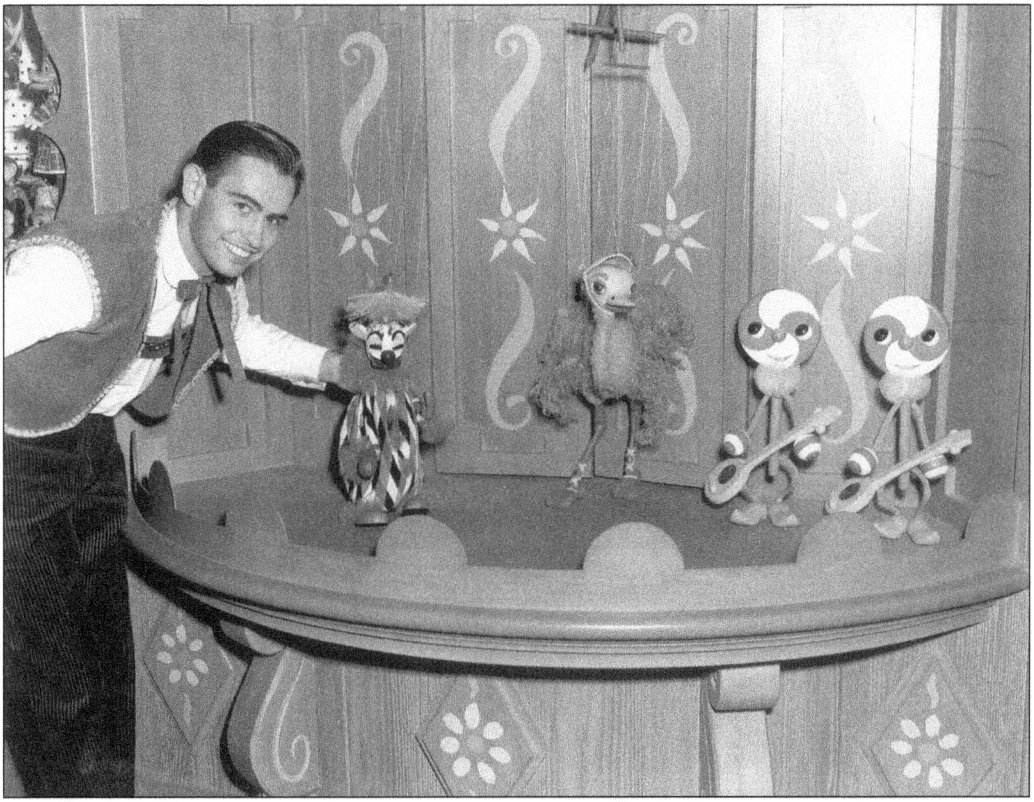

BOB MILLS AT DISNEYLAND, 1958. Bob Mills, a designer of puppets at Fairyland, was hired by Walt Disney to perform his magic at Disneyland's Tinker Bell Toy Shoppe. He did so for four and a half years, from 1957 to 1961, before later becoming a professional makeup artist in Hollywood for stars such as Glenn Close and Michael Keaton. (Courtesy of Bob Mills.)

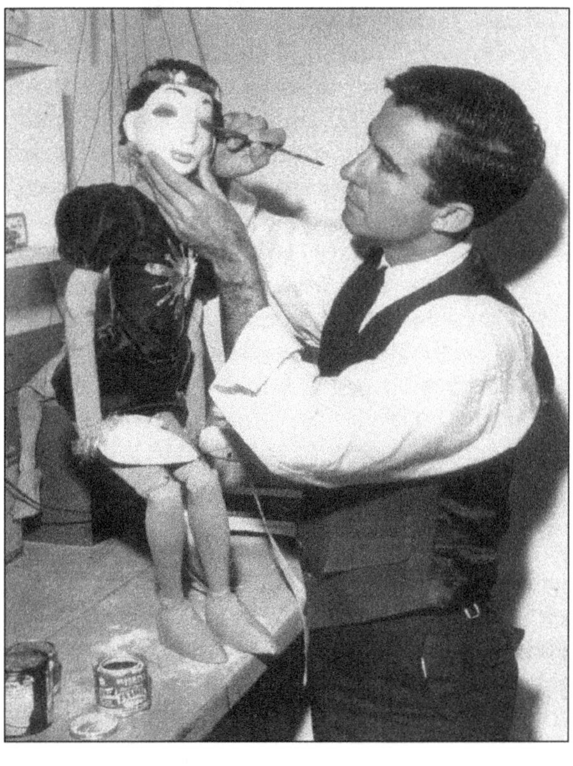

TONY URBANO IN THEATER WORKSHOP, 1959. Fairyland's second puppet director was Tony Urbano. He was also an accomplished singer, actor, and artist and soon was lured away to Hollywood. He is seen here working on a giant puppet for a symphony concert production of Ravel's *Mother Goose Suite*. Tony Urbano's puppets can be found in numerous films, including *Flight of the Navigator*, *Short Circuit 1*, *Short Circuit 2*, and *Men in Black*.

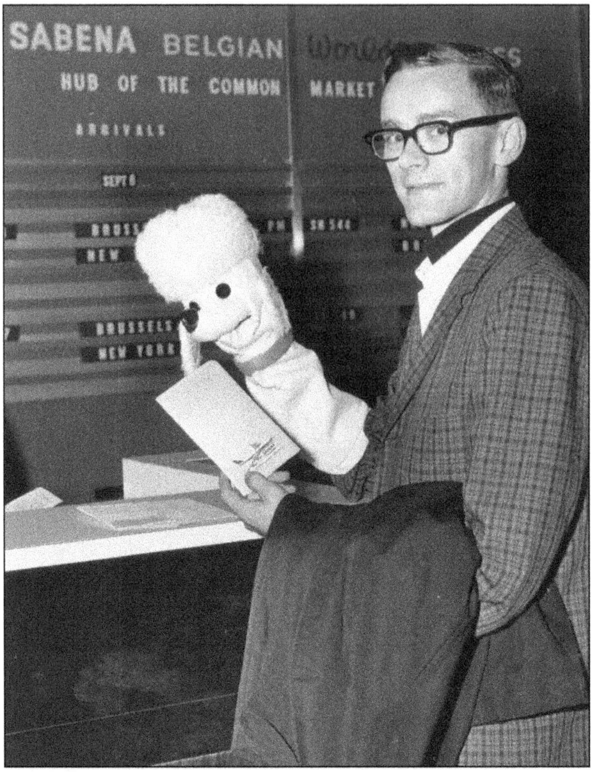

As Puppets Will Travel, 1964. Luman Coad, the park's third puppet director, is seen departing for Romania, where his Fairyland production of *A Dog's Tail* was staged at an international puppet festival. The show, entirely mimed to music, took first-place honors. Now a premier puppeteer in Canada, Coad also directs Charlemagne Press, a specialty publisher of puppetry books.

Bert at Fairyland, 1970. Lewis Mahlmann (center), Fairyland's fourth puppet director, poses with Muppet creator Frank Oz and Bert, a Sesame Street Muppet. Oz received his training at Fairyland when he was in his early teens. Mahlmann, an internationally known puppeteer, is recognized for designing puppet ballets, operas, and concert pieces for children. Twice president of the Puppeteers of America, he published five books of Fairyland puppet plays.

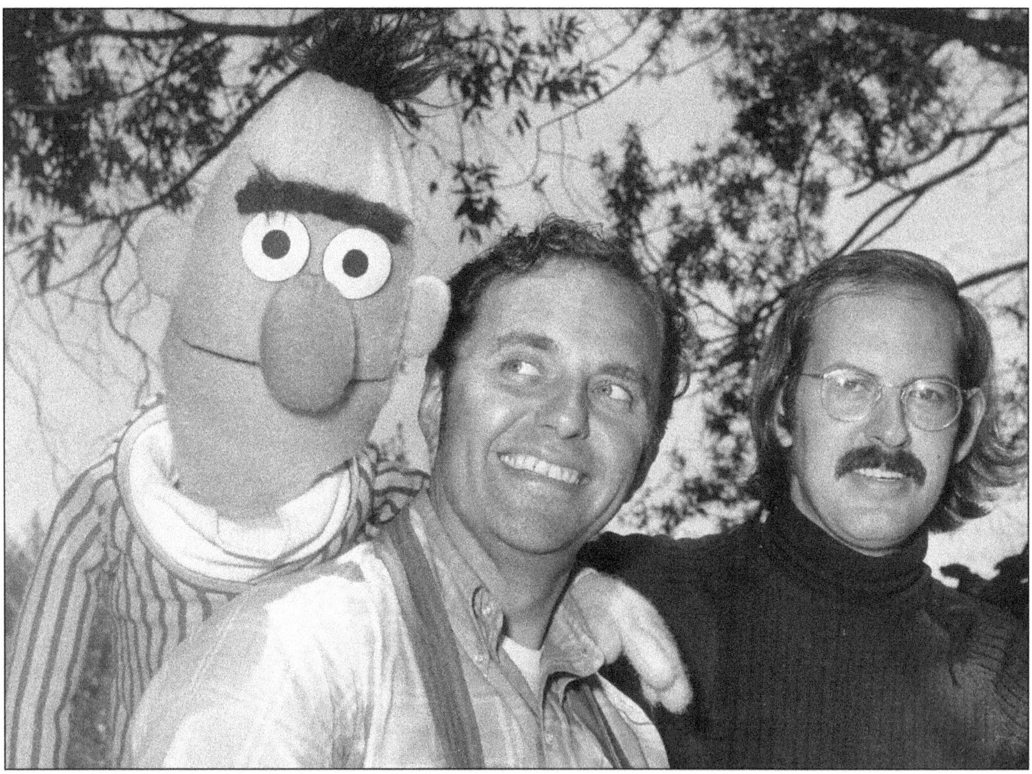

PUPPET THEATER BACKSTAGE, 2011. Randal Metz, Fairyland's fifth puppet director, manipulates the Reluctant Dragon. Metz apprenticed with Lewis Mahlmann as a child, and they eventually became business partners at Fairyland. In his career, Metz has been puppeteer at the Oakland Zoo and with circuses and has helped build puppets for Disneyland. Between them, Mahlmann and Metz have produced shows at Fairyland for over 50 years, or three generations.

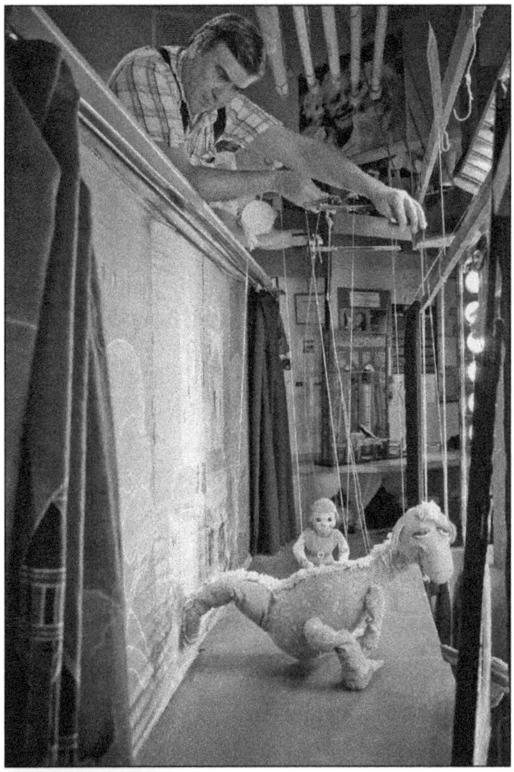

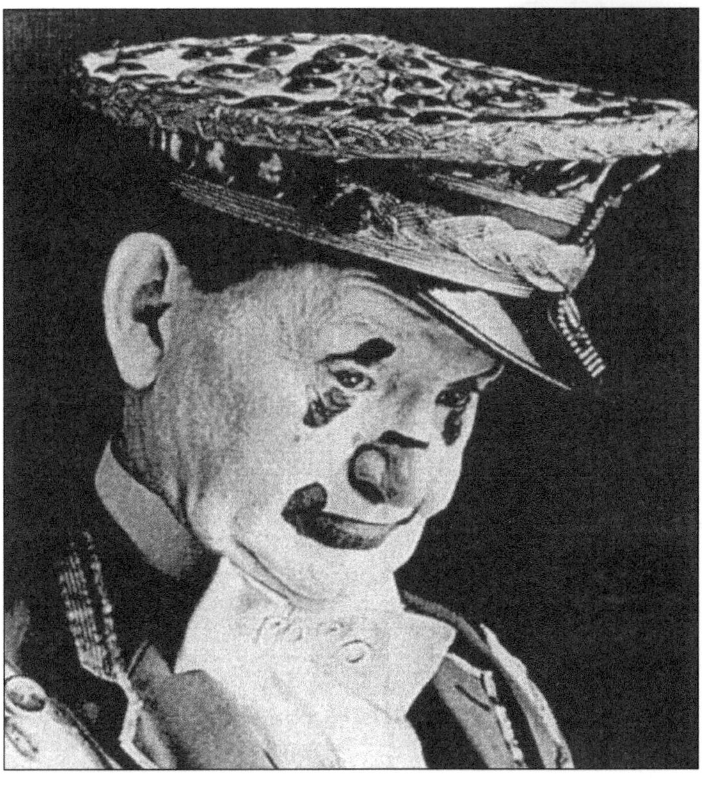

POPO THE CLOWN, 1955. For 23 years, Charles R. DeBathe, better known as PoPo, clowned for the children of Oakland. A veteran of medicine shows, circuses, showboats, vaudeville, and burlesque, PoPo enjoyed an 81-year career as an entertainer. He also traveled the world as an ambassador for Fairyland and UNICEF. This publicity photograph was taken by the renowned American photographer Ansel Adams.

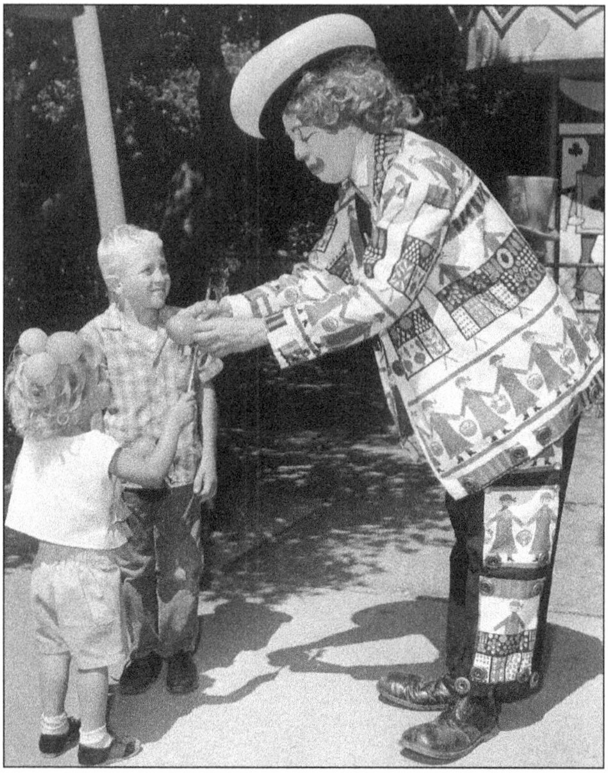

LoLo Gets in the Act, 1971. When PoPo was away from the park, his friend Adonna Houston clowned for the children as LoLo. Her father, Sam J. Houston, owned a small circus where PoPo sometimes clowned and performed with trained monkeys. After a short tour of the vaudeville circuit, PoPo and LoLo retired and settled in Oakland.

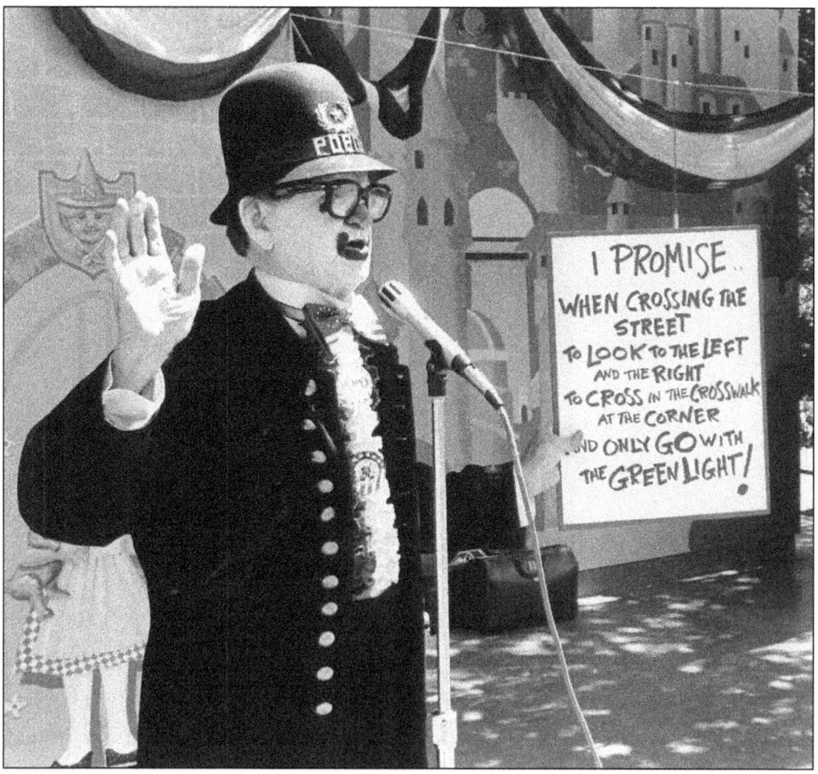

Safety First, 1975. Besides doing a clown show twice a day at the puppet theater, PoPo ran a program for traffic safety. Here he is teaching kids to cross the street safely. PoPo was also master of ceremonies for two annual events—Magic Day and Dairy Day. The latter featured a six-legged dancing cow.

Circus Hall of Fame, 1973. In honor of his long circus career, the Barnum Circus Hall of Fame Museum re-created PoPo's traveling clown dressing room and installed a lifelike wax figure. Before his career was over, people in 83 countries, 199 cities, and dozens of small islands had heard of Count PoPo DeBathe, Fairyland's "Ambassador of Fun."

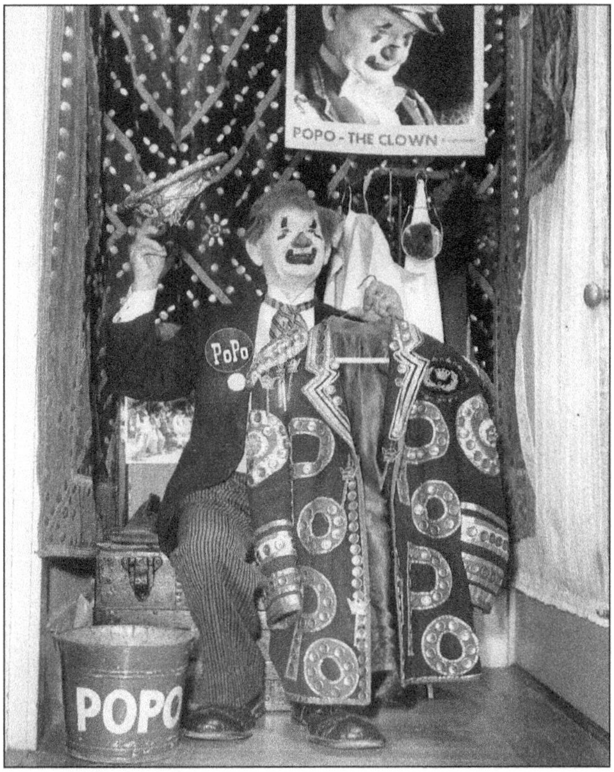

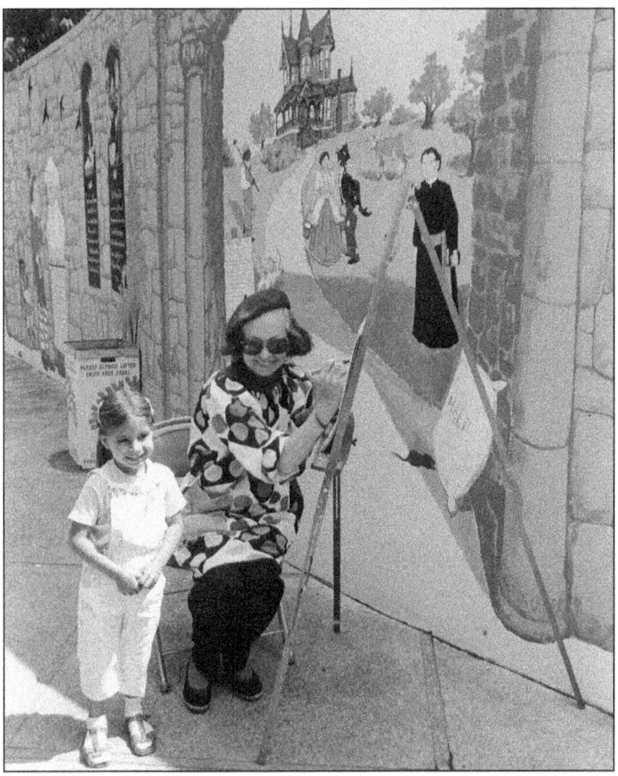

Art in the Park, 1980s. For 37 years, Marilyn O'Hare, Fairyland's artist-in-residence, conducted free weekly art contests for children, cosponsored by the Oakland Art Association. The park awarded prizes to young artists in three age groups. O'Hare's painted storybook murals can still be found throughout Fairyland.

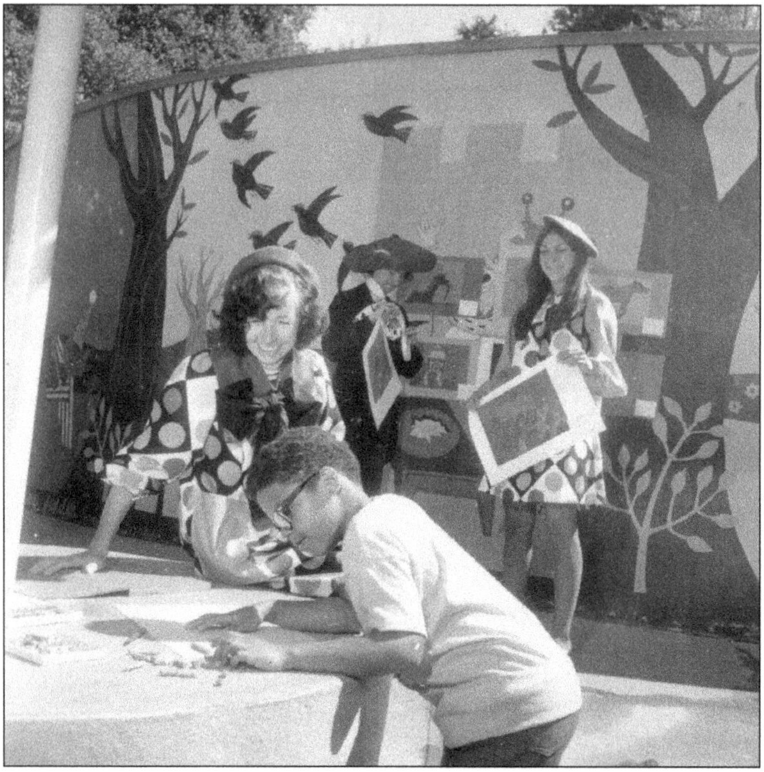

ART CONTESTS EVERY WEEK, 1973. Child artist and frequent entrant Michael Richardson Kern, a regular participant in Marilyn O'Hare's art contests, adds finishing touches to his canvas. Marilyn and her art crew, usually consisting of her five children, volunteered at the park to raise young visitors' artistic awareness. The Children's Arts and Crafts Center is dedicated to O'Hare and Kern.

FAIRYLAND HAS "PERSONALITIES," 1961. The Fairyland Personalities, established in 1960, are children ages eight to ten who volunteer to portray storybook characters in the park, to the delight of younger visitors. Each of the children in the photograph competed to win the roles he or she is playing, from Alice in Wonderland to Red Riding Hood. The program teaches life skills that helped the children excel in later life.

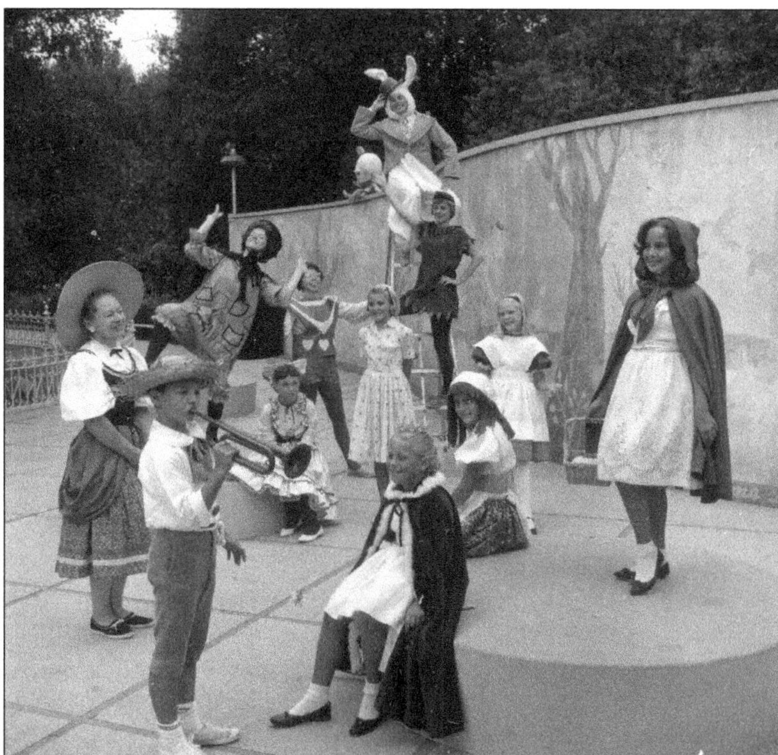

Passing on a Dynasty, 1972. From the park's inception until 1980, one lucky girl was chosen to be queen of Fairyland for a year, along with one or two princesses. These royals, along with other Fairyland Personalities, represented the park at fairs, parades, city galas, and television appearances. Here, queen Renee Dyson crowns her successor, Kathy Porter.

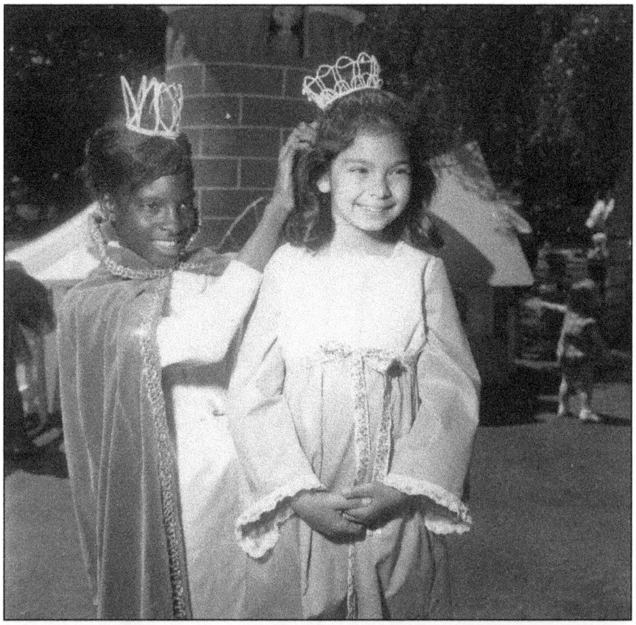

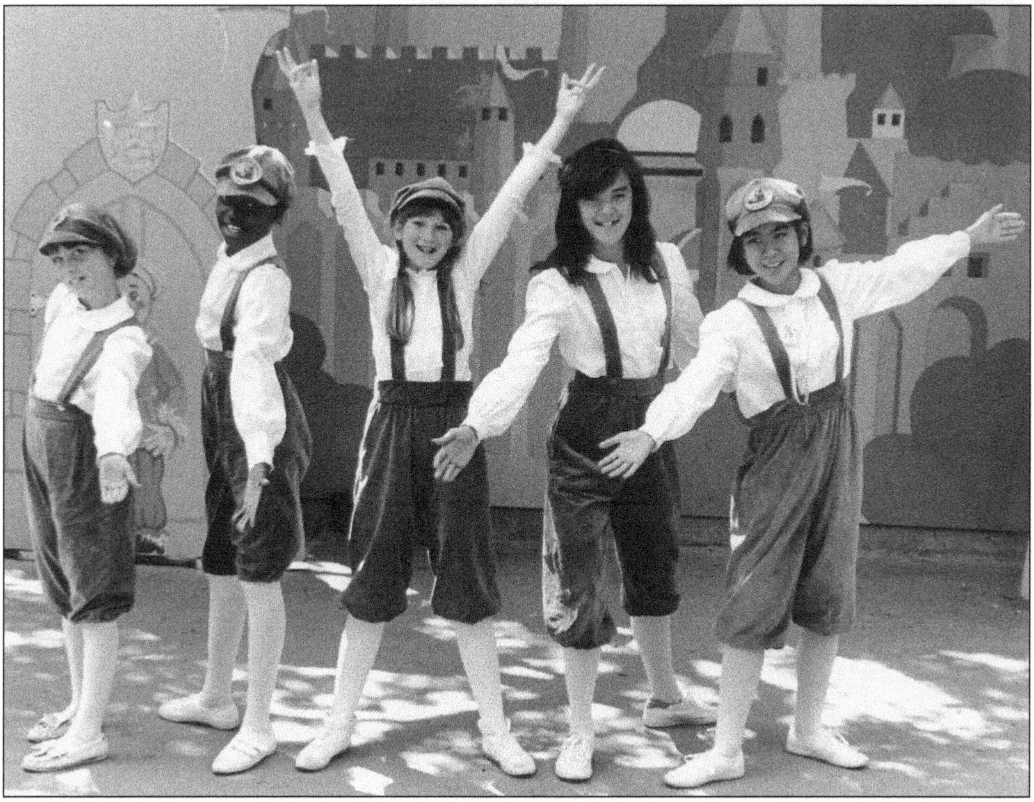

Let's Put on a Show, 1984. Out of the Fairytale Personality program arose a second troupe of slightly older children, the Mother Goose Players, who performed a musical tour of Fairyland and assisted backstage. Pictured are, from left to right, Erika Baldwin, Kamille Hudson, Alisha Monahan, Wendy Kumasawa, and Linda Sekigahama.

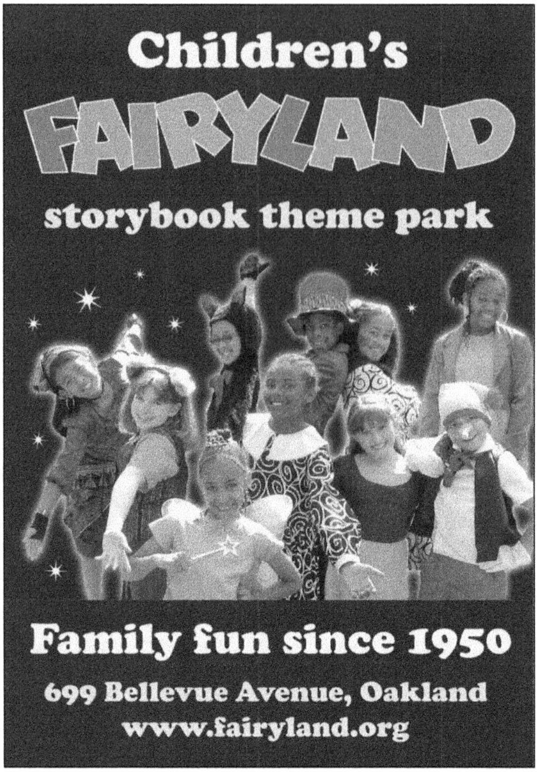

Fairyland Bus Transit Advertisement, 2007. The Fairyland Personalities evolved into a children's theater performance program that presents plays based on stories from around the world. They often appear in promotions for the park, as with this group of characters from Fairyland's original "hip-hopera," based on the Pinocchio story.

Visit Other Worlds, 2005. The Children's Theatre program is led by a professional theater director and performs plays based on tales from many cultures. Auditions for the program are held each January. Pictured from left to right, Linnaea Weld, Kelly Morrison, Jalena, and Angie Williams-Vansteenberg perform *The Monkey King's Journey to the West*, a Chinese legend.

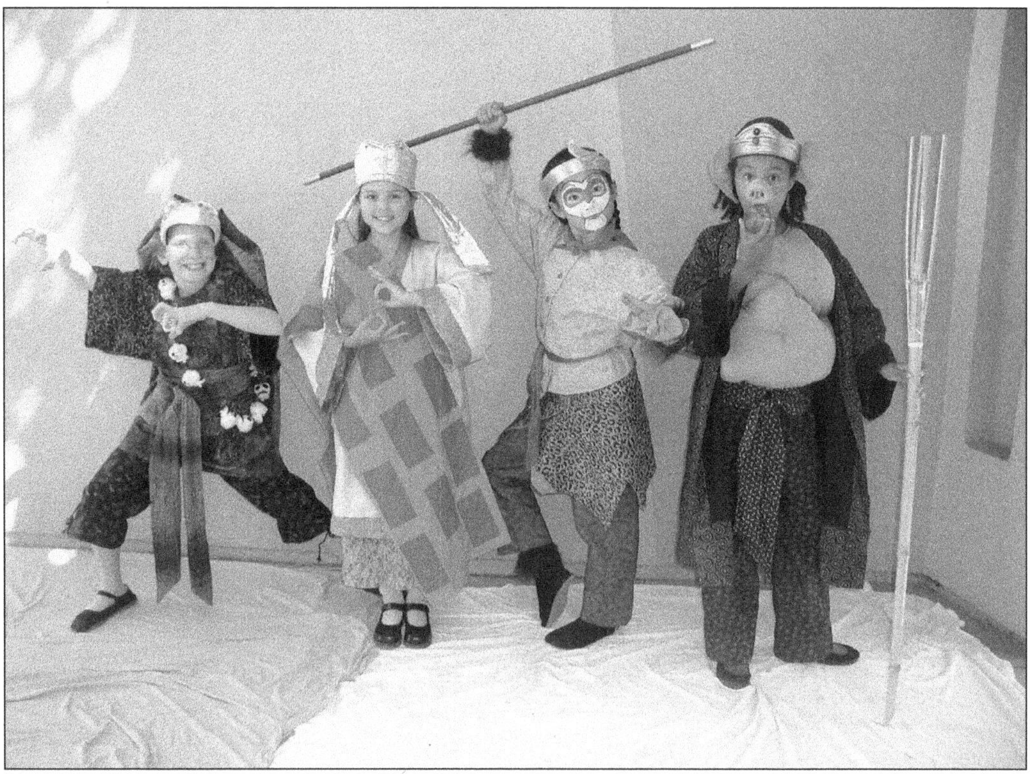

Everybody Dance!, 2006. Fairyland's primary audience is ages two to eight, but they are not too young to enjoy a rich menu of culturally diverse entertainment, from ballet and opera to live music. All entertainment is included with the low admission fee. Pictured is Bay Area reggae star Asheba dancing with young visitors and Fairyland Personalities.

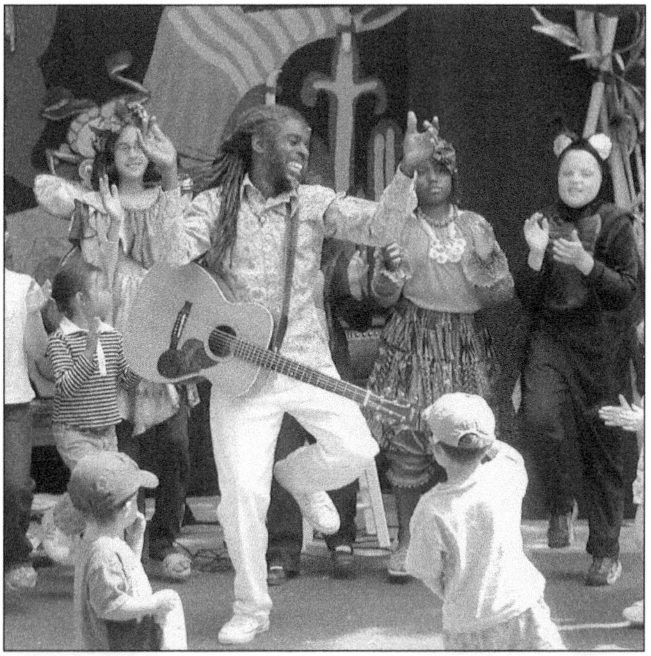

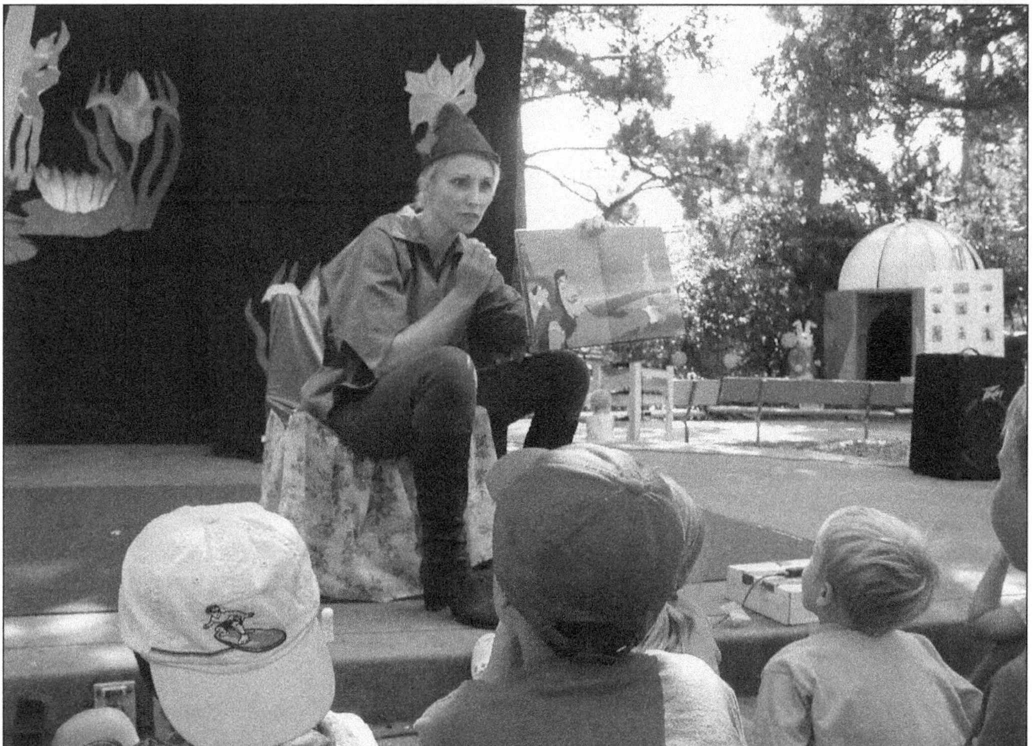

Tell a Story, 2012. Fairyland's storybook theme extends into its mission—to promote early literacy and love of literature. To that end, Fairyland often invites members of Book Pals, a group of movie, television, and stage actors, to read stories. Here, an actress portraying Peter Pan "crows" her adventures to an attentive audience.

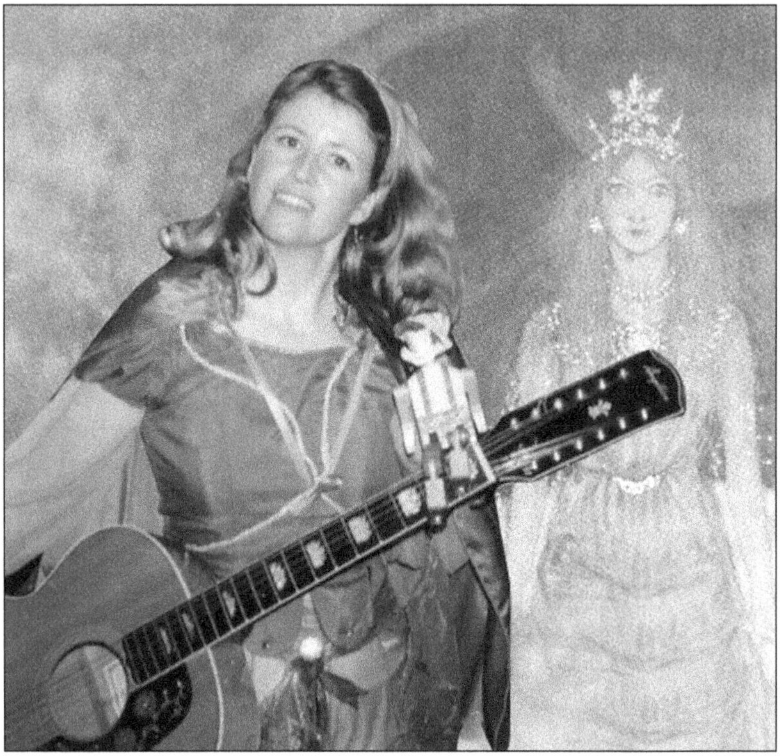

Make a Wish and Dream, 2009. Storytellers have always had a home in the park. One of the most popular is Jacqueline Lynaugh, who tells stories and sings songs as the Blue Fairy, Mother Goose, and the Snow Queen. Over a span of 35 years, Jacqueline has been active in the park as an entertainer, ride operator, and Children's Theatre director.

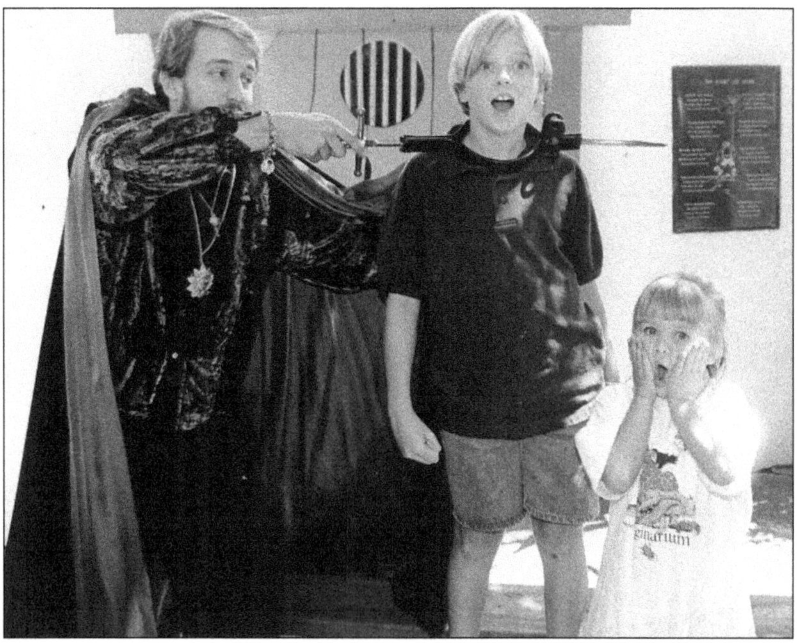

Watch This, c. 1995. Magic occurs all around in Fairyland. Entertainment favorites have always included a good magician or juggler. The bigger the illusion, the more popular it is. Here, local magician Tom Cutts passes a sword through the neck of Joel Harris, as cousin Nicki Nelson looks on, amazed, during a performance on Magic Day.

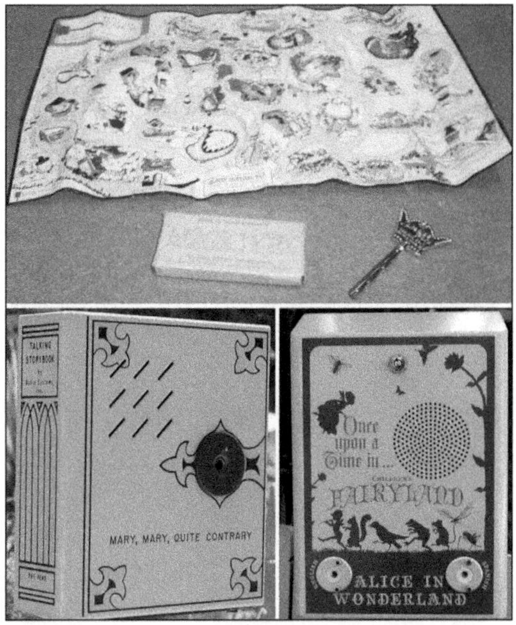

STORYBOOK BOXES AND MAGIC KEYS, 1958–2008. Fairyland's most popular and enduring invention may well be the Magic Key. Insert the plastic key into one of the talking Storybook Boxes located around the park, and one will hear a recorded rhyme or story. The key has been copied by zoos, museums, and institutions all over the country. Pictured are a 1958 gold key and map from a vending machine, along with the vintage 1960 Storybook Box (lower left) and a 2008 version (lower right).

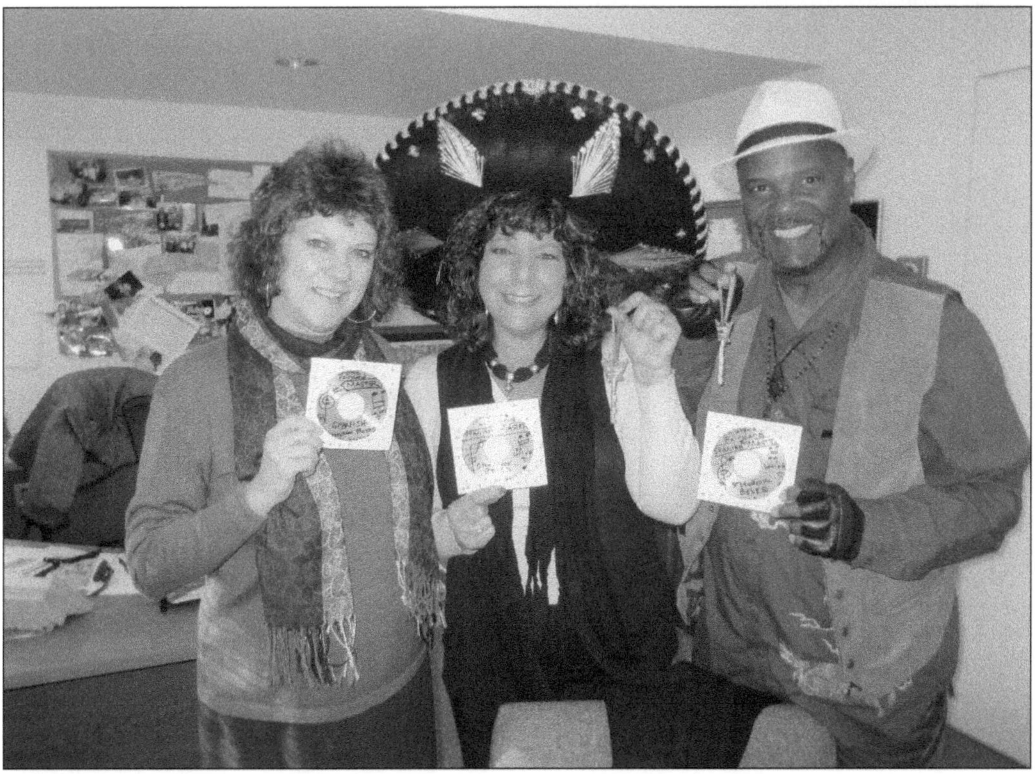

FAIRYLAND EN ESPAÑOL, 2013. Fairyland's visitors speak many languages, but until 2013, the Storybook Boxes spoke only English. That changed when composers Lori Moite and R.J. Johnson of Cotton Candy Express Music recorded Spanish versions, along with original songs, of all the stories. Here, Fairyland executive director C.J. Hirschfield accepts gold CDs of the translations from Moite and Johnson.

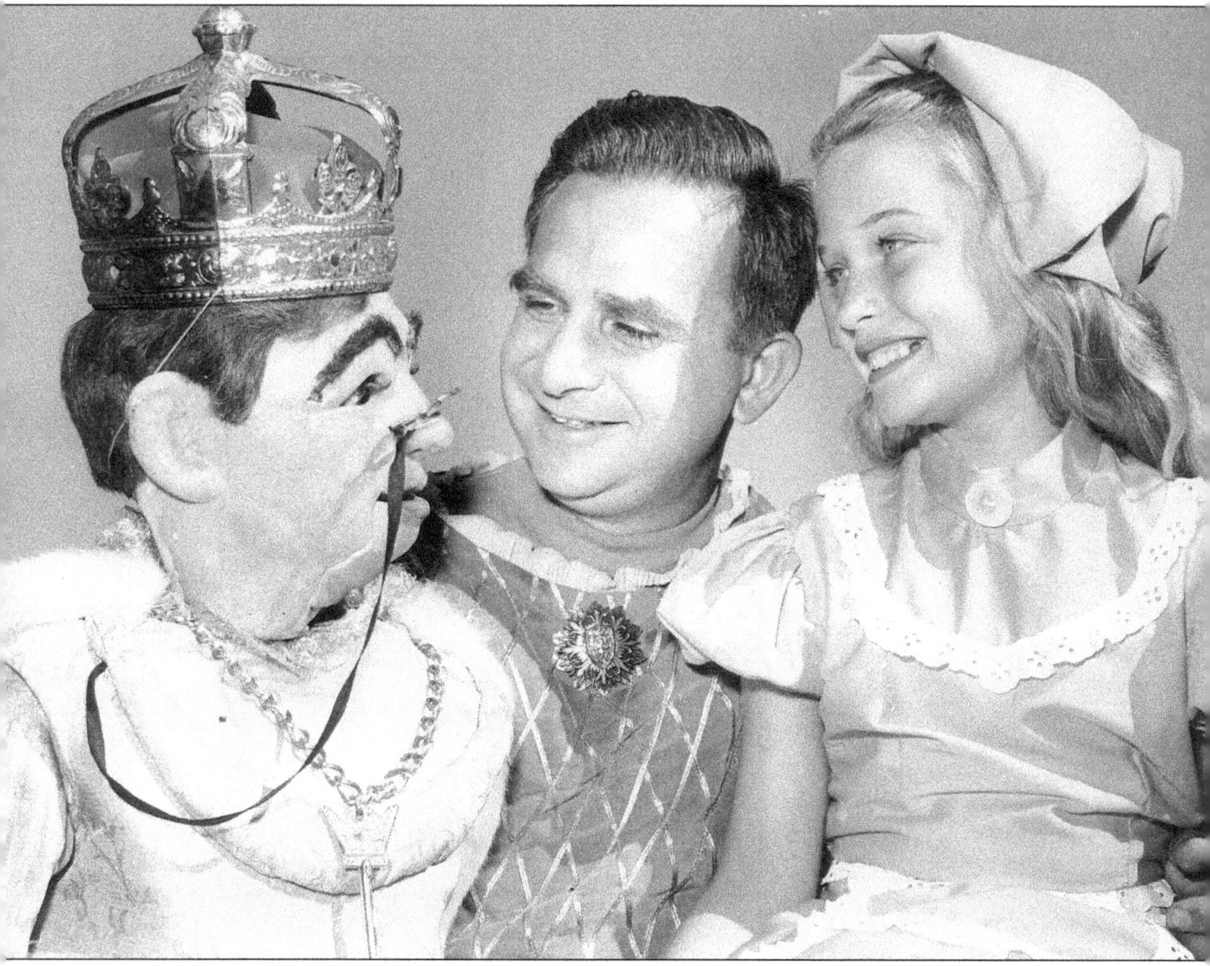

Magic Key Inventor, 1964. Bruce Sedley, inventor of the Magic Key, was a cartoon-show host on Channel 2, KTVU, for many years. A fan of Fairyland, he would announce to his audience that he and his companion, the ventriloquist dummy King Fuddle, were appearing at the park. When hundreds of families showed up, Sedley feared developing laryngitis. To save his voice while not disappointing kids, he created a gold key that when inserted into a metal box prompted a recorded tale. That was in 1958, and the rest is history. Sedley is also credited with creating the first magnetic stripe keycard. From left to right are King Fuddle, wearing a Magic Key; Bruce Sedley; and Miss Muffet (Debbie Sousa).

Six

FAIRYLAND COMES OF AGE

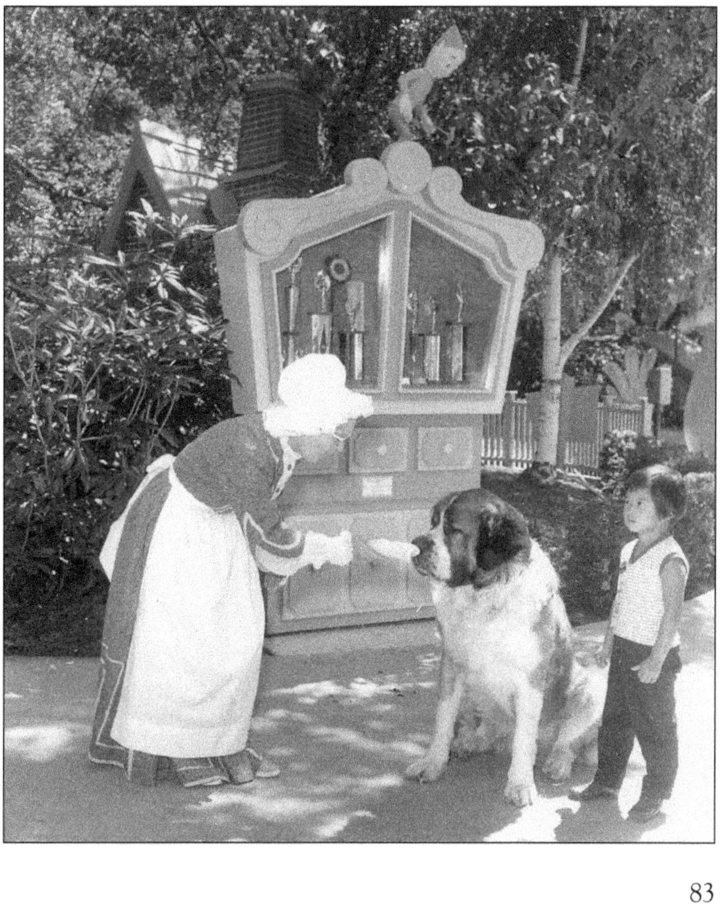

MOTHER HUBBARD'S CUPBOARD, 1967. Mother Hubbard (Merle Brothers) demonstrates to her canine companion Jamie that her cupboard is not bare—it houses trophies won by the Fairytale Personalities. Jamie, who won several awards, often pulled children in a dogcart through Bay Area streets on parade days. The cupboard is currently used for announcements of upcoming events and activities.

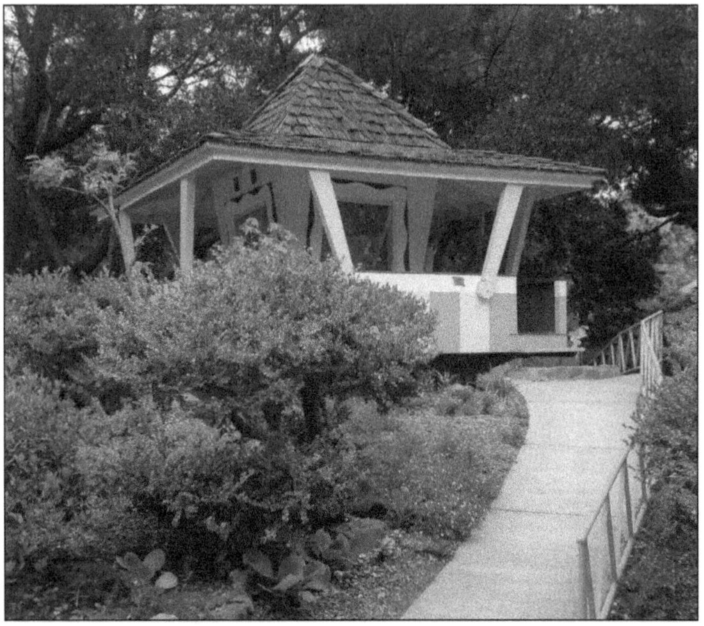

MUSICAL ALPINE MOUNTAIN HOUSE, 1975. This Swiss cottage high on a hill is the home of Meister Tinkle. The cottage was built in 1956 around a full-size piano barrel organ, made in Germany in 1880. Inserting a Magic Key activated the musical instruments. Fairyland is raising money to convert the mechanism to an electronic one.

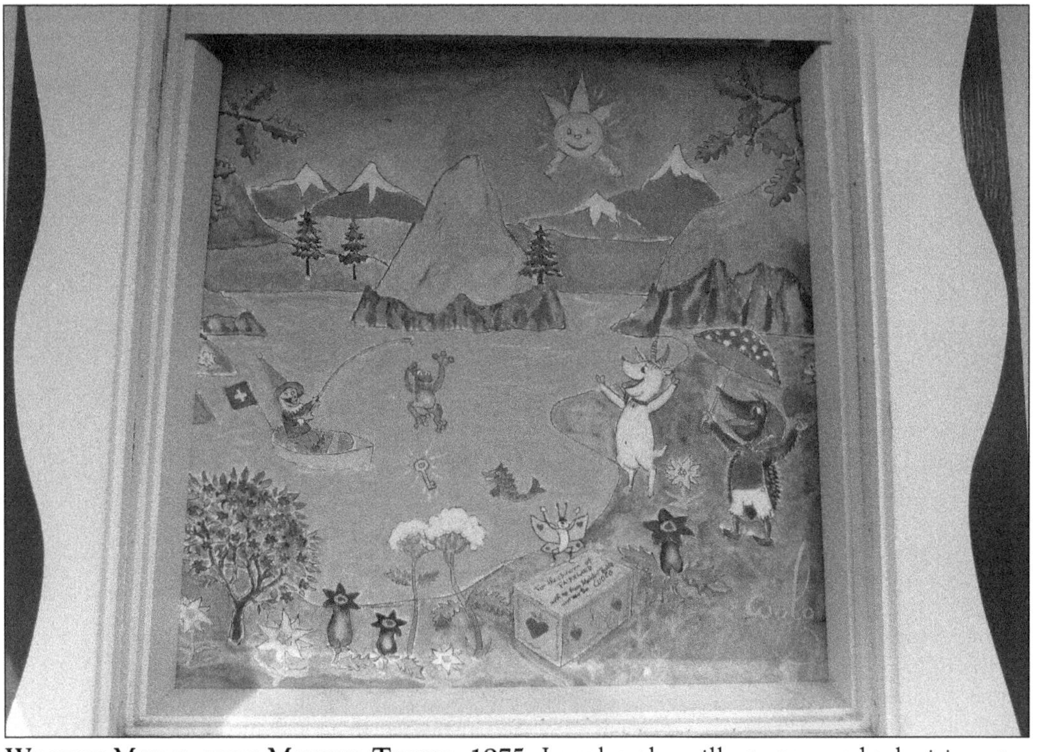

WINDOW MURAL FROM MEISTER TINKLE, 1975. Local author, illustrator, and television star Wolo von Trutzschler spun the tale of Meister Tinkle around his own popular Friendship Valley children's book series. Before Tinkle took up residence, the building was simply a decorative Swiss cottage. Meister Tinkle is the fictional creator of the Fairyland Magic Key that activates the Storybook Boxes. The three murals that tell the tale were a hand-painted gift from Von Trutzschler.

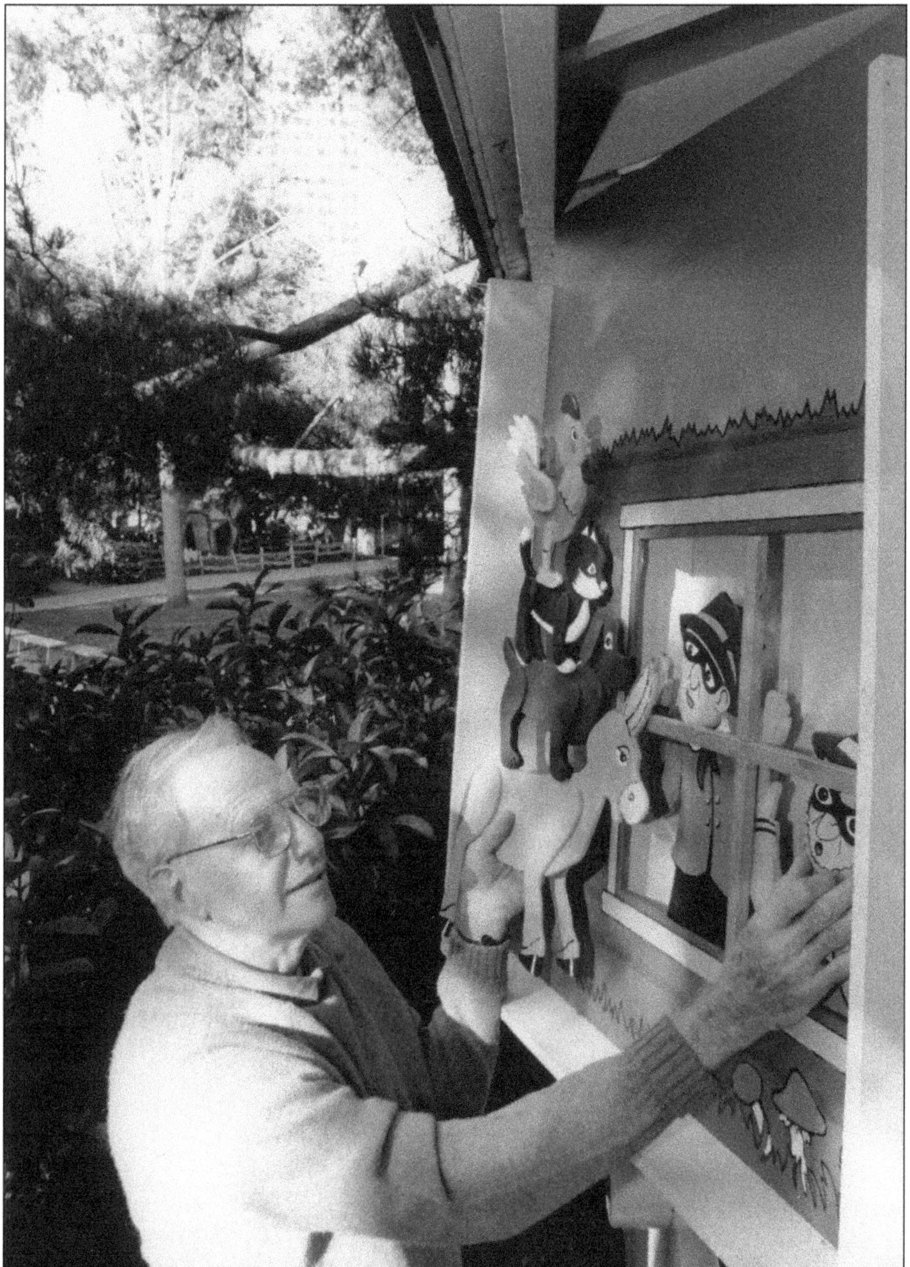

Bremen Town Musicians, 1997. By 1990, the piano barrel organ had ceased to play, and the Oakland Rotary and Sunset Music Club agreed that the Swiss cottage needed a new look. The music club favored a jazz-inspired story, and so puppeteer Lewis Mahlmann (pictured) created wooden cutouts for the four cottage windows based on the German tale of the Bremen town musicians. These new three-dimensional windows replaced the earlier Meister Tinkle murals and covered up the 1880 player piano organ. When a Magic Key triggered the jazz music, the wooden cutouts in the windows moved and acted out the story. Although the mechanics needed to make the figures come to life were never realized, the cut-out wooden windows are now interchangeable with the 1975 Meister Tinkle murals.

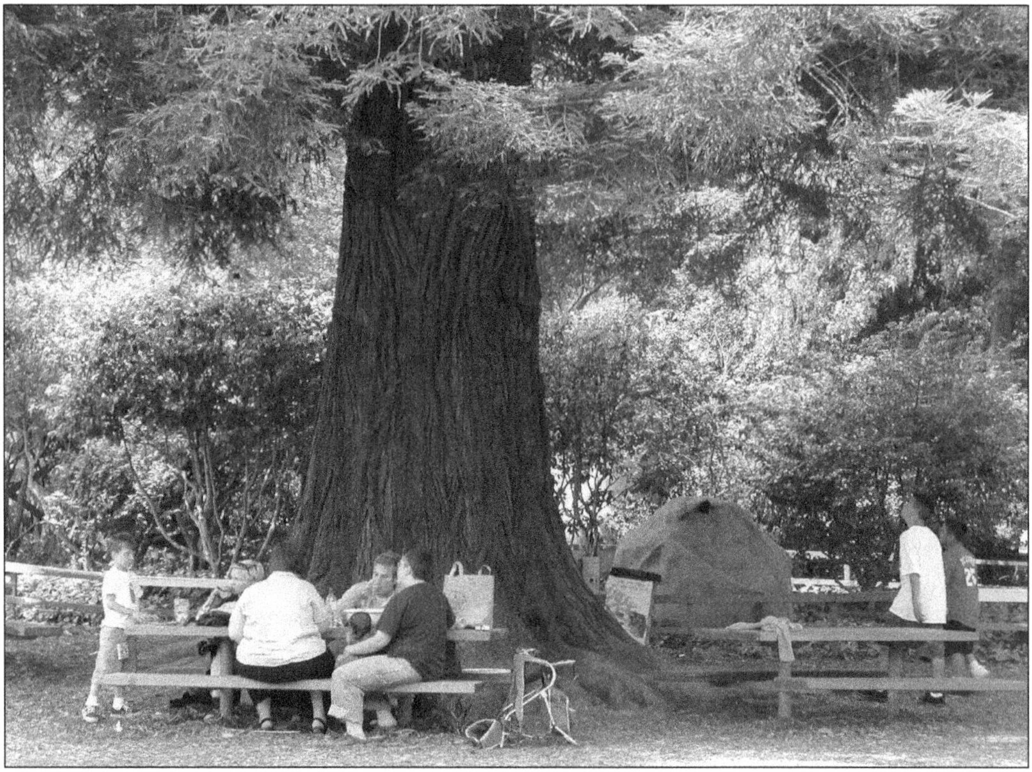

Teddy Bear Picnic Area, 1999. This wooded area, with its majestic redwood trees and view of Lake Merritt and the Lakeside Park bandstand, is used for birthday parties and informal picnics. In the summer, it is populated by dozens of family tents during Fairyland's popular family sleepovers. Evening children's concerts are also held under the trees. Painted plywood cutouts of teddy bears picnicking and playing in the forest were installed in 1984. The area's theme takes its inspiration from "The Teddy Bears' Picnic," a children's song written in 1907 that has remained popular over the decades.

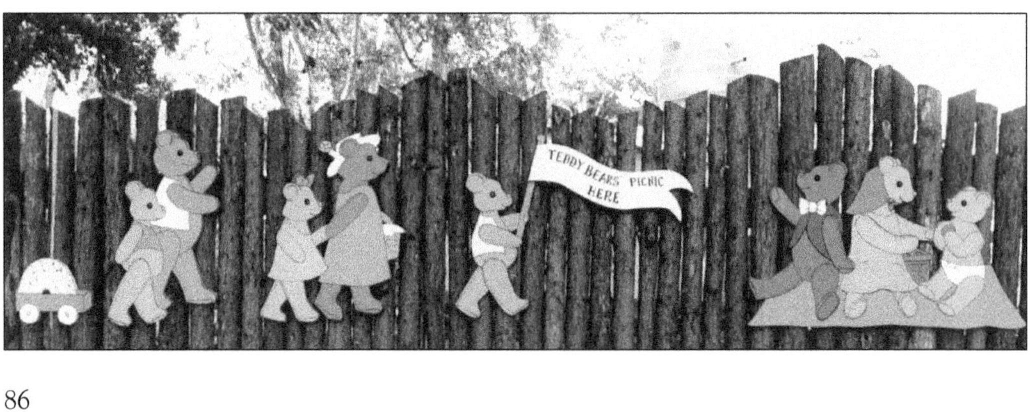

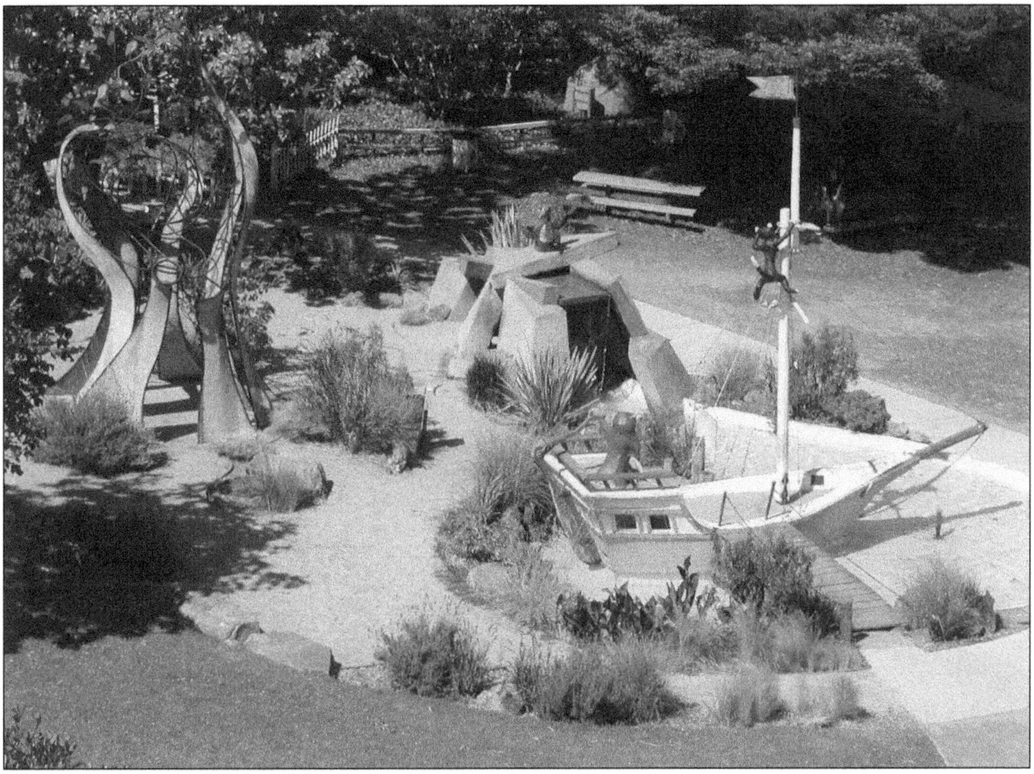

The Owl and the Pussycat, 1990s. This aerial view of the Owl and the Pussycat set gives a good sense of this play area, which was inspired by Edward Lear's nonsense verse and designed by Oakland artist Edward Schultz, who worked from William Russell Everritt's early concept drawings. The "Bong Tree," Turkey's hill of matrimony, and the Owl's pea green boat are all found anchored in the Teddy Bear Picnic Area. The setting encourages children to engage in imaginative play while adults relax under the redwoods.

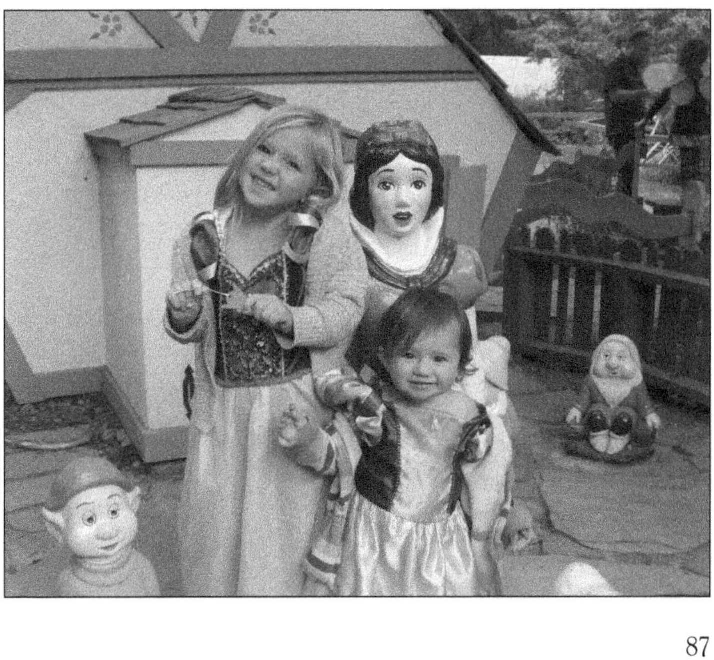

Snow White's Cottage, 2013. In 1982, Fairyland installed this colorful attraction in homage to Walt Disney and his animated fairy tale. Donated concrete garden statues pose in front of the seven dwarves' cottage, which is actually the backside of the Crooked Man's house. One can never have too many Snow Whites, as these young visitors will attest. Sage and Violet Ahern love to pretend to be their favorite storybook character whenever they visit.

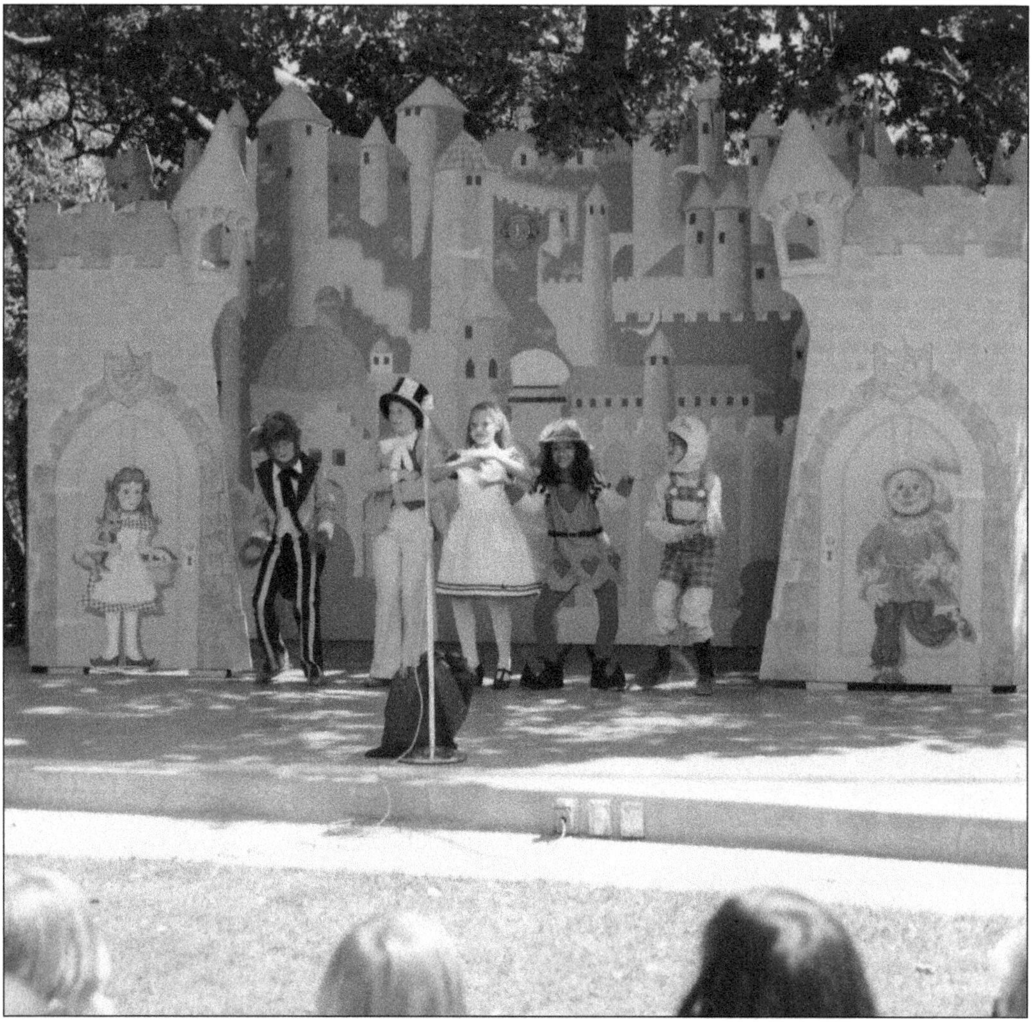

EMERALD CITY STAGE, 1999. In 1975, Fairyland added a new theater, the Emerald City Stage, as an intimate live-performance space for storytellers, magicians, clowns, and the Fairyland Personalities. Opposite the puppet theater in the Merry Meadow; this "Oz-ian" setting is used for other festivities as well. Families sit on movable benches that surround the stage; children can put their faces into the different Oz caricatures to become part of their own stories. Knowing that patrons appreciate contemporary inside jokes in some of the sets, juggler-artist Owen Baker Flynn often takes home the stage benches and voluntarily spruces them up. Pictured below is his storybook parody of the famous 1942 Edward Hopper painting *Nighthawks*.

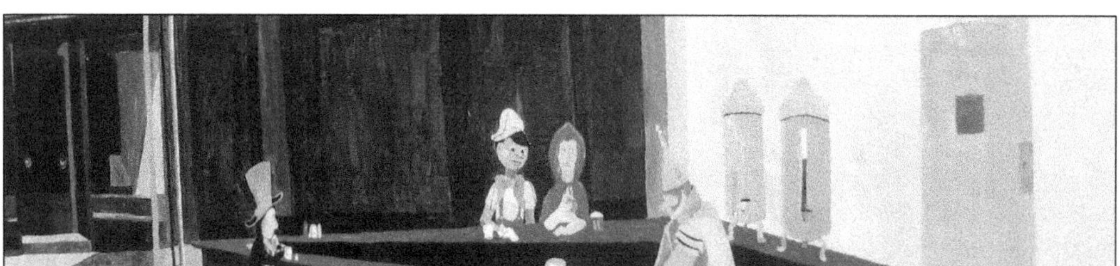

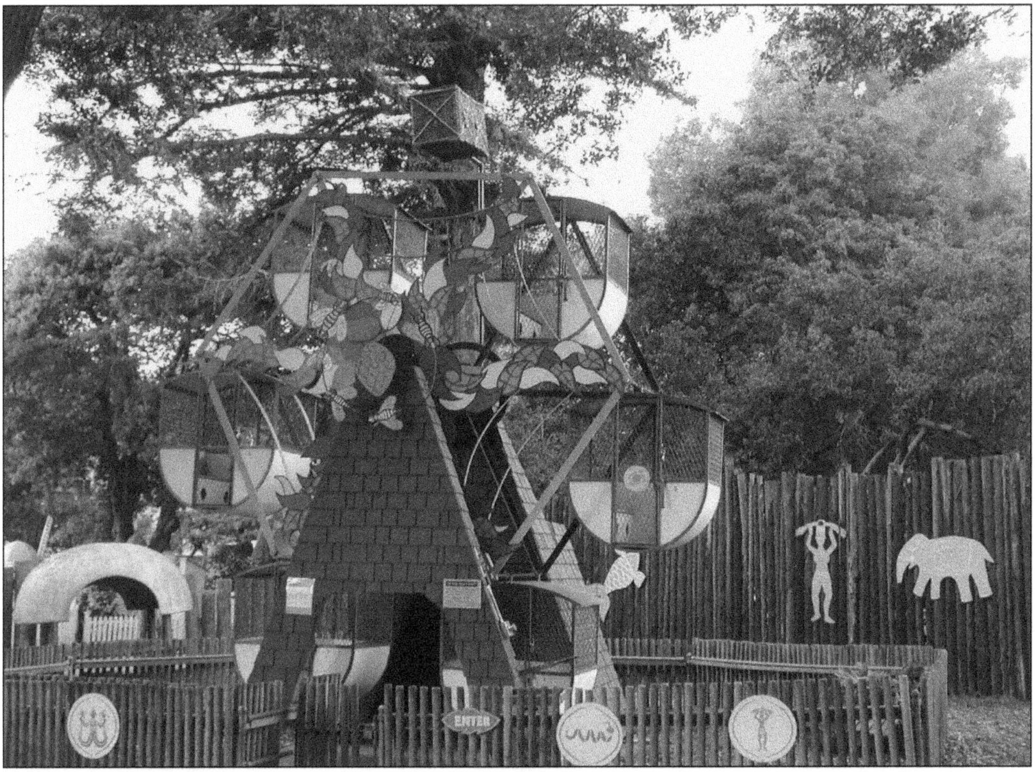

MAGIC WEB FERRIS WHEEL, 1992. The year 1975 also saw the arrival of the Anansi Magic Web Ferris wheel. Based on African legends of Anansi the spider, this reconditioned children's ride was moved from Peralta Park in Oakland when the latter's playground was revitalized. Children climb into the enclosed carriages and spin around Anansi's web trying to snatch the box of "Golden Stories" high above their heads in the treetops. Pictured in the 1972 photograph below are Fairytale Personality Eileen Weems, the Cowardly Lion, and Fed Ernest, a City of Oakland employee, holding the original Anansi Ferris wheel model by park designer Kevin O'Hare.

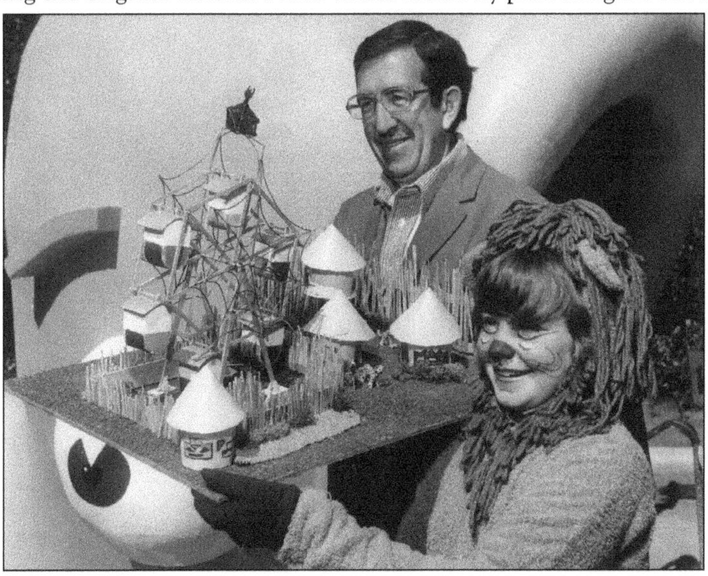

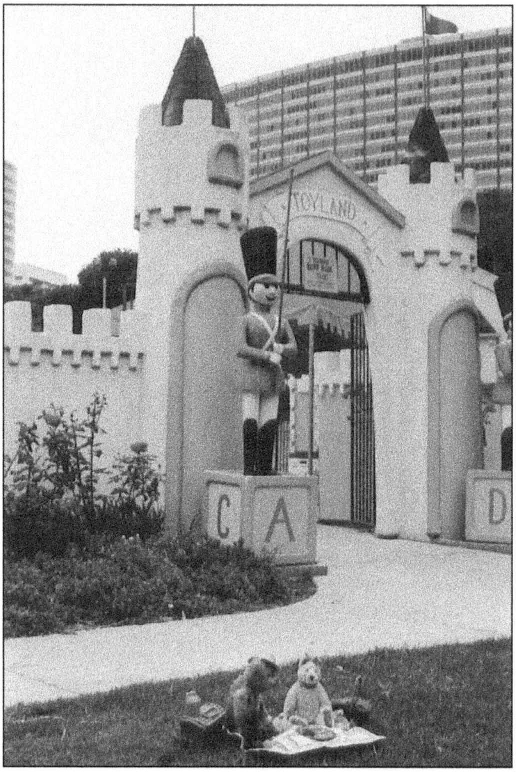

Toyland Boat Ride, 1989. Based on Victor Herbert's operetta *Babes in Toyland*, the Toyland Boat Ride opened in 1988. Originally designed as a water coaster flume ride, it underwent many cost-saving changes and evolved from a log ride to miniature bumper boats in a pond. Small battery-operated boats, supported by inflated inner tubes, propelled young sailors around the Toyland pond. The ride closed in 2004 because of restrictive new California amusement park safety standards, and it was removed in 2006 to make way for the park's new theater, Aesop's Playhouse. Note the teddy bears picnicking in the grass next to the ride? The boat ride was in the Teddy Bear Picnic Area. These children enjoy a gentle game of bumping boats while coasting through the Toyland pool.

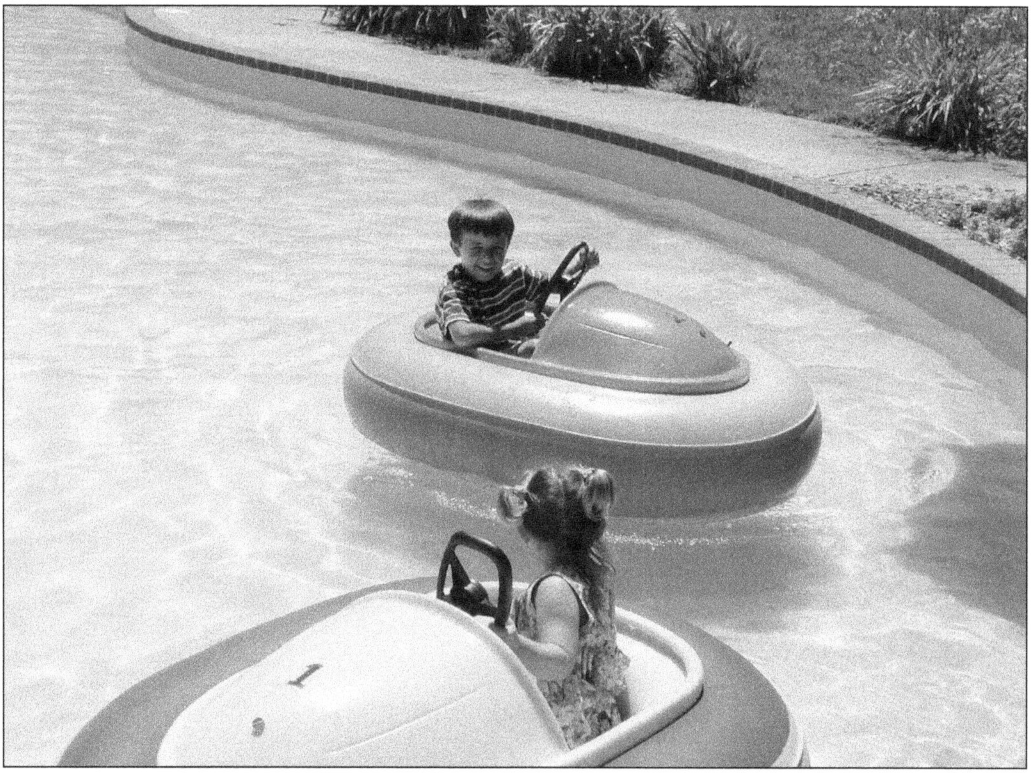

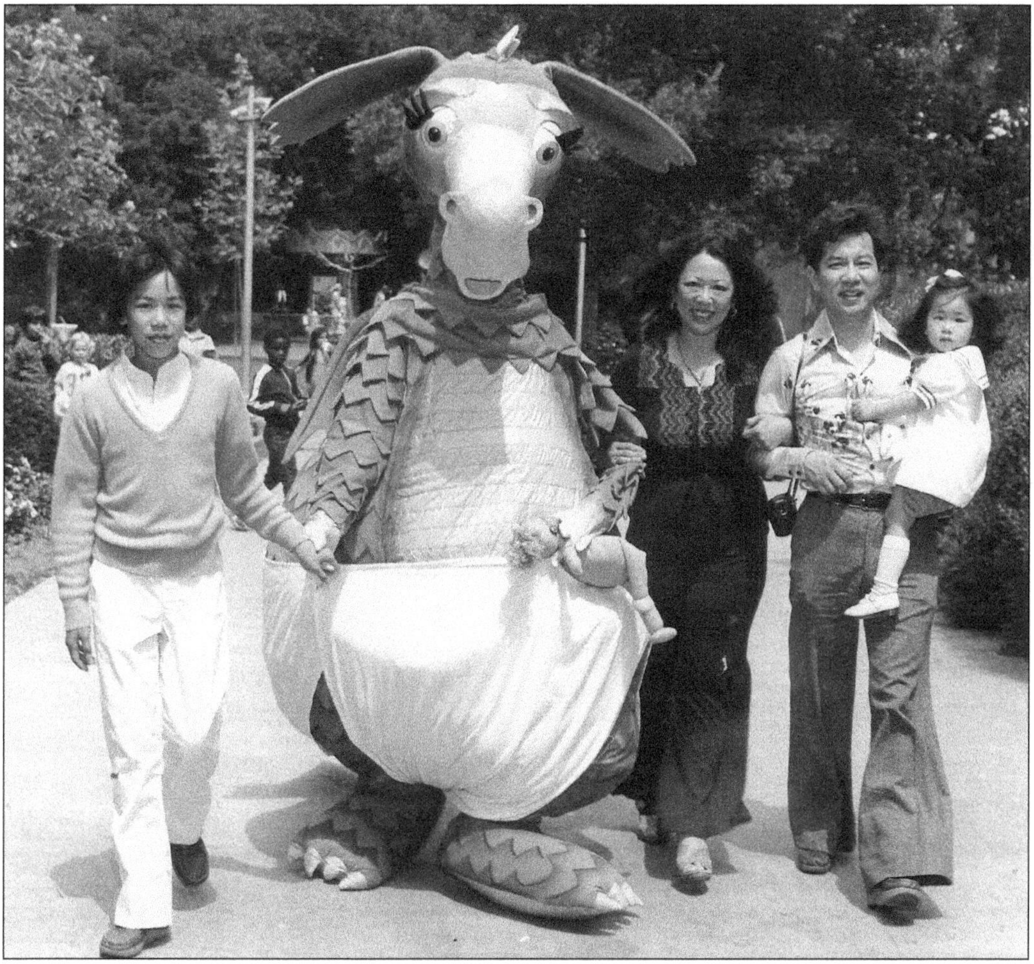

Help Lost Baby Dragon Find His Mama, 1979. Like other amusement parks, Fairyland has had a number of mascots. Here, Fairyland's first costumed character, the Lost Baby Dragon, is reunited with his sponsor's family (from left to right, Wellington Eng Jr., Shirley Eng, and Dr. Wellington Eng holding baby Alexandria). The mascot costumes were designed by Oakland district attorney and cartoonist Don Ingraham and created by puppeteer Lewis Mahlmann. Other Ingraham-designed mascots included the Purple Cow, Davey Cricket, and the never-completed Zomo the Rabbit and Donkey-Hote.

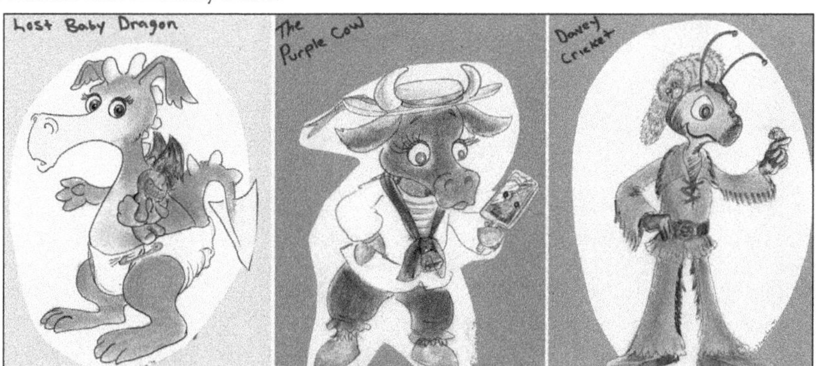

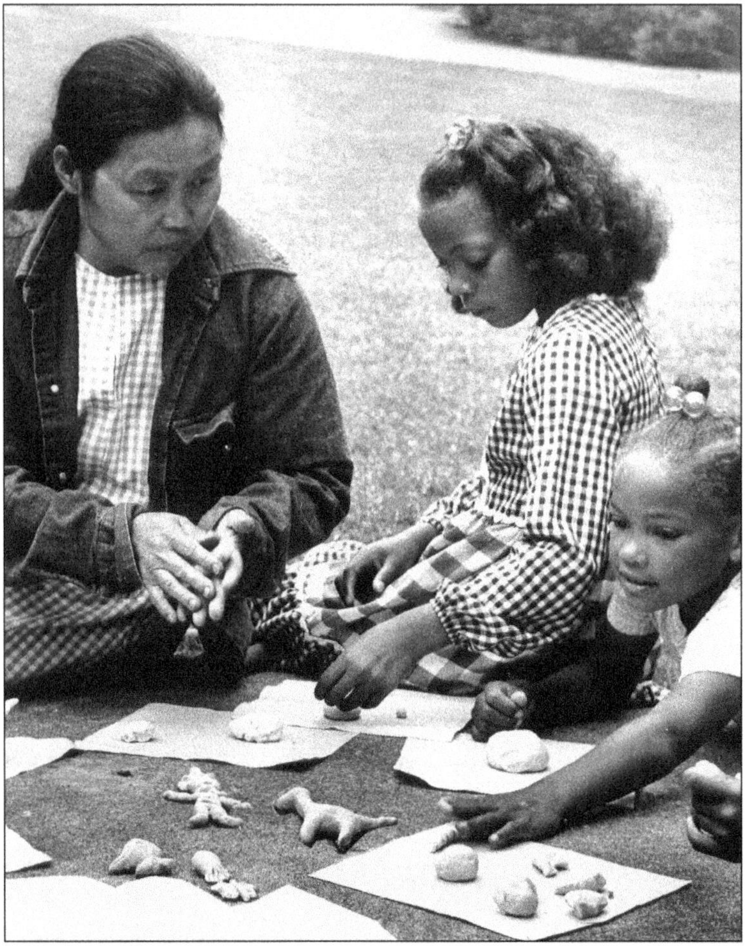

Making a Map, 1975. For Fairyland's 25th anniversary, noted Bay Area artist Ruth Asawa gave a special workshop to children in Fairyland's arts-and-crafts program. Asawa is best known for her wire sculptures and for the creation of the San Francisco School of the Arts, which now bears her name. She often sculpted in bread dough and then fired the molds for use with other media. Here, she sculpts a map of Fairyland with help from children. Working with artist Marilyn O'Hare, Asawa sculpted the main attractions; everything else was handmade by the children. The bread-dough sculptures were baked into nine sections of the map and covered with plaster to make separate molds.

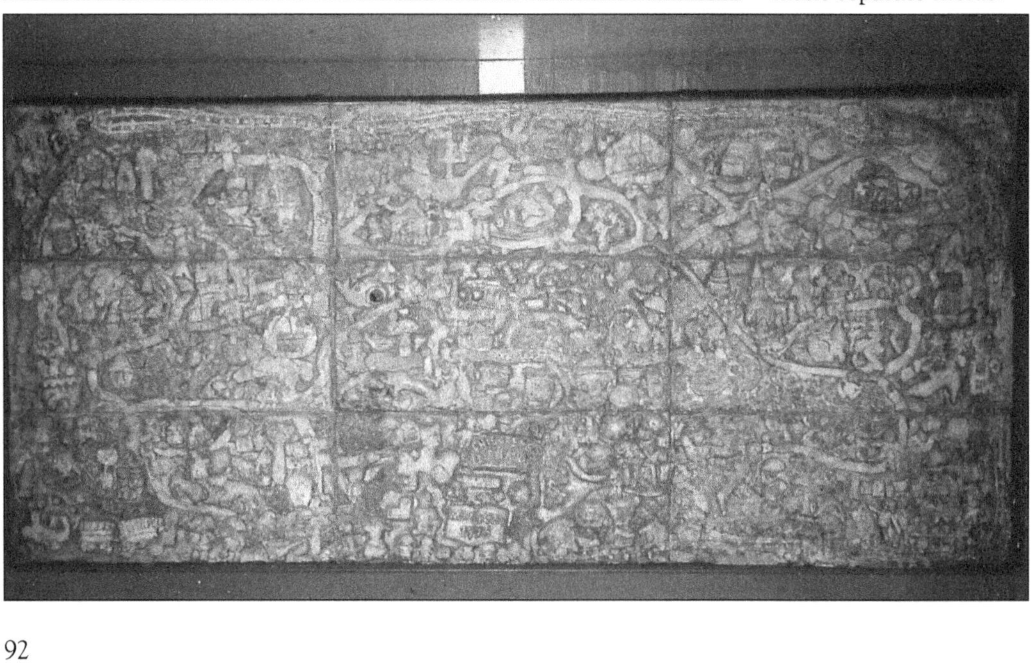

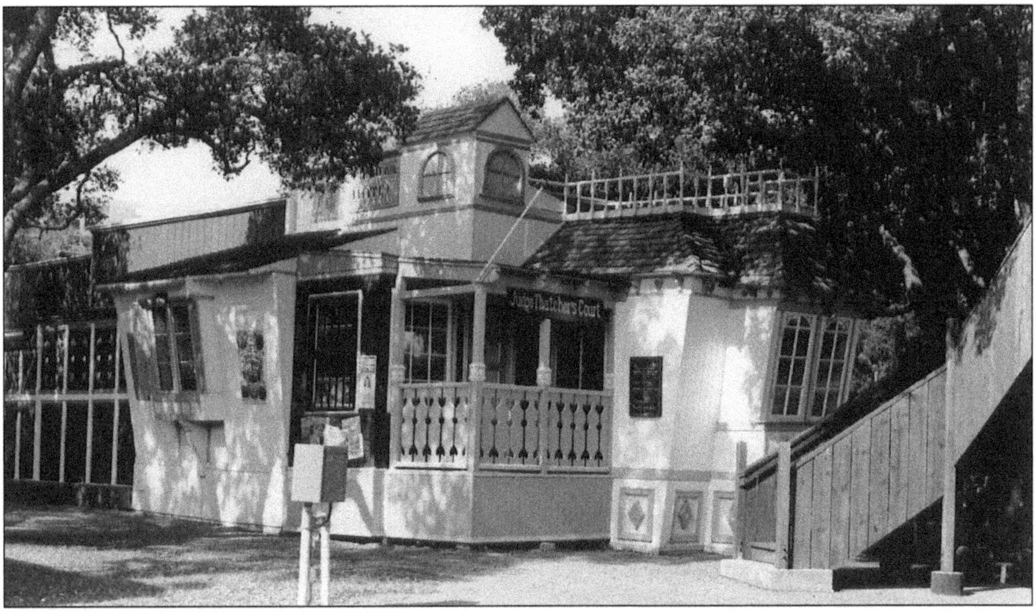

Tom Sawyer Village, 1990. Based on Mark Twain's classic novel, the village was not only a colorful set of buildings for Yankee Doodle Junction (now Old West Junction), it was also a facade for the house trailer where Fairyland's night watchman lived. When he climbed inside to the widow's peak on the roof, the watchman could see the entire park at night. These buildings were removed in 2004 and replaced with maintenance workshops. The Yankee Doodle covered bridge, pictured at right, was adjacent to Tom Sawyer Village. Opened in 1982, the bridge connects the Teddy Bear Picnic Area with the Junction, crossing over the train tracks of the Jolly Trolly Train.

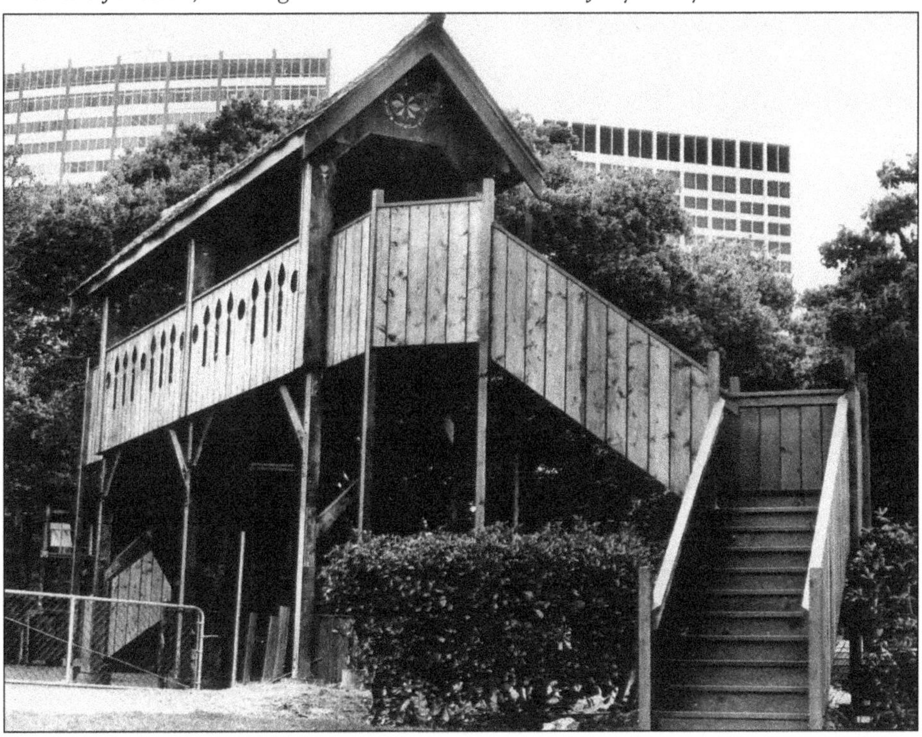

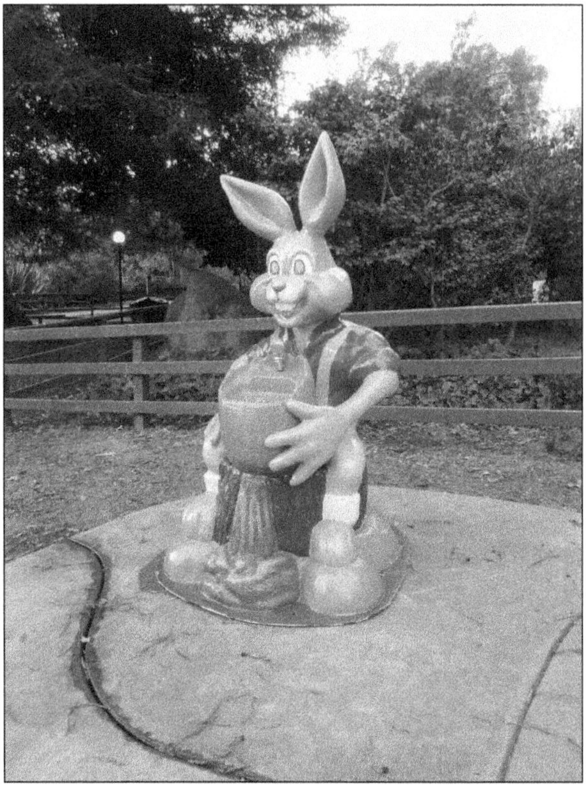

Brer Rabbit Faucet, 2012. Brer Rabbit, which debuted in 1992 at the base of Yankee Doodle Bridge, is one of the park's many unusual water fountains—in this case, a depiction of a classic American folktale hero. Today, the fountain can be found near the entrance to the Teddy Bear Picnic Area, giving refreshment to thirsty visitors.

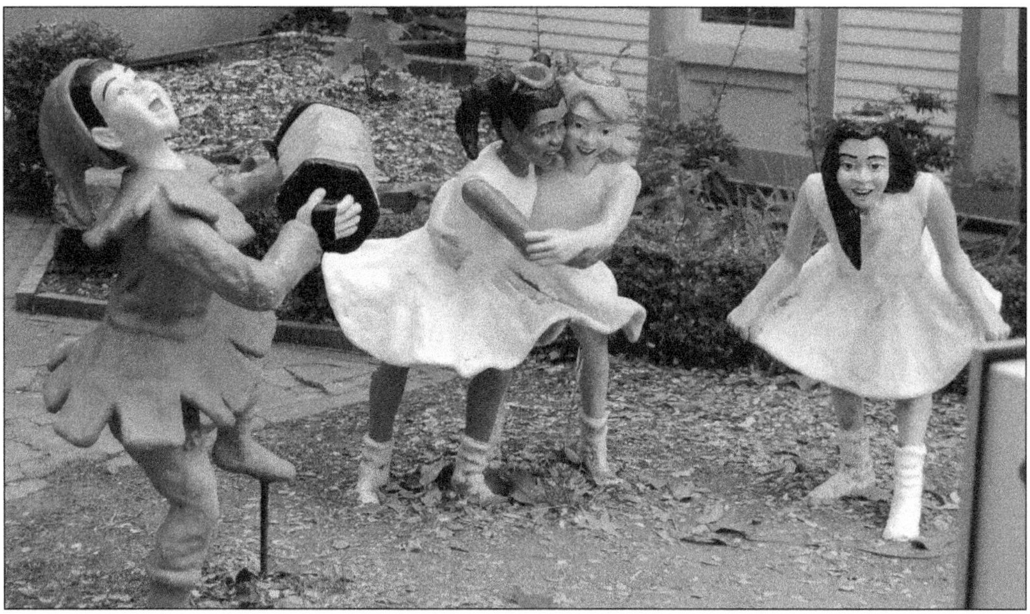

A Fairy Celebration, 1998. For many years, Oakland schools celebrated the winter holiday season with the Christmas Pageant. Each school learned one part of the pageant, then joined with other schools to present the entire piece at the Oakland Auditorium. These statues, by artist Baron Von Jabba, were sculpted from a pageant photograph and dedicated to Louise Jorgensen, who directed the pageant for 68 years.

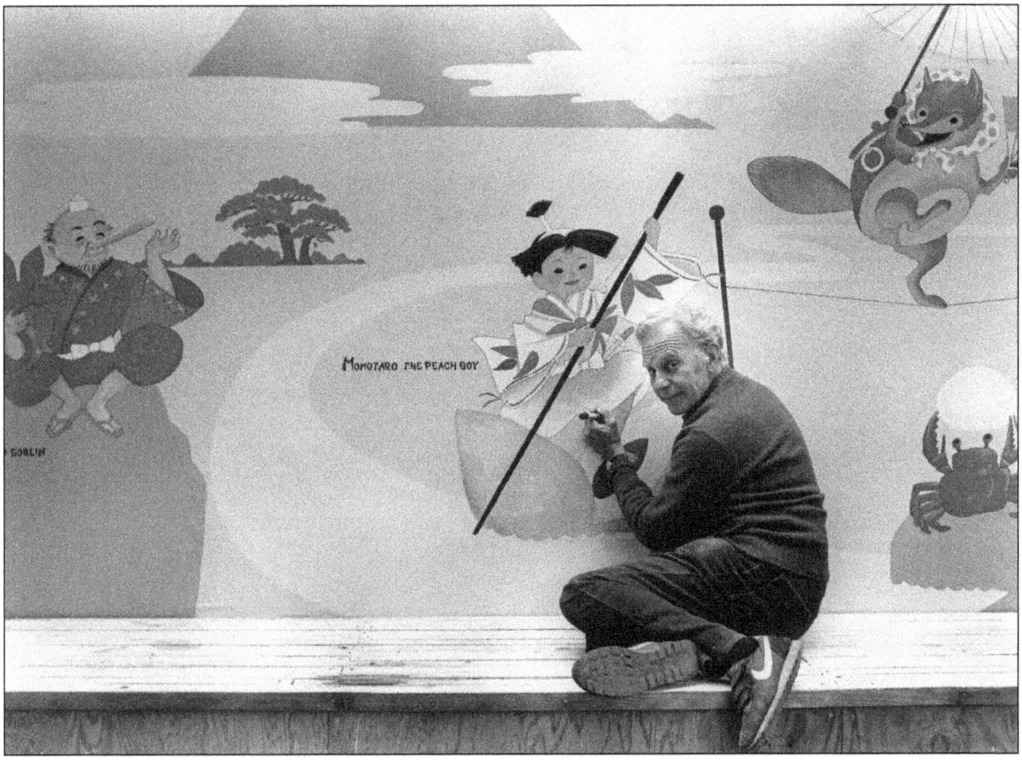

JAPANESE TEA GARDEN, 1989. Mural artist and puppeteer Lewis Mahlmann puts the finishing touches on a party area dedicated to the stories of Japan. The garden featured a mural, as well as Japanese plantings and a torii (Japanese gate). The attraction was a joint project of the Lake Merritt Lions Club and the Fukuoka-Hakata Lions Club of Oakland's sister city in Japan.

JAPANESE TEA GARDEN BIRTHDAY AREA, 2015. This set was redesigned and refreshed with murals by Shannon Taylor, Fairyland's art and restoration director. When not being used for parties or other catered events, the party area is a quiet place to enjoy a snack or a conversation.

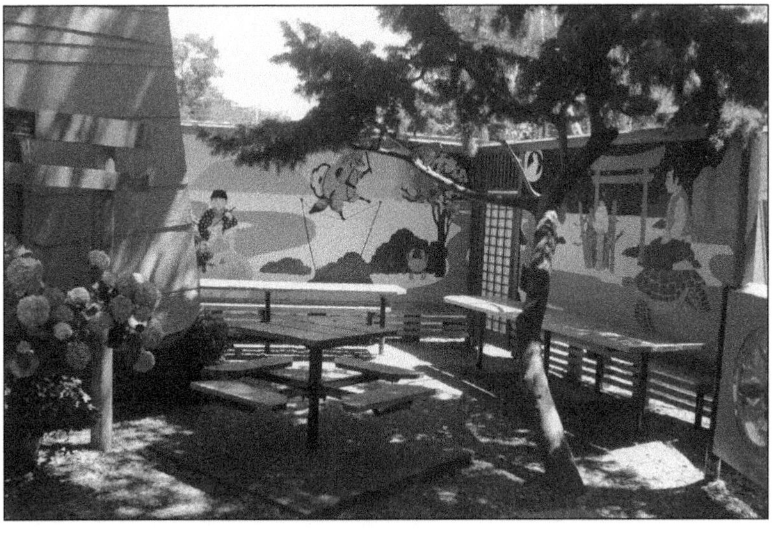

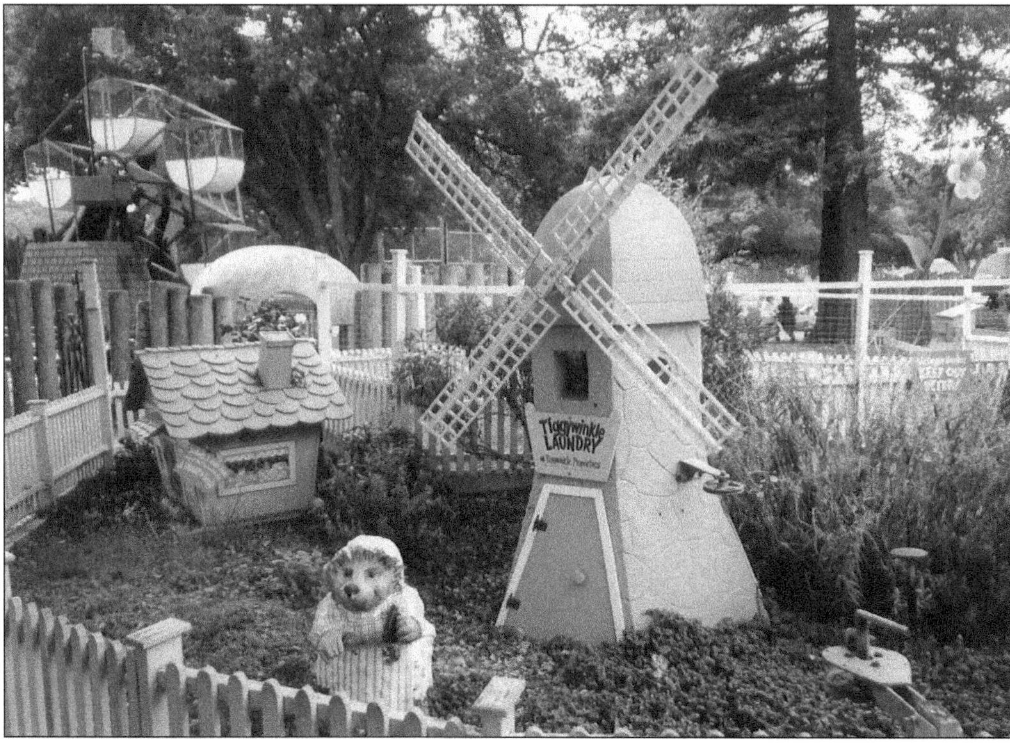

Peter Rabbit Village, 1995. In 1993, the park opened one of its largest play areas, Peter Rabbit Village, based on stories by Beatrix Potter. These new animal houses connected the Peter Rabbit set with Goosey, Goosey Gander. The design was by puppeteers Lewis Mahlmann and Randal Metz, with animal statues by Larry and Kevin O'Hare. Representatives from the World of Beatrix Potter theme park, who hold the rights to Potter's work, loved the set so much that they granted Fairyland the right to use the characters and buildings. Pictured are Miss Tiggywinkle's windmill laundry, the mouse house, Jeremy Fisher's cottage, and the Ginger and Pickles Curio Shoppe.

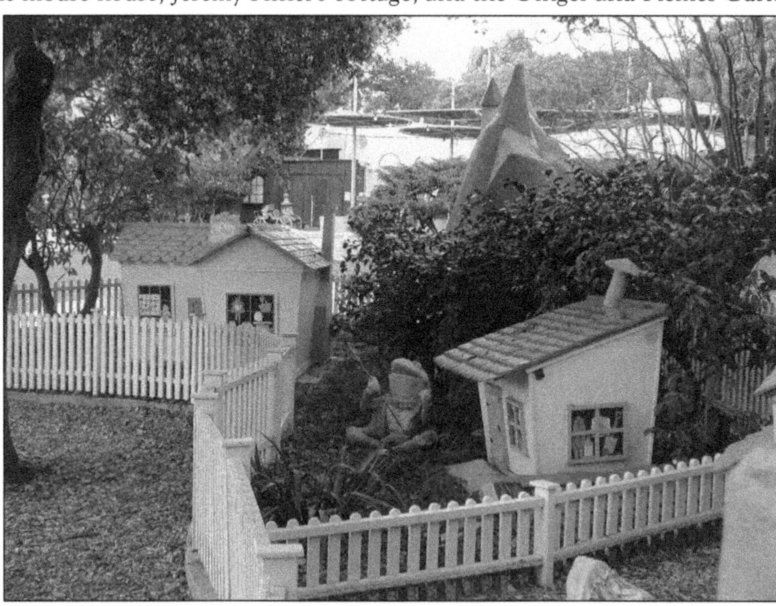

Seven

Eventful Events

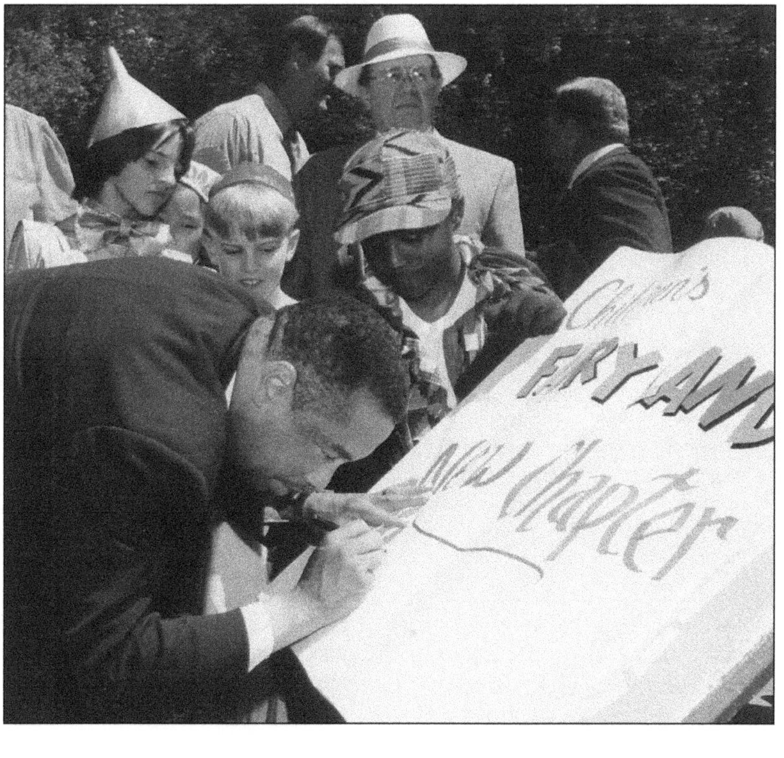

A New Chapter, 1994. One of the most significant events in Fairyland's history took place in 1994, when the City of Oakland approved Fairyland's restructuring as a nonprofit corporation, enabling the park to be managed independently. Here, Mayor Elihu Harris signs a new page in Fairyland's story, with onlookers Katie Krimetz (Tin Man), Bryan Weimer (Aladdin), Paul Wilson Jr. (Anansi), and board member Roland Smith.

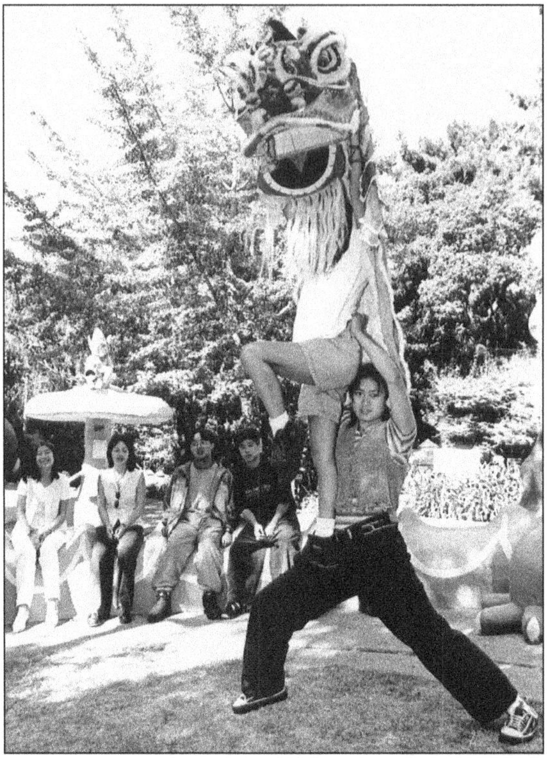

CHINESE NEW YEAR FESTIVITIES, 1998. Fairyland celebrated the Chinese New Year in style with members of the Asian Youth Services Dancing Team. Children made kites and faux firecrackers; storytellers told traditional Chinese tales. And everyone received a free fortune cookie! Through art, dance, and theater, Fairyland celebrates many of the cultures represented in the San Francisco Bay Area.

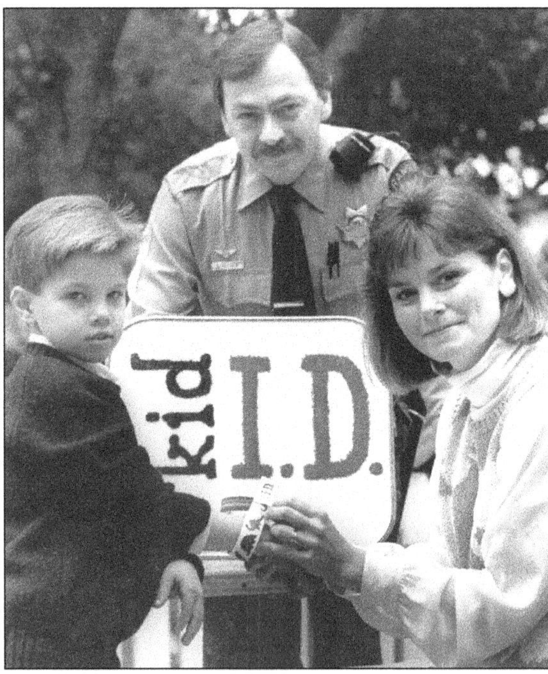

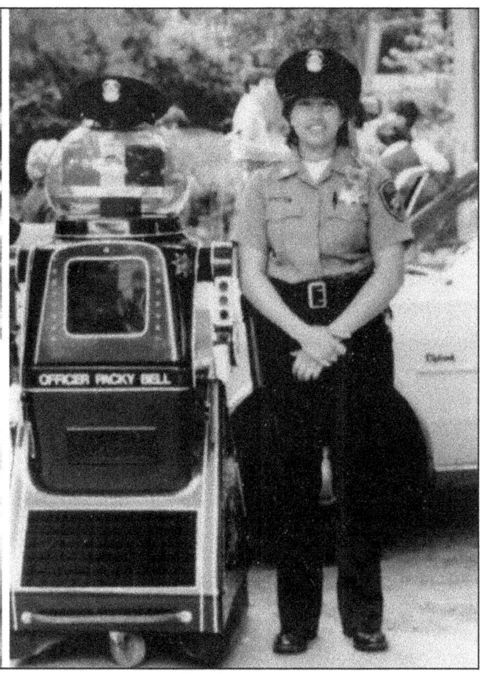

PUBLIC SAFETY DAY, 1980S. This event promoted police, fire, and educational programs in the city of Oakland. In these photographs, park ranger Rick Hayden and representatives of Kid I.D. (left) show off safety security bracelets while Oakland Police explorer Peggy Esposito and robot officer Packy Bell teach traffic safety.

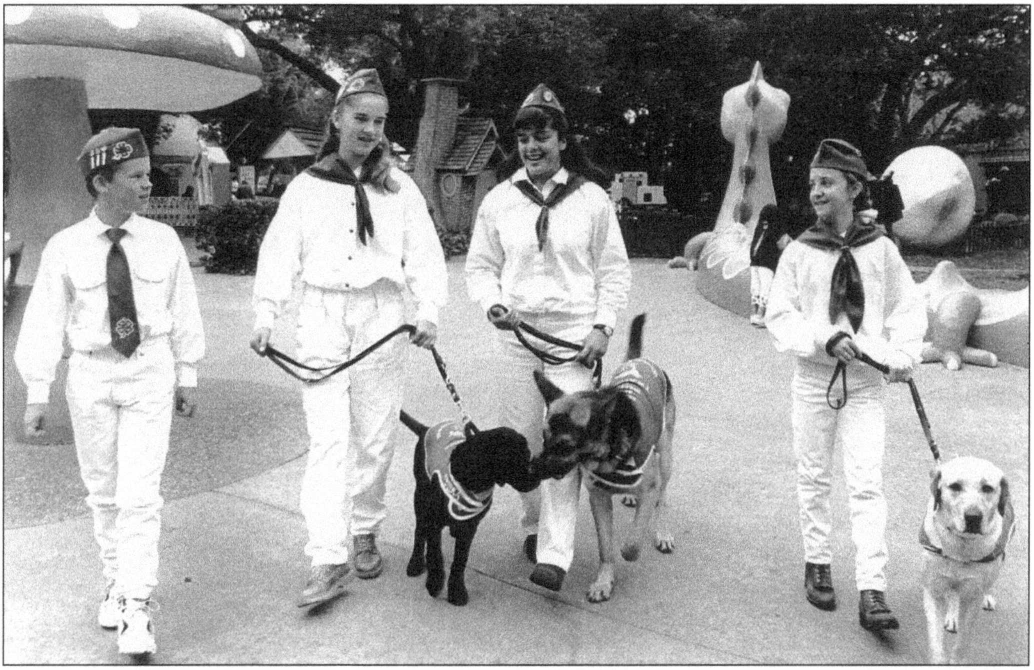

4-H Day, 1995. Members of the 4-H Guide Dog Organization—the four H's stand for head, heart, hands, and health—show off their canine trainees. Each year, final tests for guide dogs for the blind were held at Fairyland; the dogs were tested on their ability to follow commands and ignore increasing stimuli. Other festivities included snail racing, earthquake safety, and "Chemicals R Us."

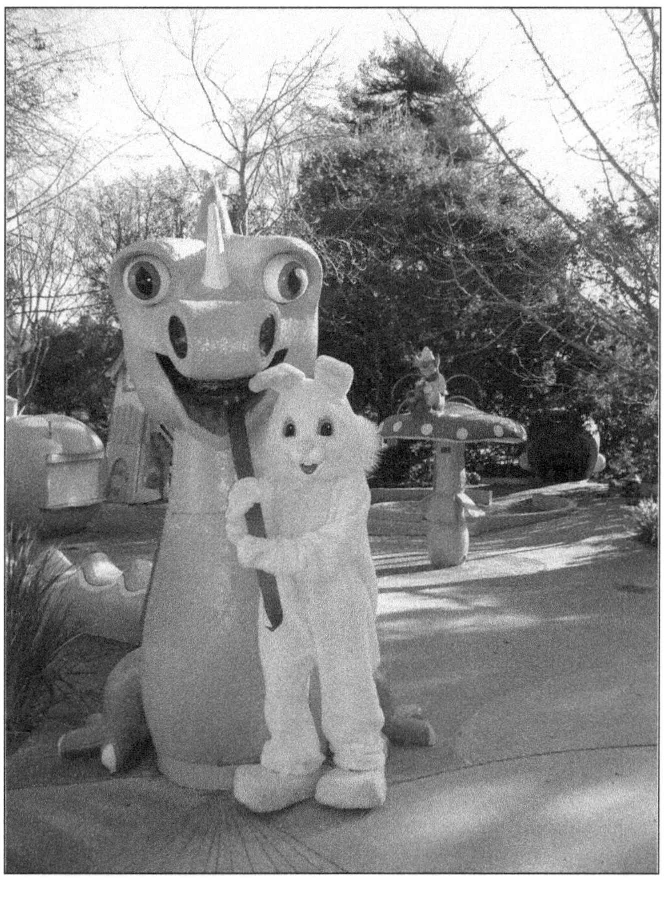

Springtime Festivities, 2000. Peter Cottontail is a regular springtime visitor to the park. Special spring activities have included egg dyeing, making baskets out of construction paper, and egg rolling (with the nose) in a race across the Merry Meadow. In recent years, Bunny Weekend has featured the bunny-costumed, walk-around characters Critters by the Bay and the Tap-Dancing Easter Bunnies, a local troupe.

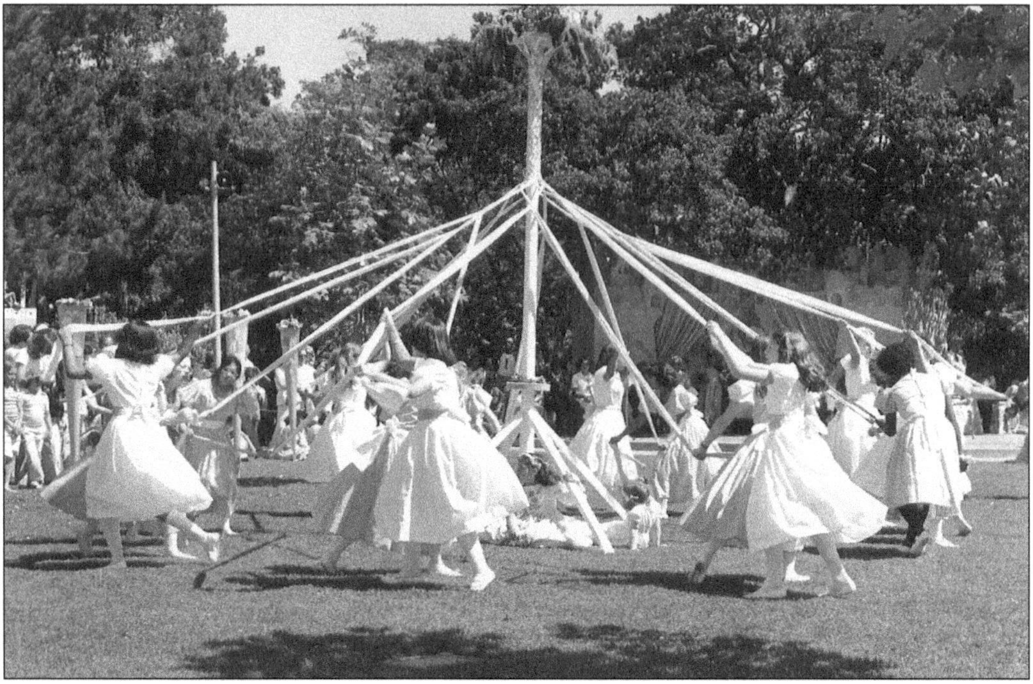

May Day Festivities, 1977. These dancers from the City of Oakland Parks and Recreation Department weave colorful ribbons around a maypole under the direction of Louise Jorgenson. For many years, during the park's May Day/Coronation festivities, the young dancers would share the maypole dance with young visitors to Fairyland. The City of Oakland built four maypoles that were placed throughout the city.

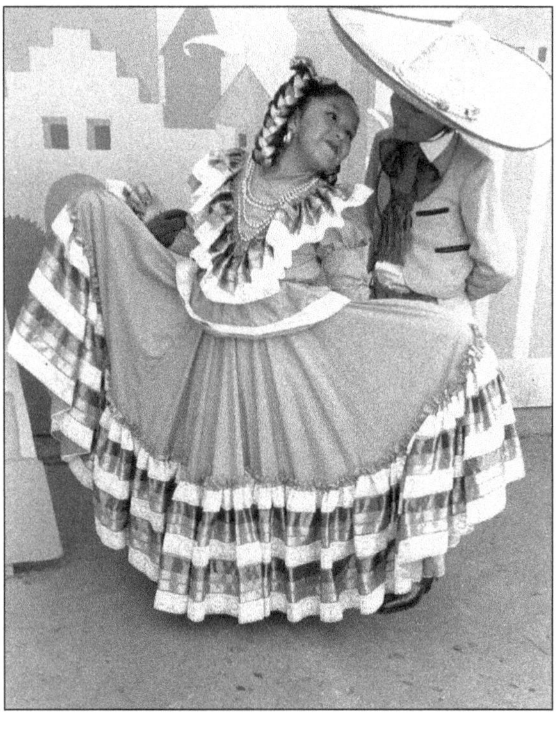

Cinco de Mayo, 1991. Two young members of the Ballet Folklórico Guadalajara de Oakland demonstrate their traditional dancing talents on the Emerald City Stage. Highlights of this fiesta included Mexican music, storytelling, traditional dances, and free sombreros for all park visitors. Fairyland also celebrates other cultural occasions, such as Black History Month, with specially themed events.

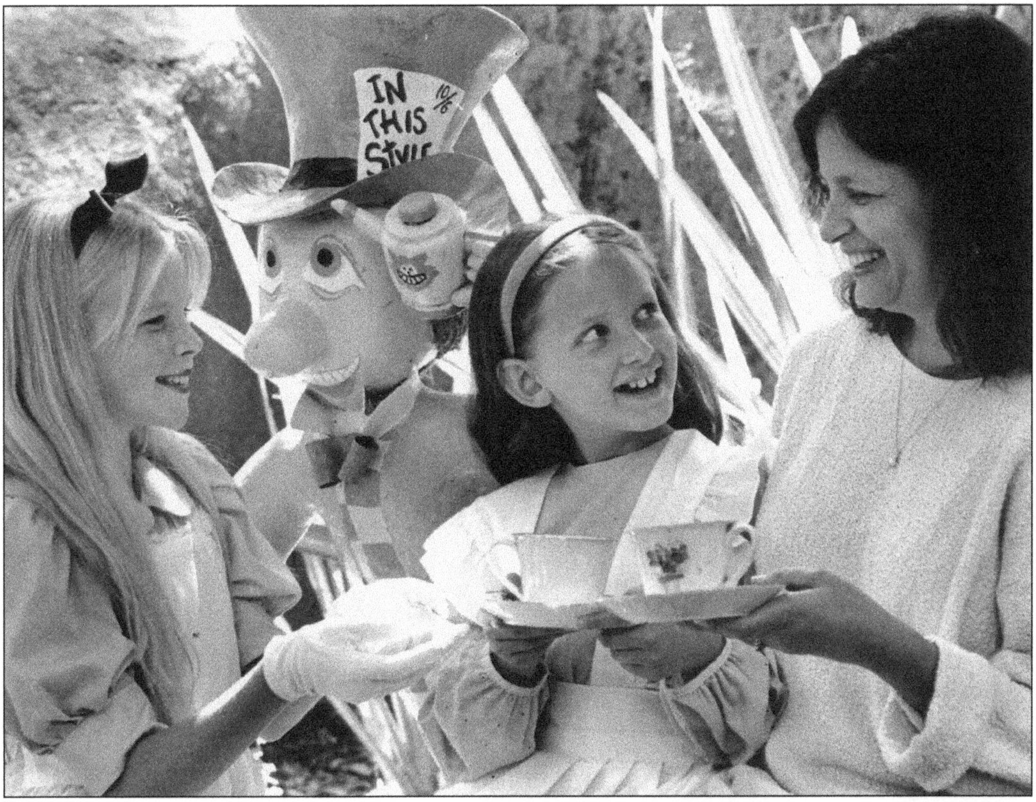

MOTHER'S DAY TEA PARTY, 1992. All mothers were invited to attend a Mad Tea Party with Alice, the Mad Hatter, and the Queen of Hearts. Families sat at a long table; Wonderland characters served imaginary tea and cookies while pushing guests down the buffet to a new seat. Every mother received a flower. Here, Alice (Angela Hangartner) serves tea to Jenna Diestler and her mother, Sherry.

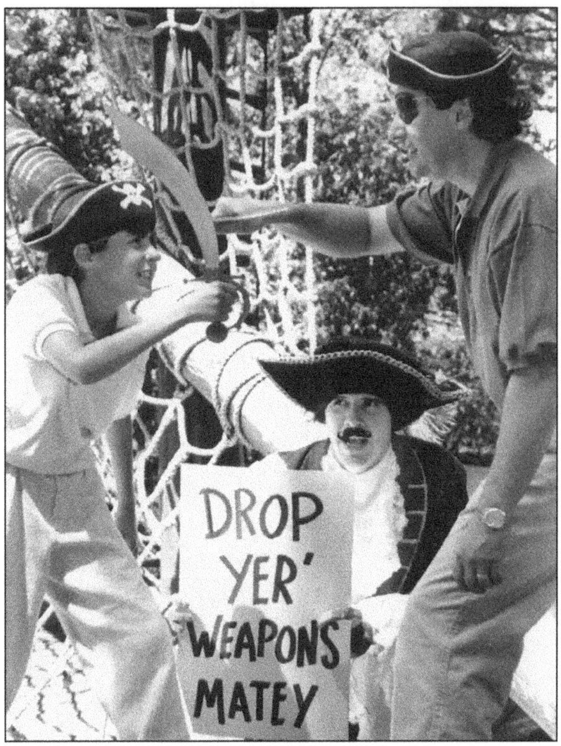

FATHER'S DAY PIRATE GAMES, 1995. Father's Day featured pirate games and races with Captain Hook and his crew. Families learned to dance a sailor's jig, speak like a pirate, walk a plank while carrying water, and engage in a swordfight. Each swordfight winner received an eye patch and a temporary tattoo. Here, Tony Moglia duels with son Matthew while Captain Hook cheers them on.

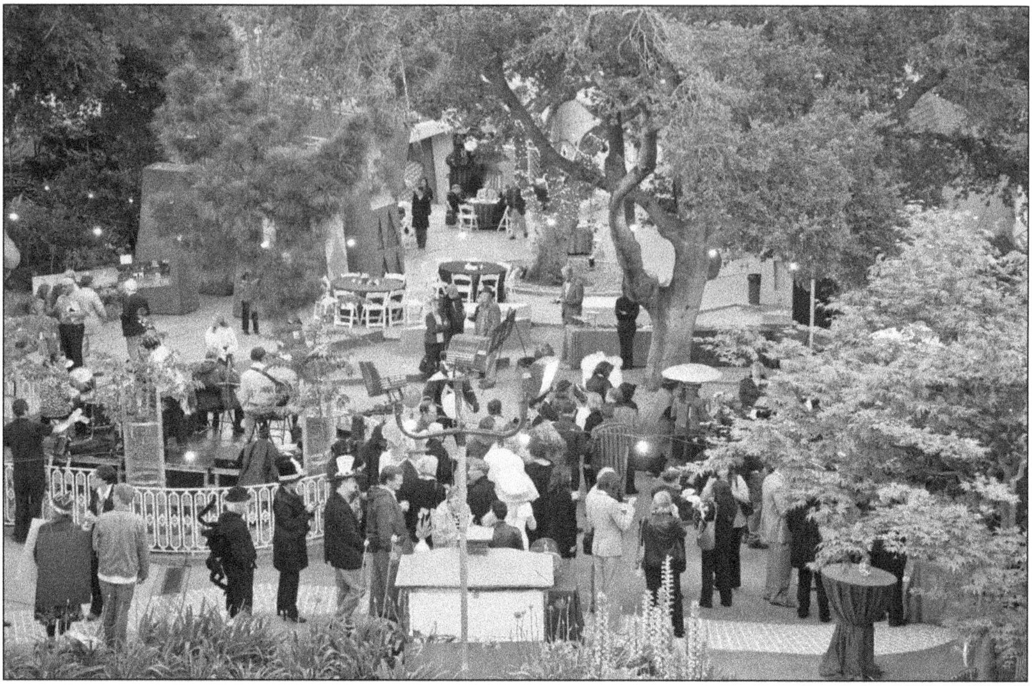

A NIGHT IN FAIRYLAND, 2012. After hours, Fairyland becomes an enchanting playground for grown-ups. Since 2007, the annual fundraising gala has been held after dark in the park; it is an opportunity for adults to dress up in costume, dine and drink, bid on donated items, and dance under the stars. Past themes have included "A Villain-thropic Evening," "Happily Ever After," and "Beauties and Beasts." In 1996, before the gala was held at Fairyland, one of the auction prizes was "queen for a day"; here, winner Elizabeth DeFeo looks astonished as Merlin (magician Tom Cutts) performs feats of wizardry.

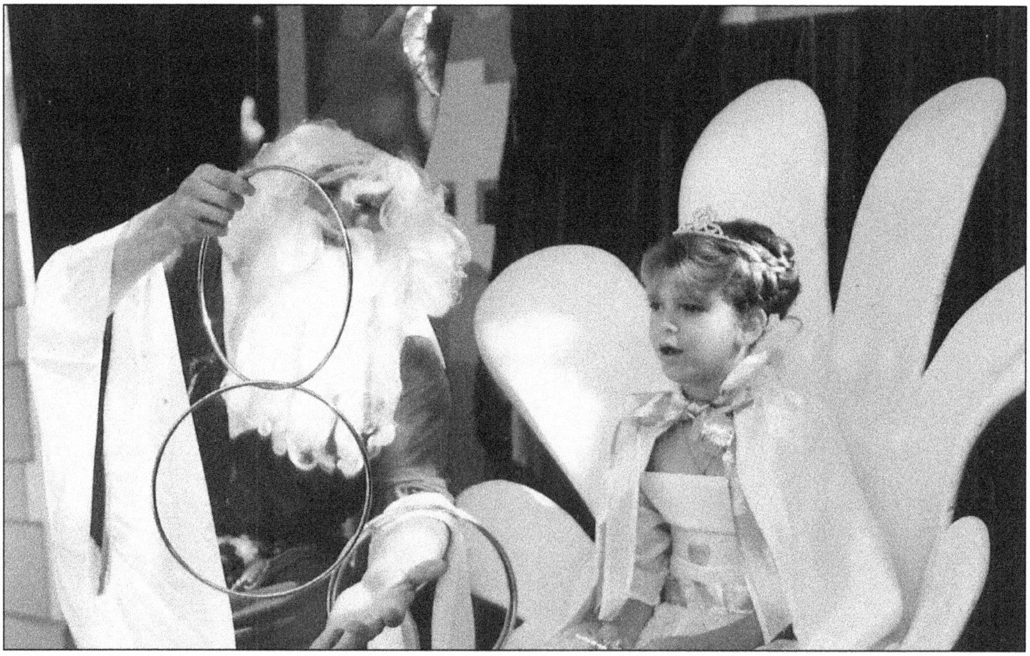

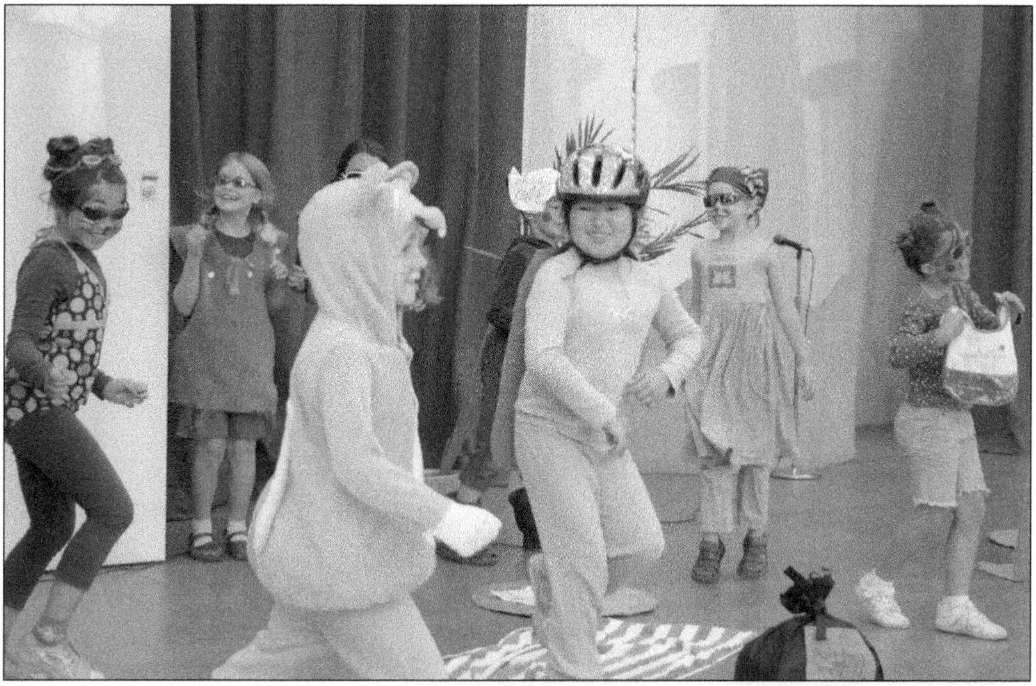

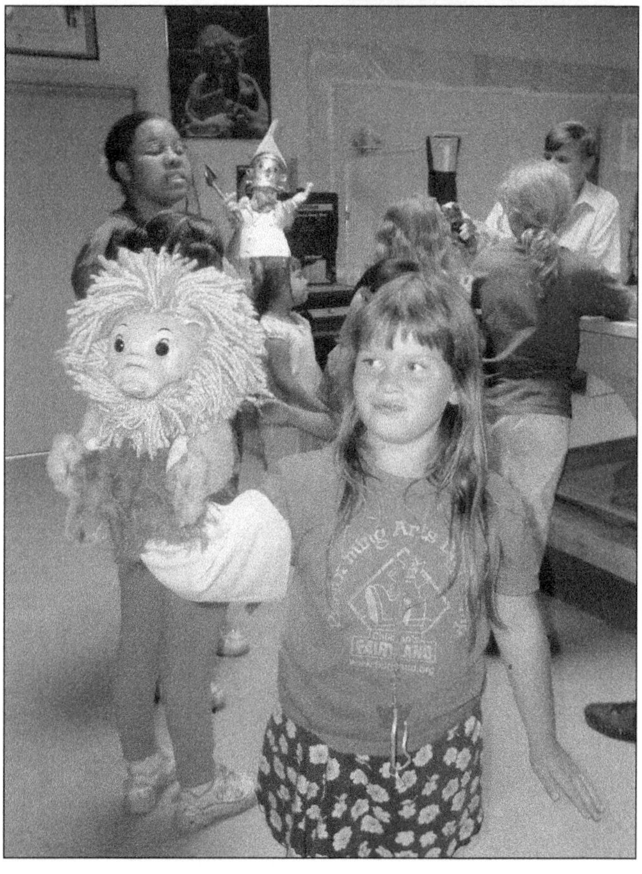

SUMMER CAMP IN FAIRYLAND, 2011. Fairyland's weeklong Performing Arts Summer Day Camp began in 1996 as a circus camp that taught stilt walking, juggling, and clowning. The program evolved to cover performing arts in general, exploring a different culture each week, with an imaginative theme such as superheroes or pirates. Children explore the park, create craft projects, get to know the animals and gardens, and produce original plays that they perform for their families at the end of the session. A highlight of the week is sneaking backstage to watch the puppet show from behind. Above, one group of campers performs their play; at right, another group learns about puppetry backstage at the puppet theater.

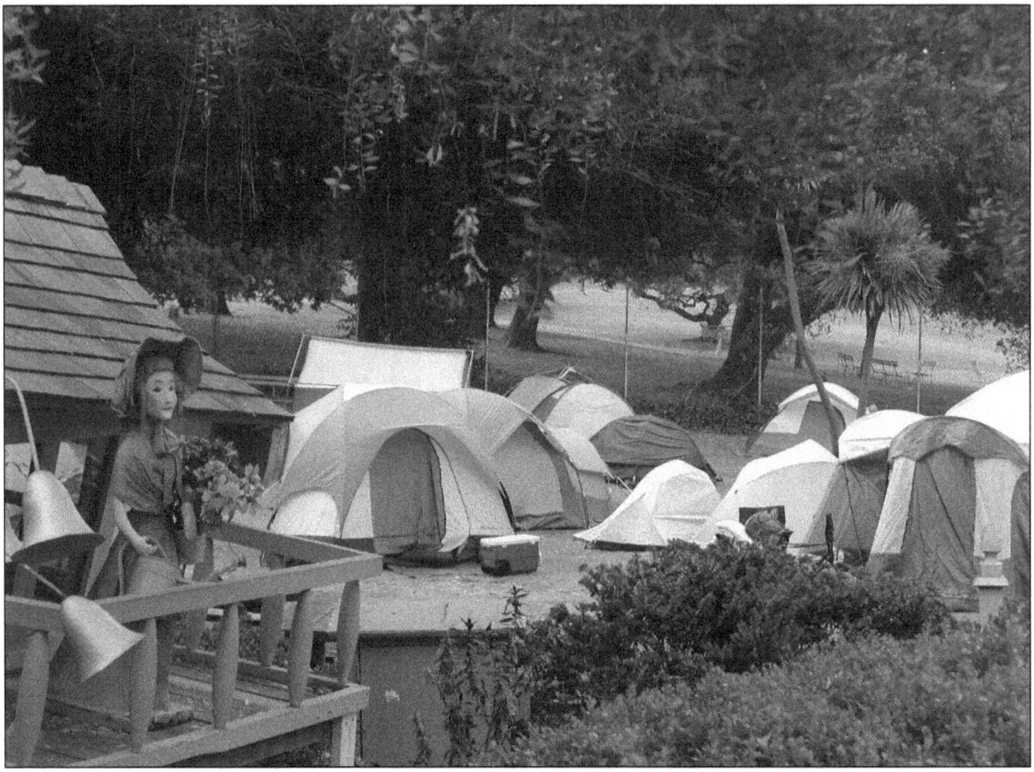

Fairyland Overnighters, 2010. Each summer, hundreds of happy campers spend a night under the stars at Fairyland. Families arrive at 5:45 p.m.; after the Fairy Gates close at 6:15, they are served dinner and invited to enjoy special after-hours entertainment, as well as free run of the park (including all rides). Soft music awakens the campers the next morning, and they are treated to breakfast at the Johnny Appleseed Café before checkout. "Magical," "safe," and "special" are words that parents use to describe the experience of camping in this urban environment. These family tents are staked in the Teddy Bear Picnic Area, with Mary, Mary standing guard.

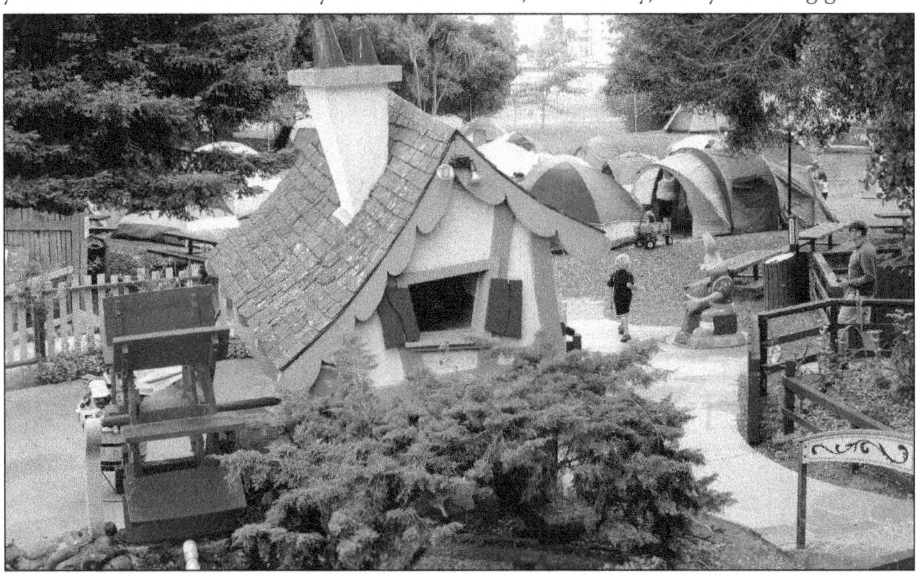

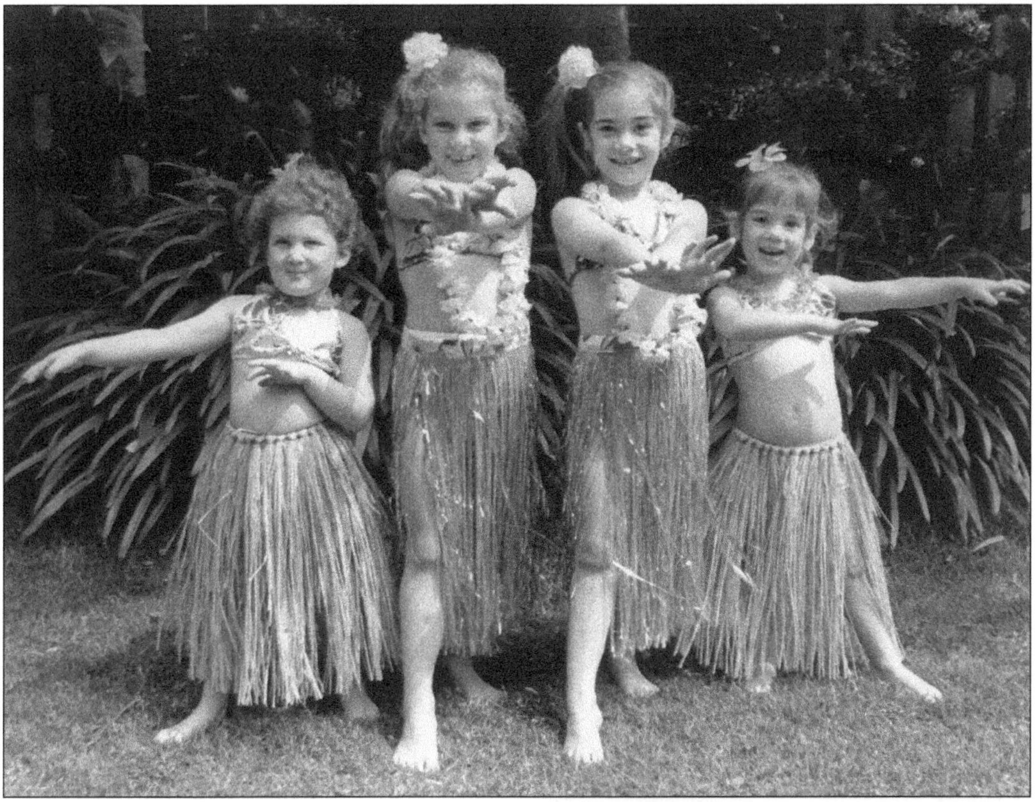

Hawaiian Day, 1996. Visiting hula dancers Heidi and Lindsey Bergen and Alexis and Jessica Sclamberg demonstrate their moves for the children of Fairyland. Other Hawaiian Day activities included fire dancers, tropical bird shows, sand-castle contests, and paper lei making. The event took advantage of abundant local resources for traditional Hawaiian arts.

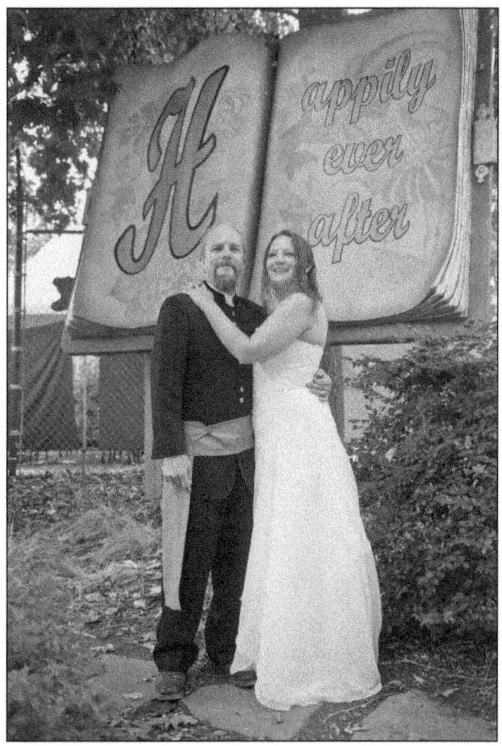

Happiness in Fairyland, 2000s. Andrew and Sarah Nardinelli celebrate their wedding at Fairyland. A relatively new tradition, Fairyland weddings, engagement parties, and vow-renewal ceremonies have proved a popular way for couples to re-create happy childhood memories while starting a new "happily ever after" in a romantic storybook setting.

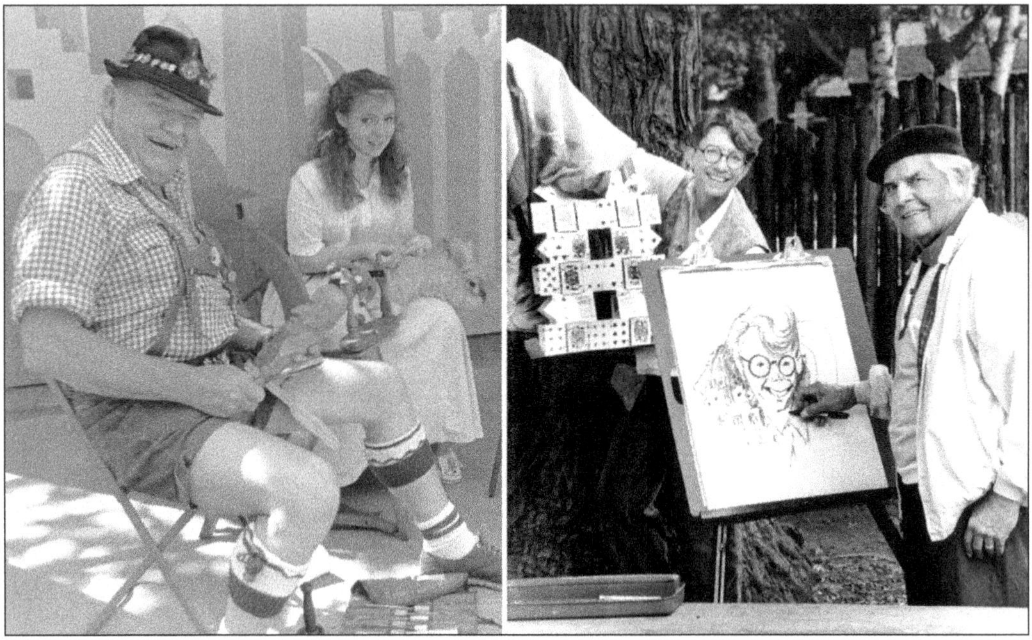

Summerfest Weekend, 1994. Summerfest was the weekend for storytellers, magicians, and artists of all kinds to share their skills with children. There were free demonstrations of all types of art forms, including woodcarving (Robert Dean Woods), yarn spinning (Rachel Lieberson), magic (Blake Maxam), and sketching (Larry O'Hare).

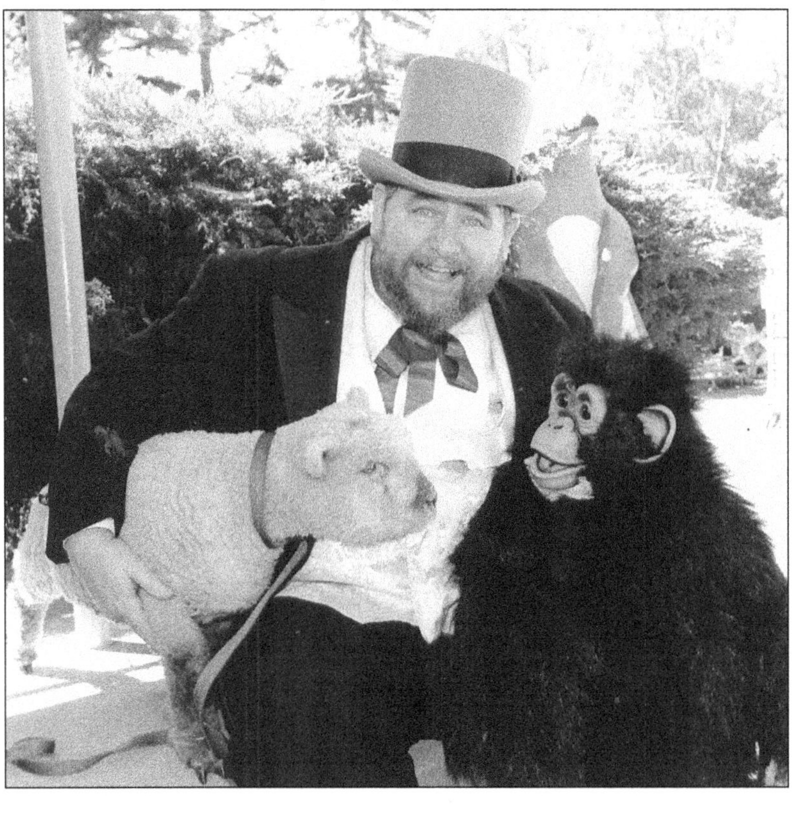

Doctor Dolittle Day, 1989. Doctor Dolittle visited the park once a year to teach the proper care of animals. One year, he hosted Thanksgiving Day for the Animals, and children helped make a holiday meal for their favorite creature. The doctor, Ron Johnson, pals around with Chee-Chee his puppet chimpanzee and Woolikins the baby lamb.

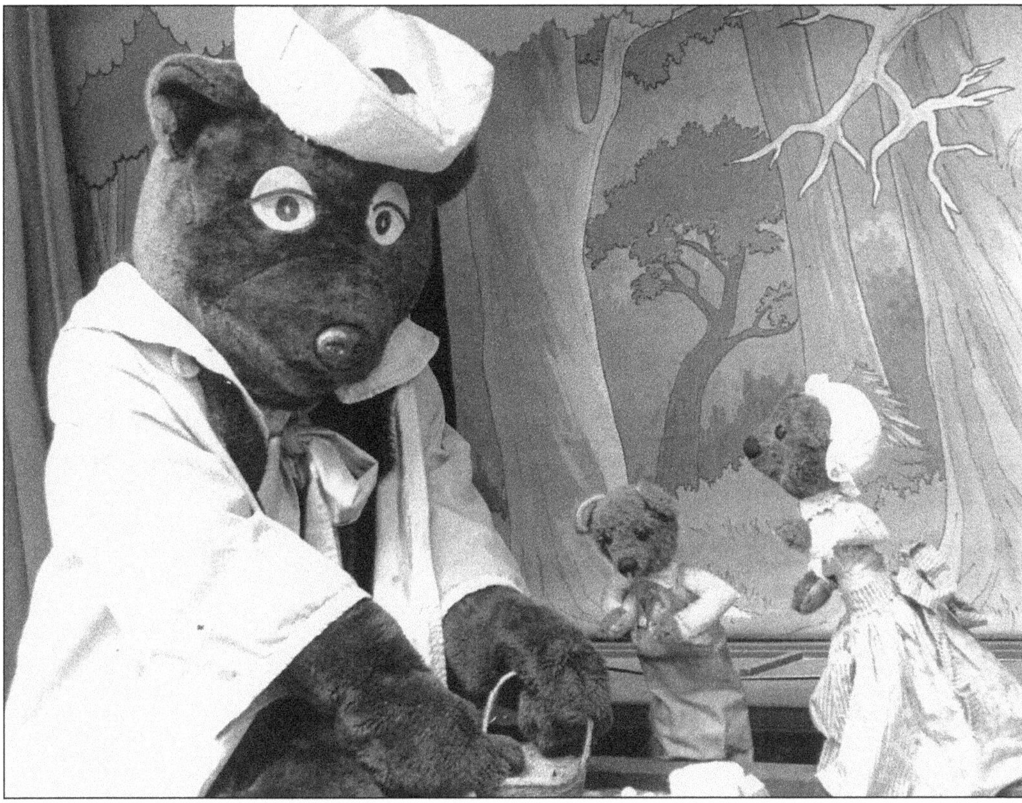

TEDDY BEAR PICNIC DAY, 1988. Farnsworth the Bear, Fairyland's mascot, is here to lead the children and their teddy bears to a secret place for a picnic. Children who brought their stuffed-bear friends to the park received free stickers, discounted admissions, and bear hugs from Farnsworth. Today, plush animals and hand puppets are popular items in the Magic Lantern Gift Shop.

HOSPITAL DAY, 1990. A collaboration with Children's Hospital of Oakland, this event taught children what to expect in a doctor's office or hospital. It featured a play area with medical gadgets, storytelling, and theatrics. Children brought their favorite toys to the doll emergency hospital to have them "healed."

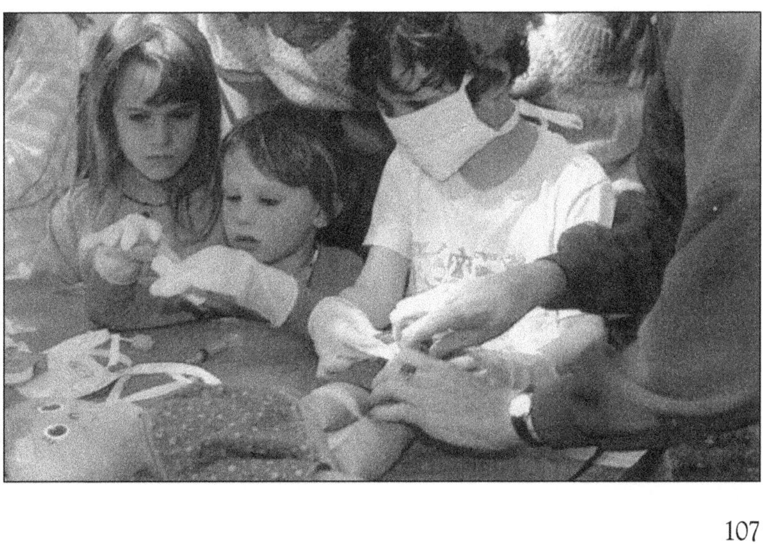

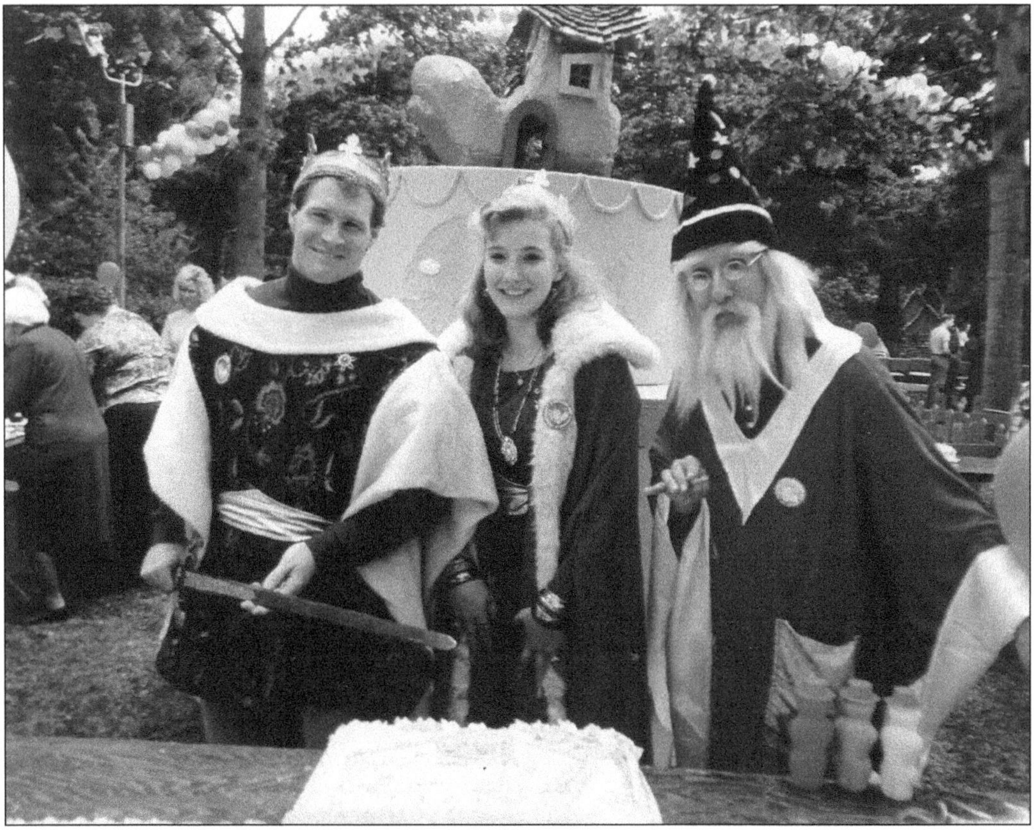

Fairyland's Birthday Party, 1990. Fairyland's September birthday has been the occasion for festive themed events, including a 1990 Camelot party at which King Arthur (Joel Schlader), Queen Guinevere (Allison Kastama), and Merlin the Wizard (Blake Maxam) cut Fairyland's cake with the legendary sword Excalibur. For Fairyland's 20th birthday in 1970, the park invited former Oakland puppeteer and director Frank Oz of the Muppets, who trained at Fairyland's Storybook Puppet Theater when he was a teenager, to visit the park and bring his Sesame Street friends Bert and Cookie Monster. A few hundred guests were expected, but thousands showed up. Here, park host Darryl Ferreria clowns with Cookie Monster at the puppet theater.

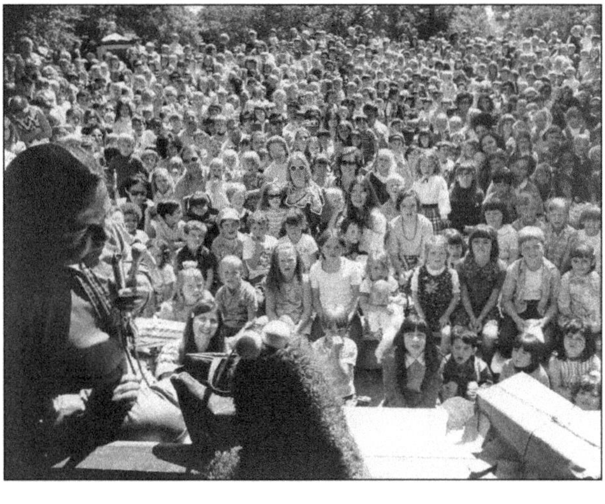

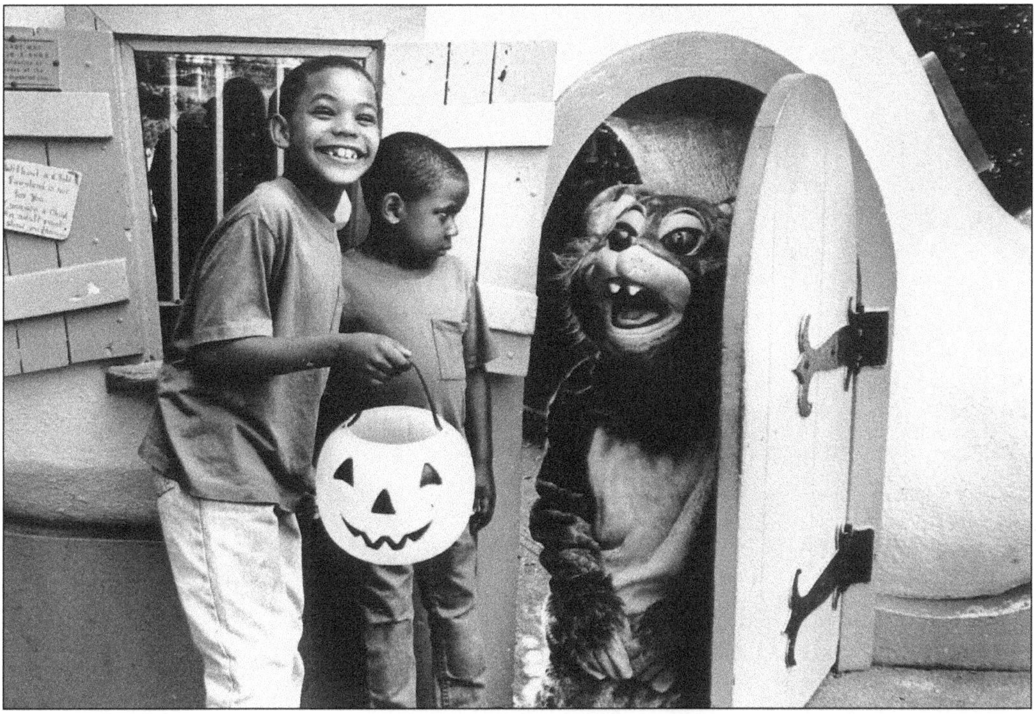

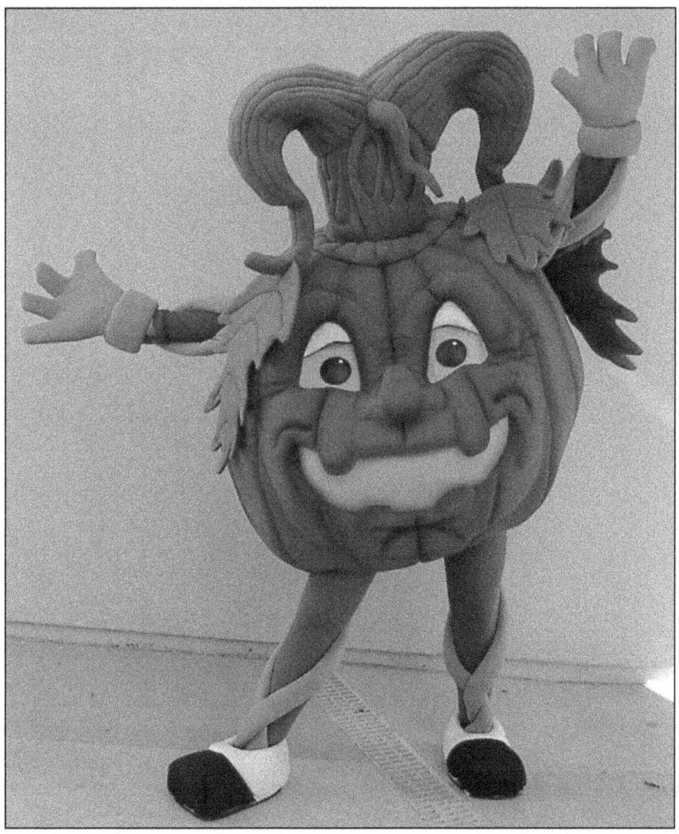

Jack O'Lantern Jamboree, 1995. "More delightful than frightful!" is the slogan for Fairyland's annual Halloween event, a tradition since 1978. One of the first Halloween events of its kind in the Bay Area, the jamboree has been imitated at other parks, as well as in malls and schools. Attractions have included a haunted tunnel, a pirate school, storybook-themed train rides, and a spooky carnival. Treat stations are located throughout the park, and goody bags are included with park admission. It looks like one visitor is ready for Halloween candy! His brother is less certain. Just don't "wolf" down the treats, advises the grinning pumpkin mascot.

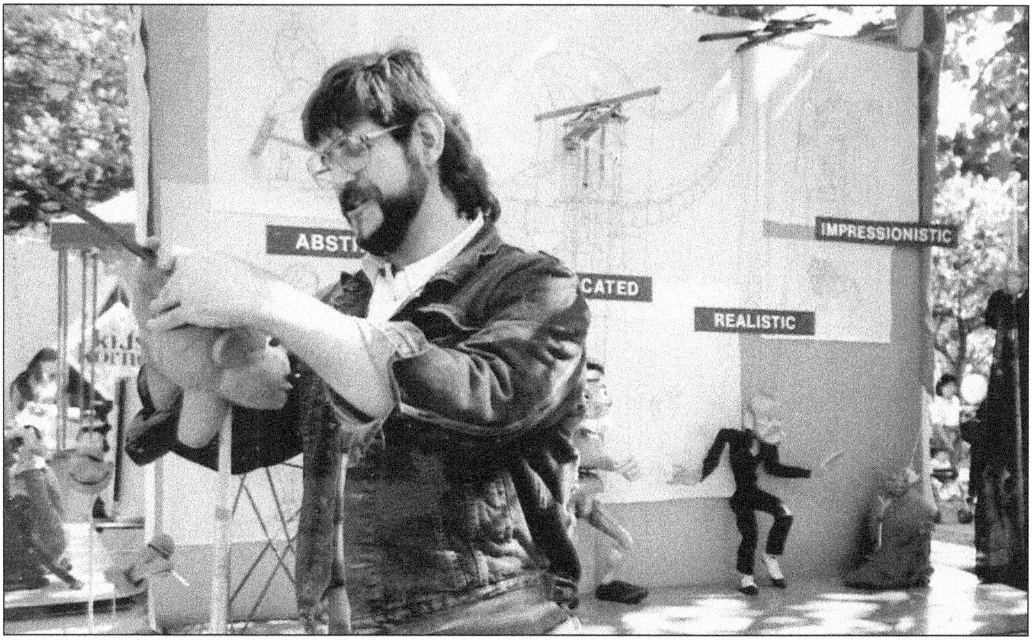

Puppet Fair Weekend, 1995. Cosponsored by the San Francisco Bay Area Puppet Guild, the weekend features puppet shows, a puppet history display, and puppet-making instruction. In 2016, Fairyland's puppet theater celebrated 60 years of continuous operation. In the photograph, puppeteer Richard Steven Weber demonstrates how to carve a marionette like Pinocchio.

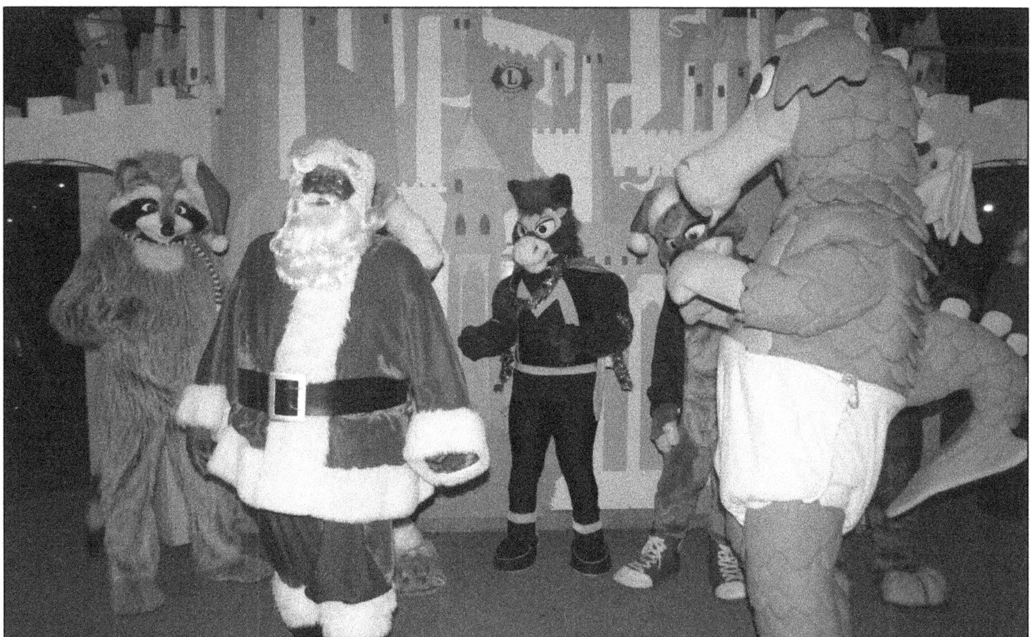

Fairy Winterland, 2008. Santa (Ron Zeno), the Lost Baby Dragon, and Critters by the Bay, walk-around animal characters, greet holiday visitors. For two weeks each December, Fairyland holds holiday festivities that culminate in a Santa parade under twinkling fairy lights. Depictions of holiday traditions from around the world are another highlight.

Eight

Toward Tomorrow

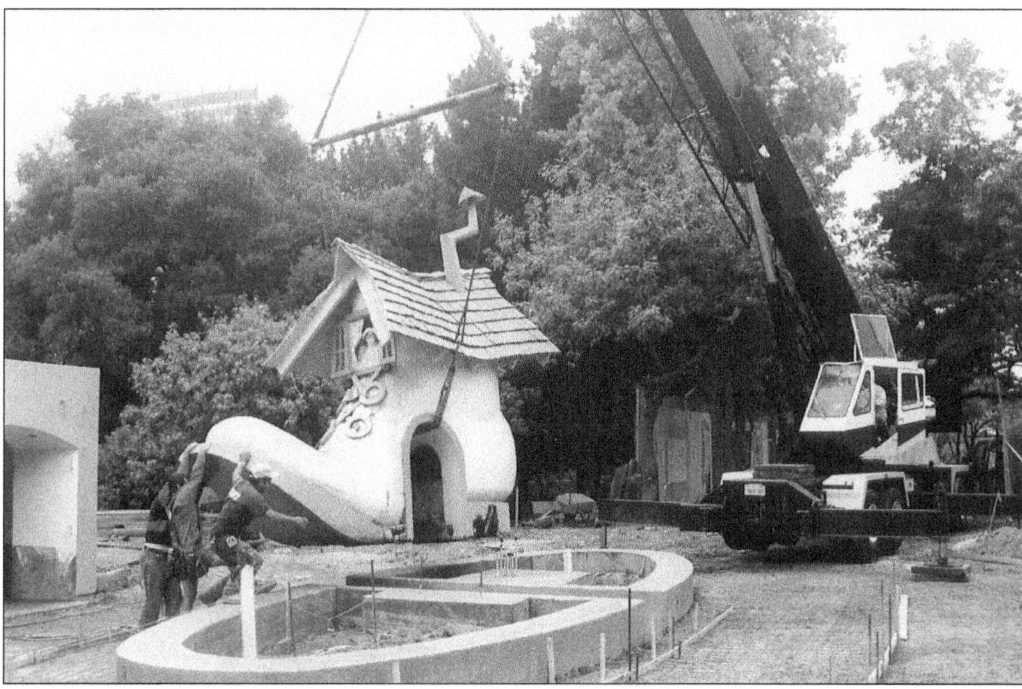

Move That Shoe!, 2000. Construction workers carefully lift Fairyland's iconic first set with a crane and place it on its new footprint. Although it is no longer used as a ticket booth, the shoe was repositioned in front of the park's new entry gates so that visitors could still pass through it to enter the park. The Shoe can also be seen by traffic on Grand Avenue, a busy thoroughfare.

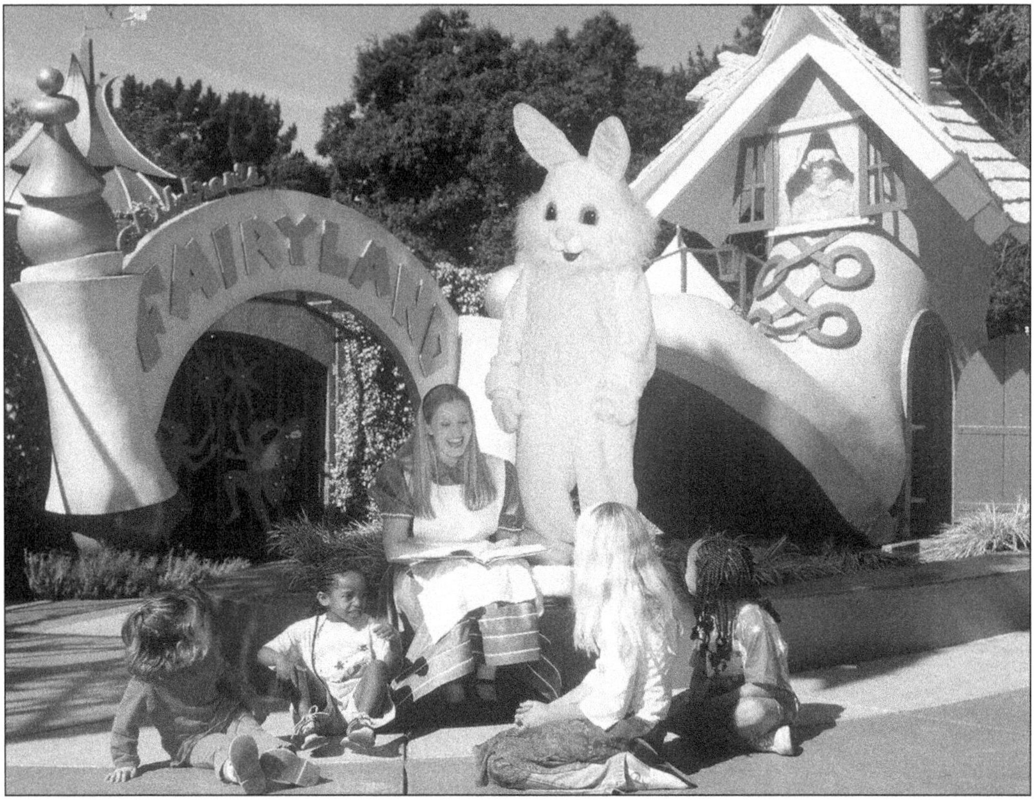

Follow That Rabbit, 2002. Alice (Rebecca Lyons) reads to children about the secret entrance she found into Wonderland. But the White Rabbit plans to take them instead down into the new magical gates of Fairyland. Fairyland has always strived to help those who would most benefit from the park's language-rich environment, and so each year, it subsidizes 16,000 family members at low or no cost.

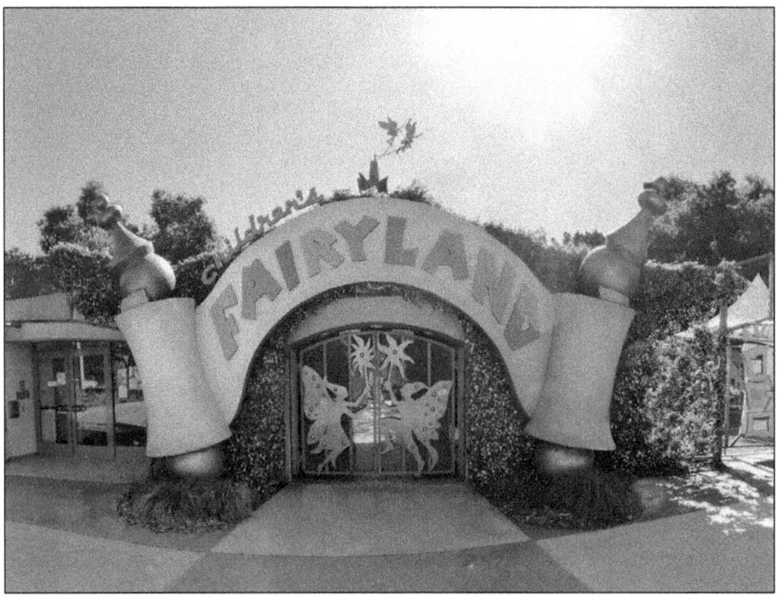

Fairy Gates, 2001. These are the magical gates that allow visitors to enter the world of childhood dreams and literature. The side entrance to the Magic Lamp Gift Shop can be seen to the left of the giant scroll. Aladdin's Genie, who towers above the entrance, is currently in the bottle and not visible. Can that really be tiny fairies flitting and flying above the scroll?

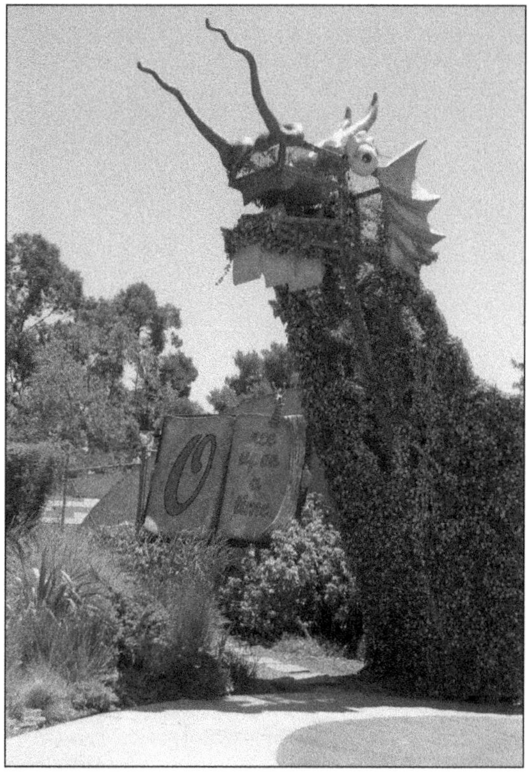

Topiary Dragon, 2005. The Garden Dragon, a wire sculpture covered in climbing ivy, guards the Fairy Gates at the park's entrance. On the dragon's sides are large books inscribed "Once Upon a Time" and "Happily Ever After," the classic beginning and ending of many children's tales all over the world.

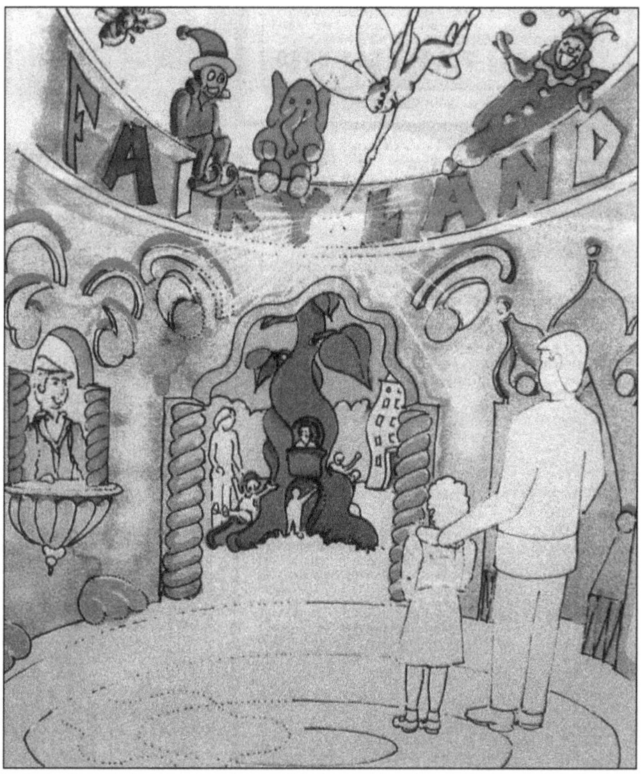

Park Entrance Concept, 1998. This is of one of many designs created by Ace Architects principals Lucia Howard and David Weingarten for a major park redesign. The drawing shows the view past the ticket booth into Fairyland. Jack and the Beanstalk's twisty slide, seen in the center of the image, did not survive past the concept phase.

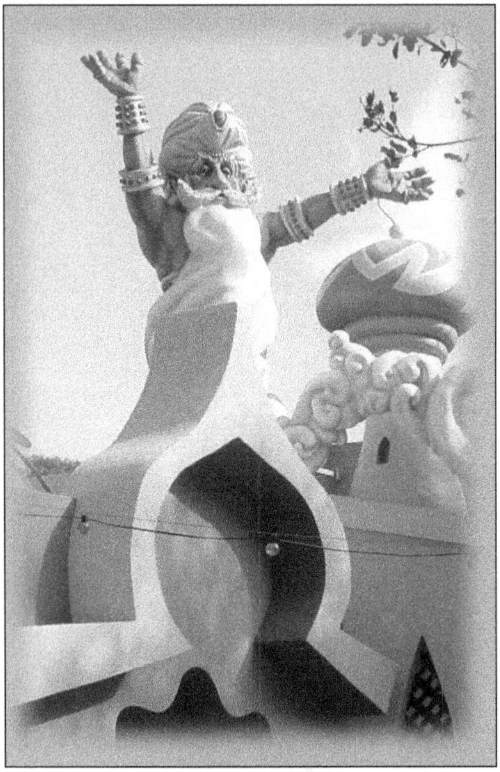

Magic Lamp Gift Shop, 2005. The gift shop, situated just inside the Fairy Gates, is presided over by the Magic Genie and Aladdin on his carpet. All of the fiberglass figures around the entrance were designed and built by Mario Chiodo of Chiodo Entertainment. Chiodo grew up in Oakland and frequently visited Fairyland as a child; he wanted to leave an example of his talents for his own children to enjoy for many years. The plaza architecture represents elements from all corners of the globe: the gift shop echoes Arab motifs, a Pacific Asian gate frames the Happy Dragon, and a set of African arches beckons the visitor to other adventures.

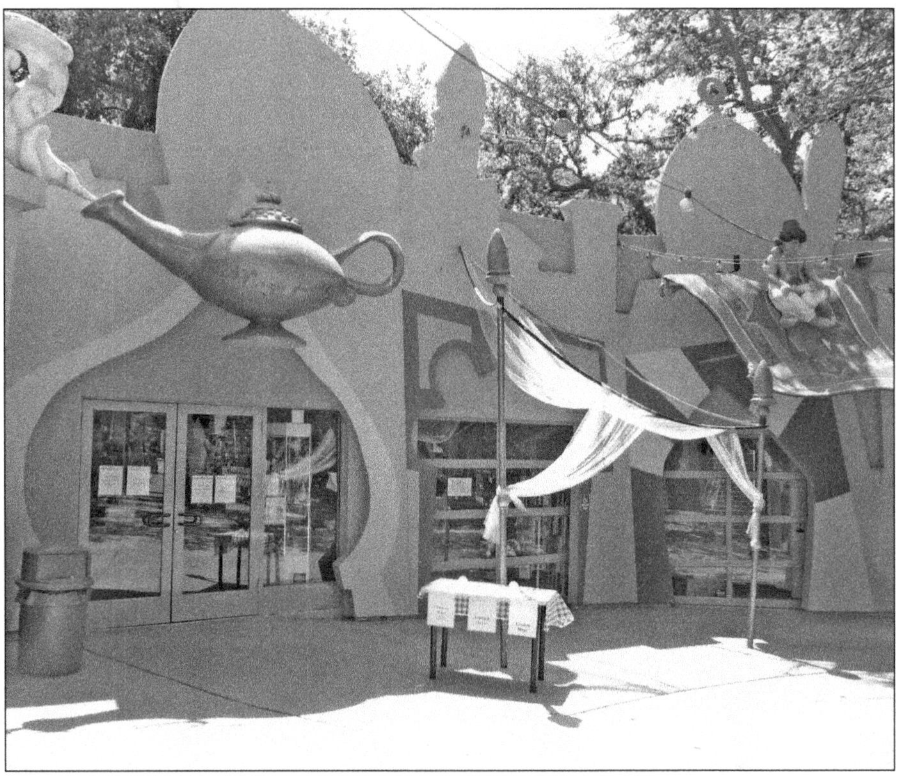

Dragon Slide and Chinese Tea House, 1990 and 2014. In 1962, architect William Russell Everritt gave Fairyland his last and finest design. A gift from father and son businessmen Milton and Joe Shoong and the Shoong Foundation, the elegant Dragon Slide rises 32 feet in the air, with the "floating" Chinese Tea House at its side. From the teahouse—the highest point in Fairyland—a visitor can survey the entire park. The teahouse's airy appearance is deceptive: it is constructed from 13 tons of cement and many tons of steel. The slide was refurbished once in 1990; in 2014, Milton Shoong's sister Doris underwrote a second two-month restoration of this popular attraction.

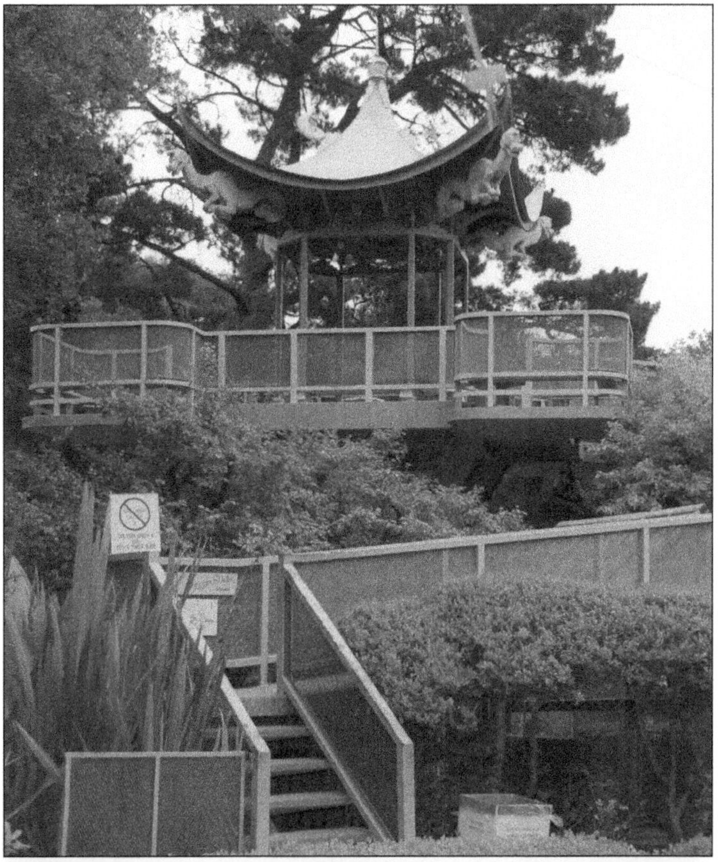

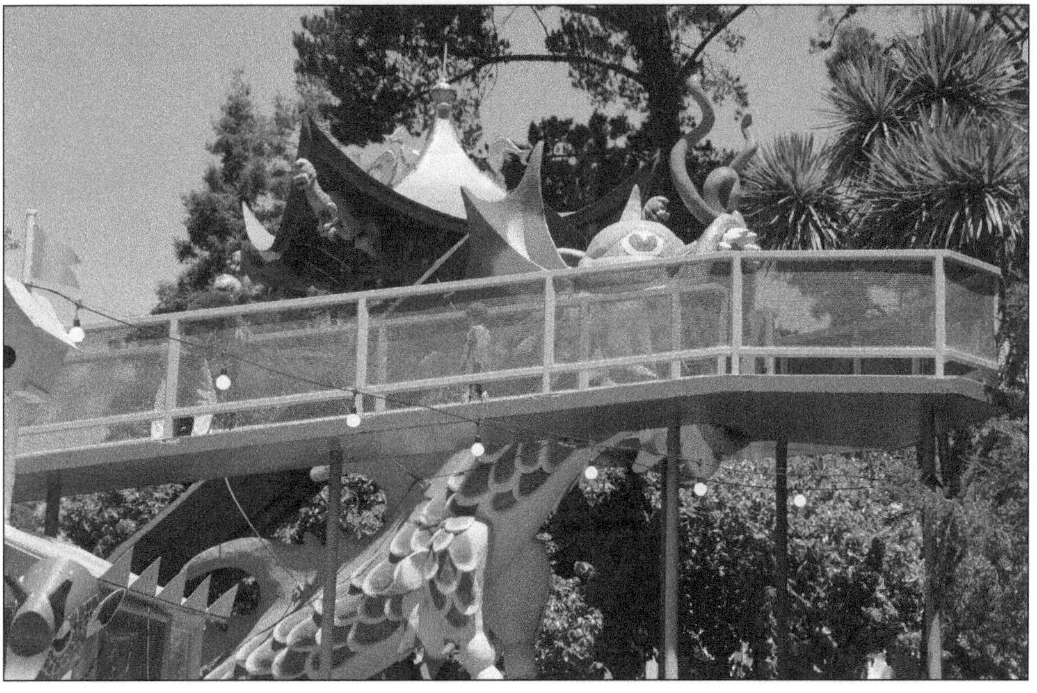

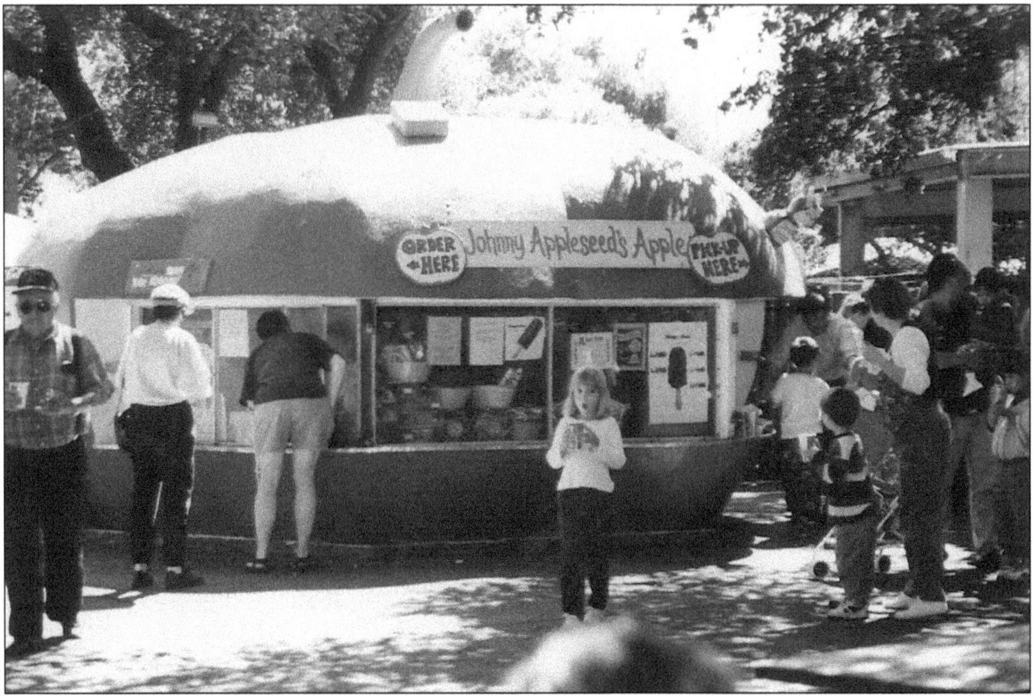

Johnny Appleseed's Café, 1997 and 2005. The Fairyland café started life in 1960 as the Big Pumpkin Food Stand, as its squash-like shape suggests. In 1995, the pumpkin was painted red and transformed into Johnny Appleseed's apple, with sculpted worms added for whimsy. The structure's small size limited its functionality, so in 2001, Ace Architects of Oakland created a new building, J.A.'s Good Eats, capable of handling large catered parties, as well as serving family-friendly fare to daily visitors. In 2016, the café added a pizza oven. The original pumpkin/apple structure still stands in the picnic area, which is part of Old West Junction, a set that celebrates folklore, tall tales, and legends of the American West.

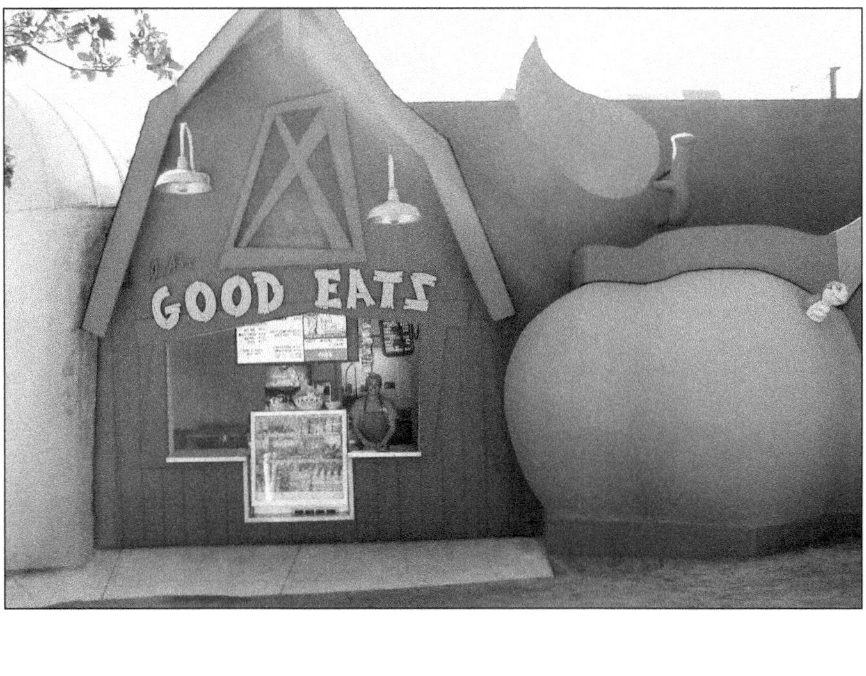

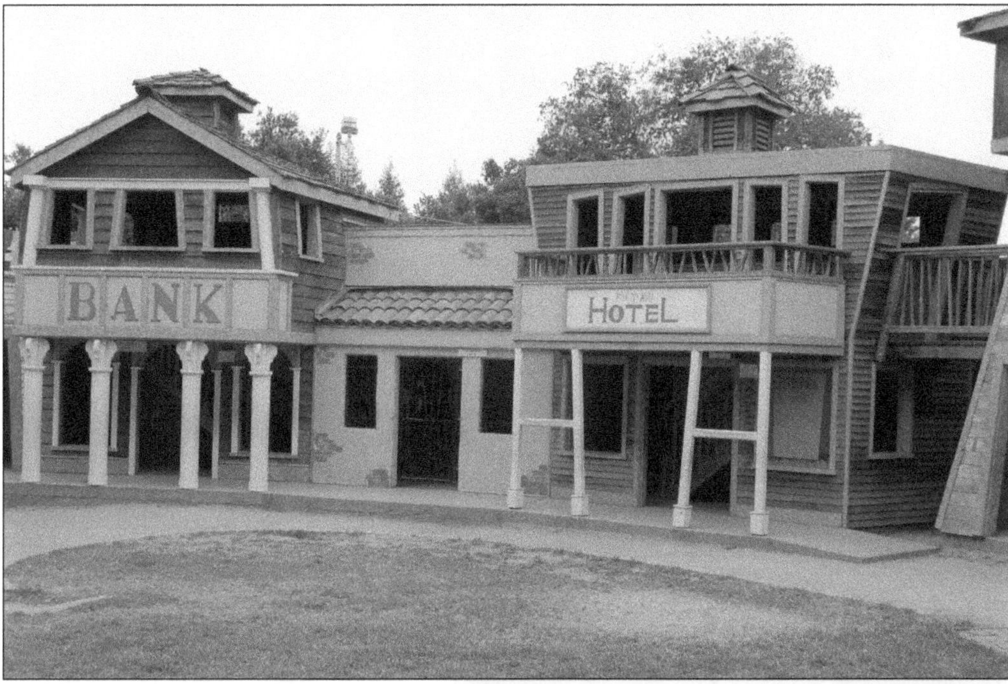

Old West Junction, 2005. Originally conceived as Yankee Doodle Junction, this set underwent many design and theme changes before opening in 2005 as Old West Junction. It contains a livery stable, a water-tower slide, and pony figures—all of which encourage children to act out fantasy play. The Jolly Trolly Train passes through and behind the buildings. During the annual Jack O'Lantern Jamboree in October, the set becomes a ghost town. The jail, located between the bank and the hotel, provides a convenient "time-out" area for children and parents alike. During special after-hours events for adults, the junction has hosted DJs and dance parties.

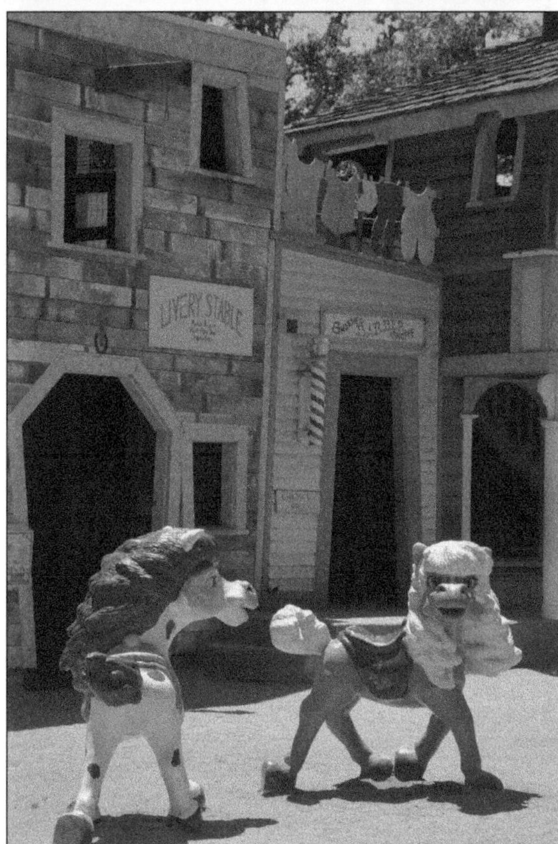

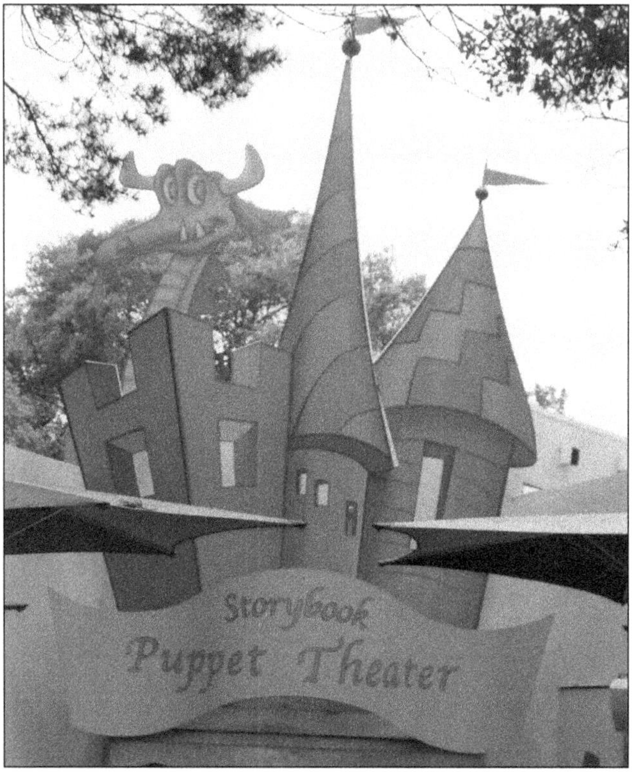

STORYBOOK PUPPET THEATER ADDITIONS, 2006. For the puppet theater's 50th anniversary, Ace Architects designed an extension to William Everritt's original 1956 design. A higher ceiling in the main building allows for larger scenery; a new workshop and storage facility provide added workspace. The new taller ceiling is masked by a dragon and castle that make the open book appear to be a classic children's pop-up book. The workshop is located in an annex designed to look like a pile of books being investigated by a pair of bookworms. Each of the titles painted on the volumes is that of an actual book of fairy tales or puppetry lore.

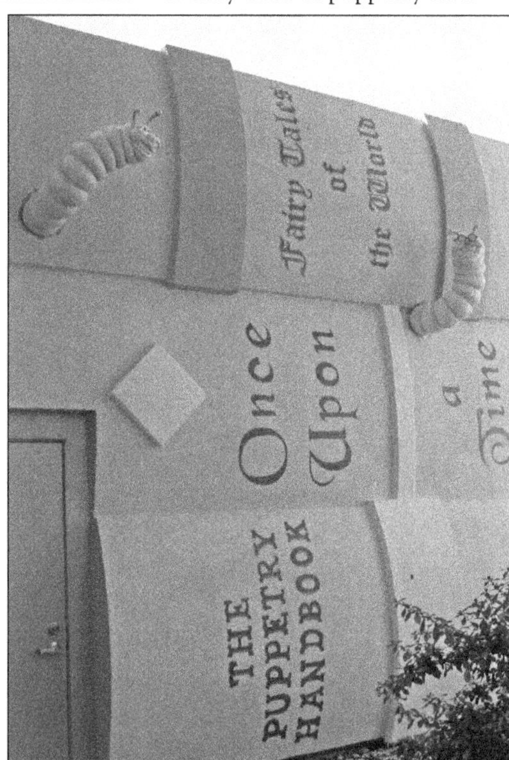

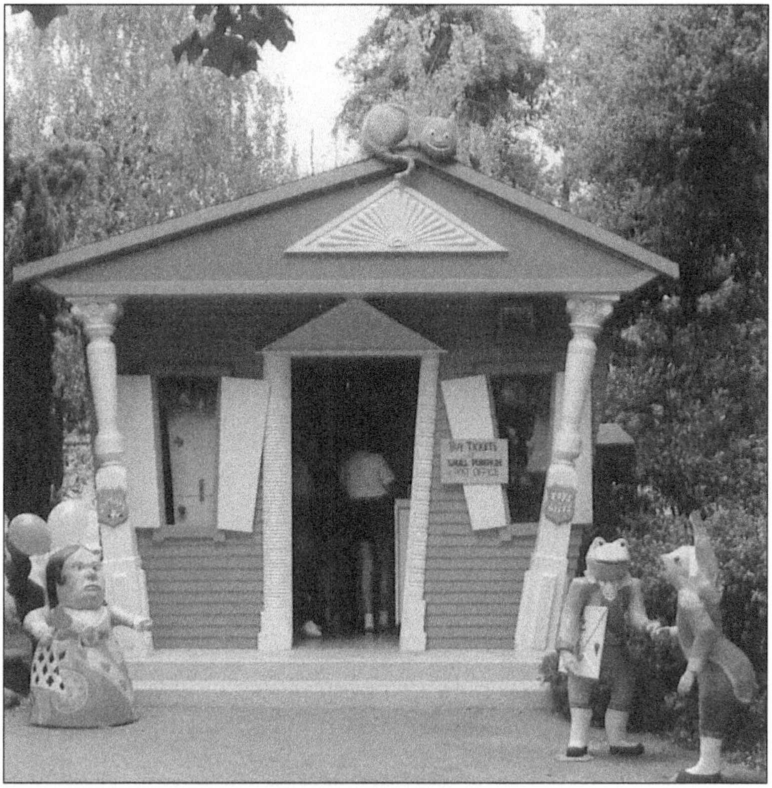

Duchess House, 1990. The Duchess House gift shop, which opened in 1960, catered to birthday party rentals with small affordable gifts. This unusual building was recycled from pieces from older Oakland Victorian buildings, such as the pillars. The fiberglass figures of the queen and her fish and frog footmen were later moved to the Alice in Wonderland Tunnel.

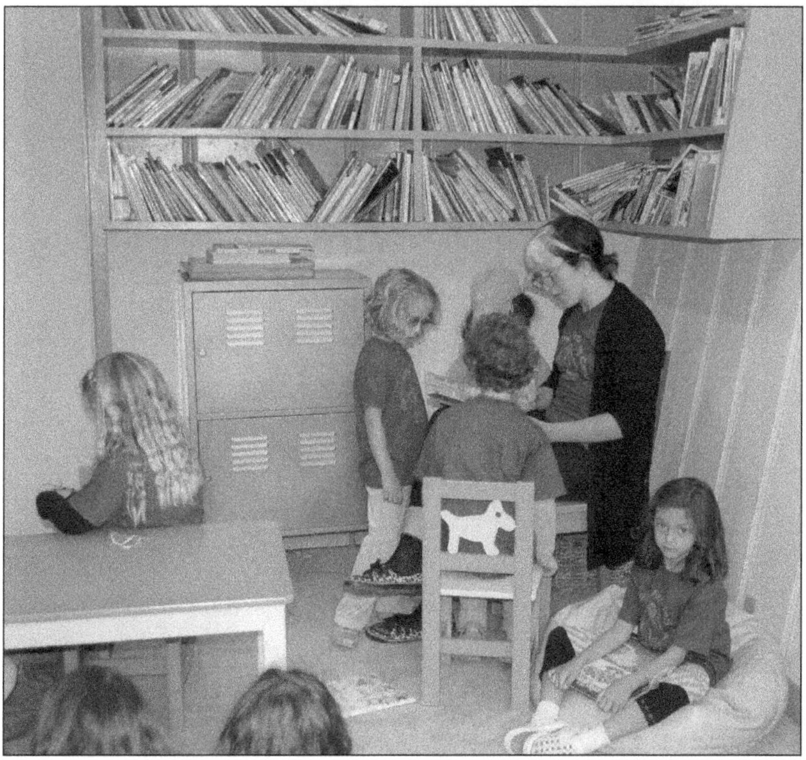

Alice's Reading Room, 2008. In 2001, the Duchess House was turned into Alice's Reading Room with the help of a grant from the Ebell Lakeview Women's Club. By 2014, volunteer librarians were helping to catalog new books and hosting weekly story times for toddlers. In the photograph, camp counselor Lauryn Kerr tells stories to Fairyland summer campers.

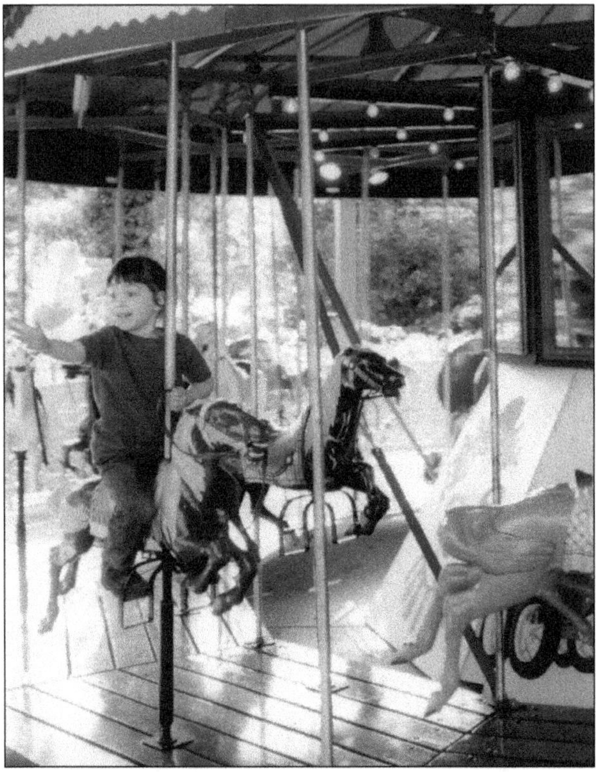

FLECTO CHILDREN'S CAROUSEL, 2003. This charming, small-scale merry-go-round was donated in 2002 by the Flecto Paint Company of Oakland, which had used it to advertise its brilliant paints and finishes at trade shows. At Fairyland, the carousel was hand-assembled by members of the Lake Merritt Breakfast Club on the site of the onetime Walrus and Carpenter Seal Pond. In 2016, the carousel was extensively refurbished thanks to support from Rust-Oleum, which had acquired Flecto. The horses were removed, stripped, and repainted in a brilliant new palette. The scenic panels in the center, which hide the motor, are now adorned with images of famous mythological horses from around the world.

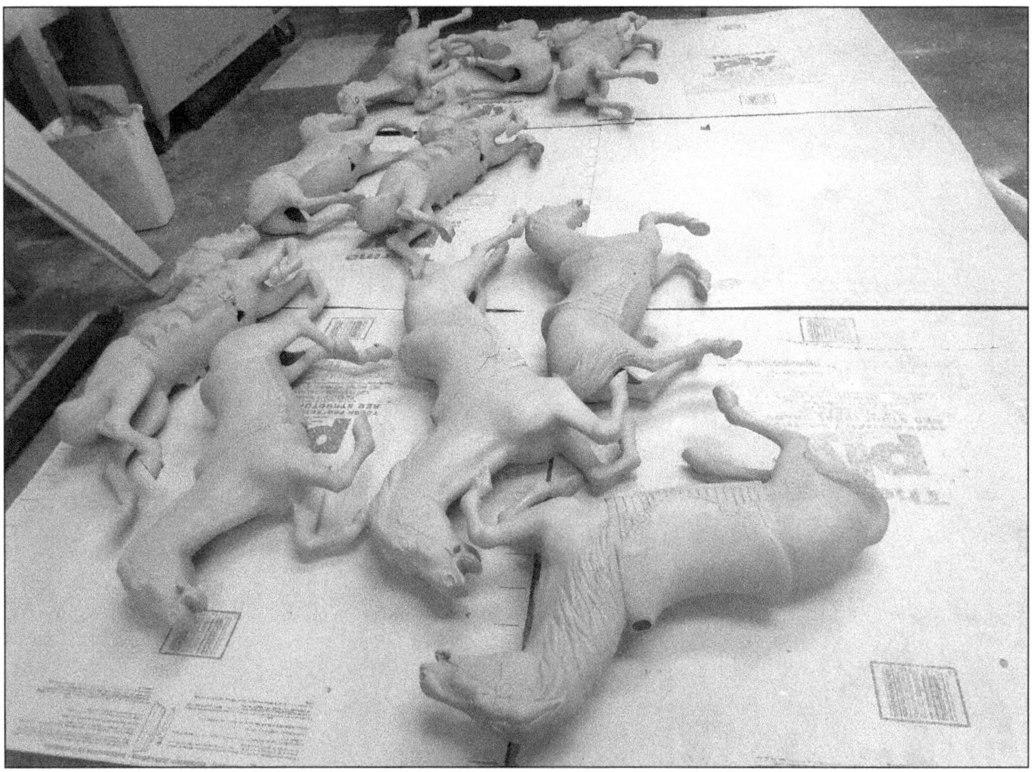

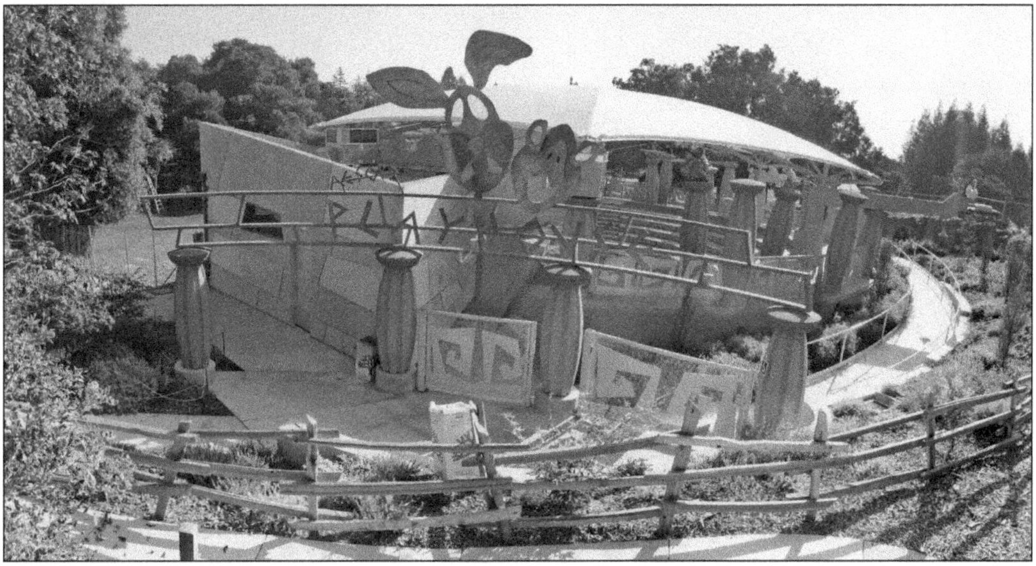

Aesop's Playhouse Amphitheater, 2008. Fairyland opened its third live-performance theater in the spring of 2008 on the site of the old Toyland Boat Ride. Inspired by Aesop's fables and designed by Ace Architects of Oakland, with original fiberglass figures and motifs by Scientific Art Studio of Richmond, the theater has two performance stages on opposite sides. One faces the semicircular covered seats and is used for Fairyland Children's Theatre performances and other live theater; the other, an outdoor stage, faces the Teddy Bear Picnic Meadow. The theater also accommodates community theater performances, as well as social functions and dances. In this view of the covered theater, a member of the Oakland Ballet Company performs for an audience.

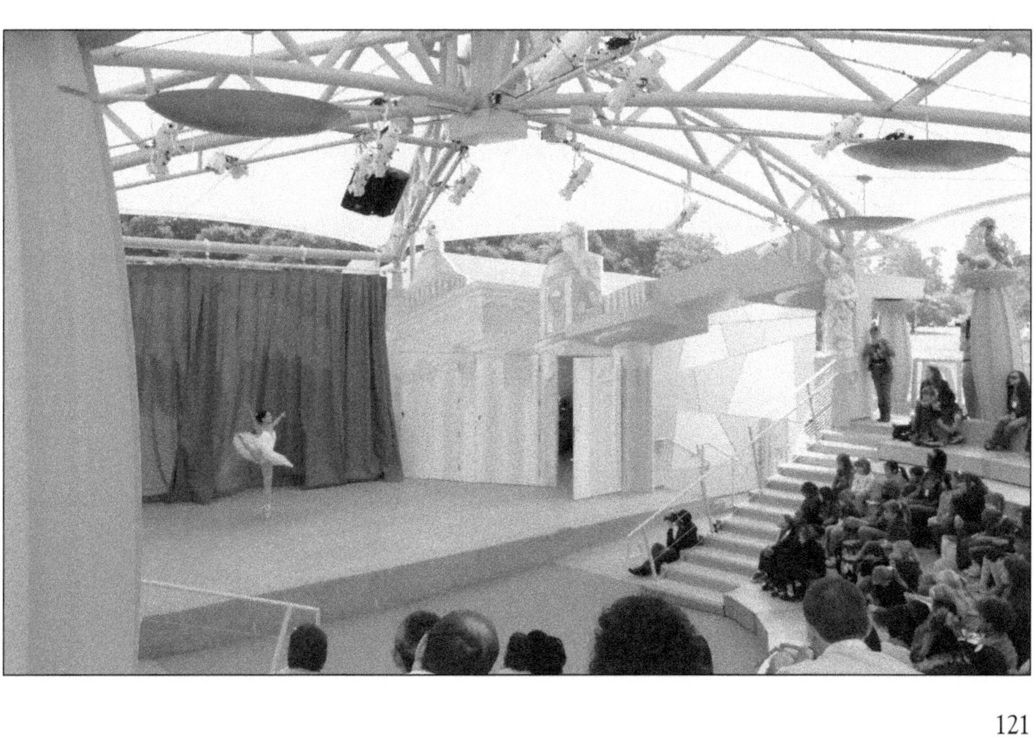

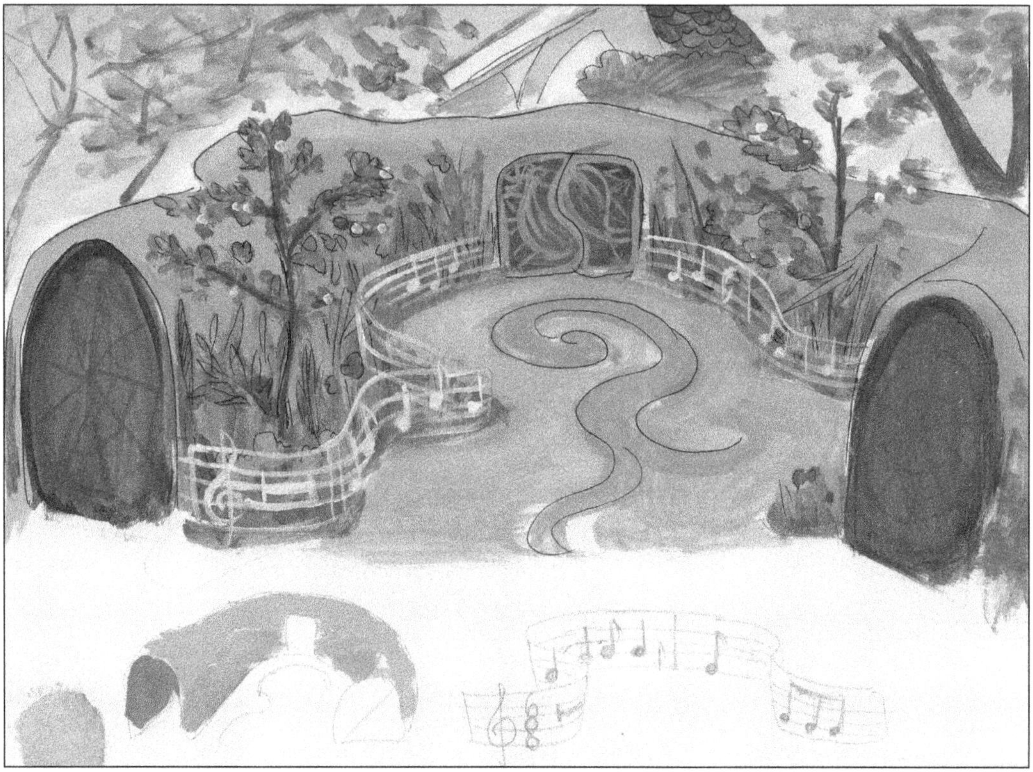

Fairy Music Farm Concept, 2008. The $3 million bond measure that allowed Fairyland to expand the puppet theater and create Aesop's Playhouse also funded the Fairy Music Farm, a repurposing of the Thumbelina Tunnel. Opened in 1956, Thumbelina had featured insect displays such as an ant colony, beehive, and worm farm; it closed in 1990. One condition of the bond expenditure was that it be used for a project by local artists; the Fairy Music Farm—the fantasy is that fairy music helps plants grow—became that project. The tunnel interior is adorned with fairy murals and playable musical instruments. (Even the benches and bridges are musical instruments!) Pictured inside the tunnel are, from left to right, designer Lynn-Rachel Altman, instrument maker Daniel Schmidt, muralist Biliana Stremska, and composer Richard Jenning.

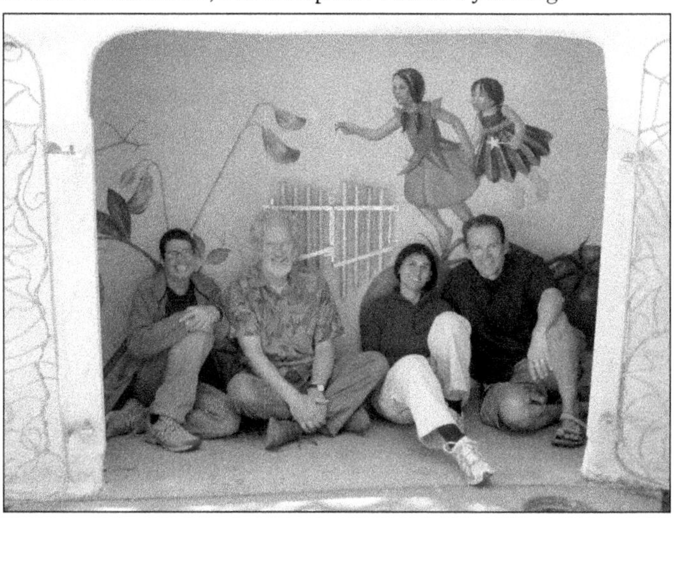

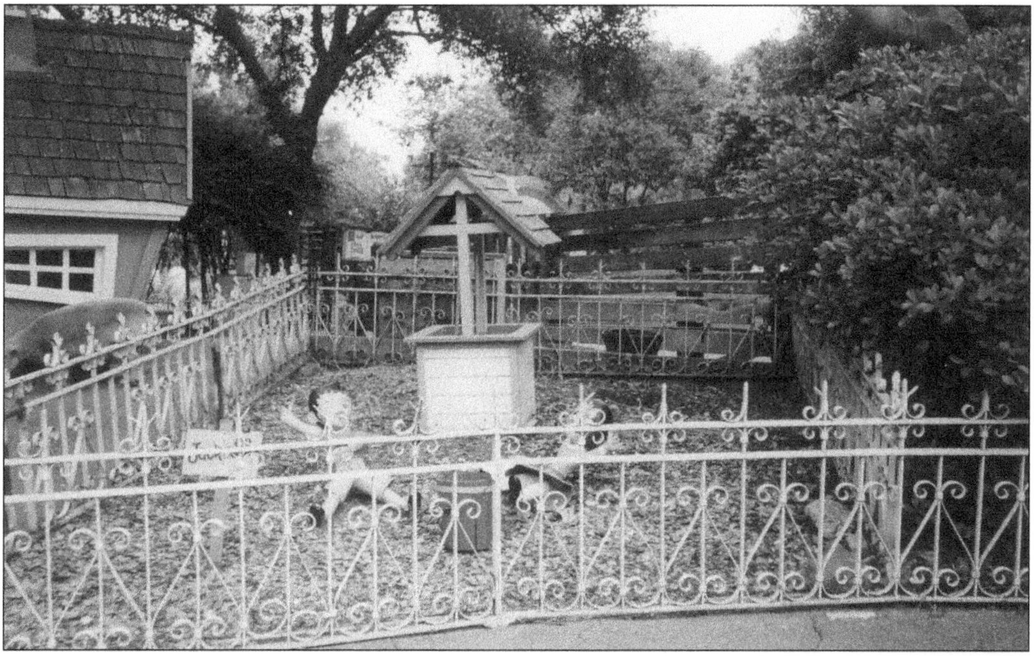

JACK AND JILL, 1990S. These well-known nursery rhyme characters have appeared all over Fairyland. Here, they are in the nursery rhyme area of the park, near Humpty Dumpty Wall. In 1959, Jack and Jill was a drinking faucet atop a hill in the Merry Meadow. Children climbed up the hill to get a cool drink from the "well" (a running water fountain).

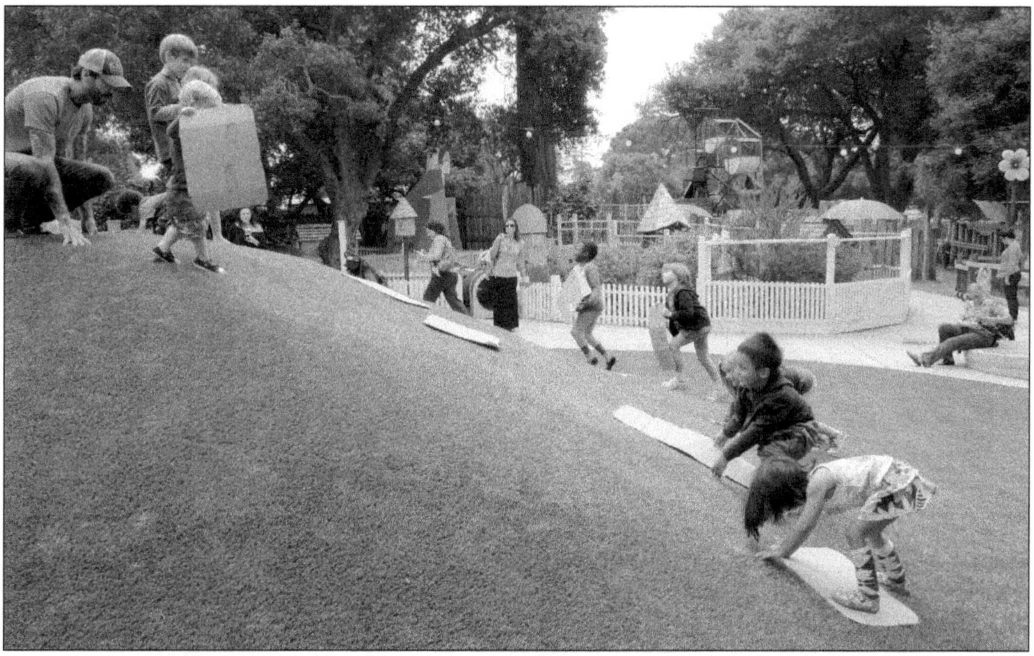

JACK AND JILL HILL, 2012. The latest incarnation of Jack and Jill is Jack and Jill Hill, a small rise covered in synthetic turf and equipped with recycled cardboard squares for sliding. It is the simplest of attractions—no instructions or technology are required because children know instinctively what to do—and yet one of the park's most popular.

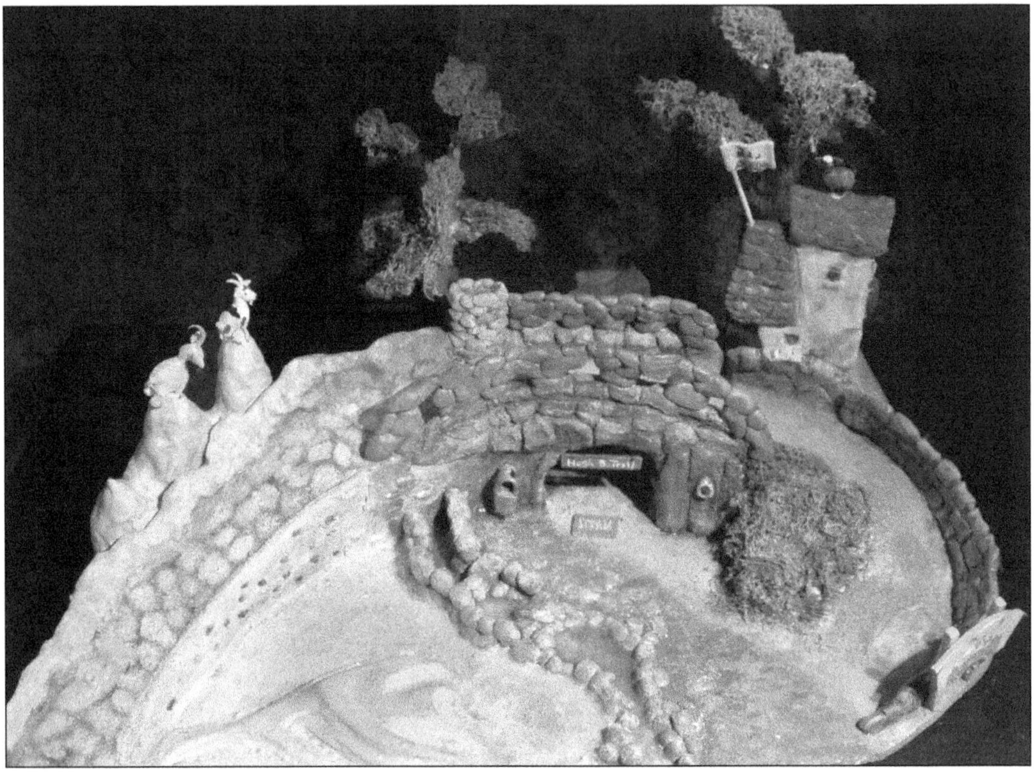

THREE BILLY GOATS GRUFF MODELS, 2014. William Everritt's original 1950 design has been thoroughly reimagined in this new set based on the classic tale of the three billy goats and the troll and created with support from Annette Kevranian and Anthony Winland of Method 42 Productions, a scenic and event production company in Santa Clara. The set features a tunnel, a troll bridge and lair, and figures of the three goats. Where the original set included live baby goats, in the 2016 version they are replaced by sculpted figures, and children are encouraged to imagine themselves as goats or a troll and invent their own stories.

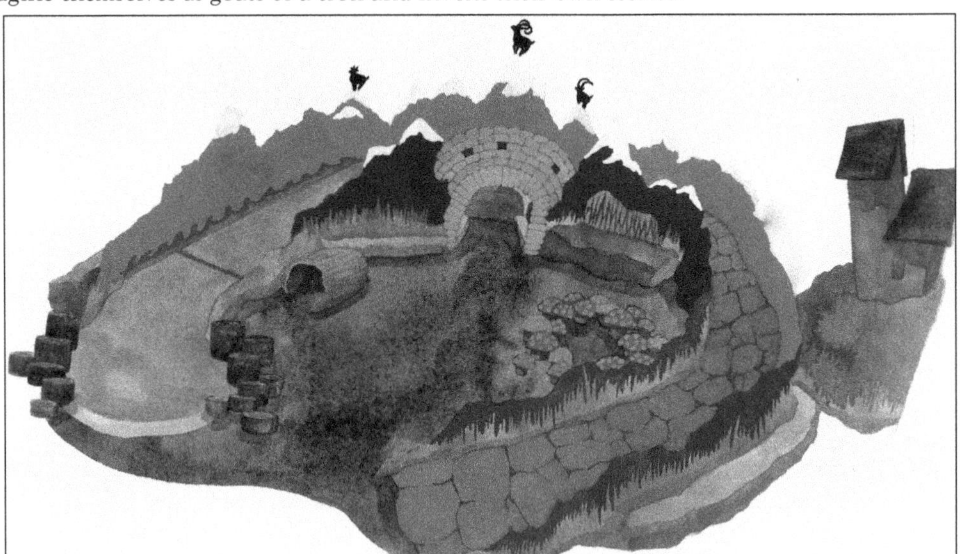

ANOTHER WAY IN?, 2005. A little girl tries to capture a bubble, perhaps in hopes it will carry her over the gates of Fairyland. Oswald the Bubble Elf's bubbles sometimes escape the park and float out into the street. The windows of the Fairyland administrative building, adjacent to the gift shop, are all circular, a design echo of the bubbles.

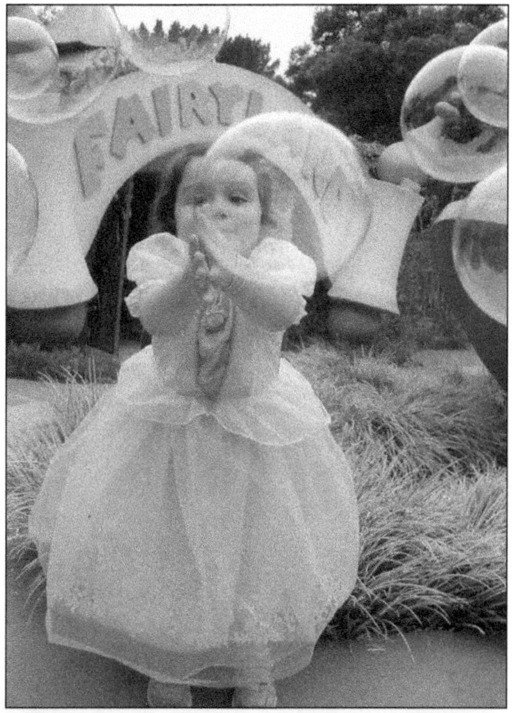

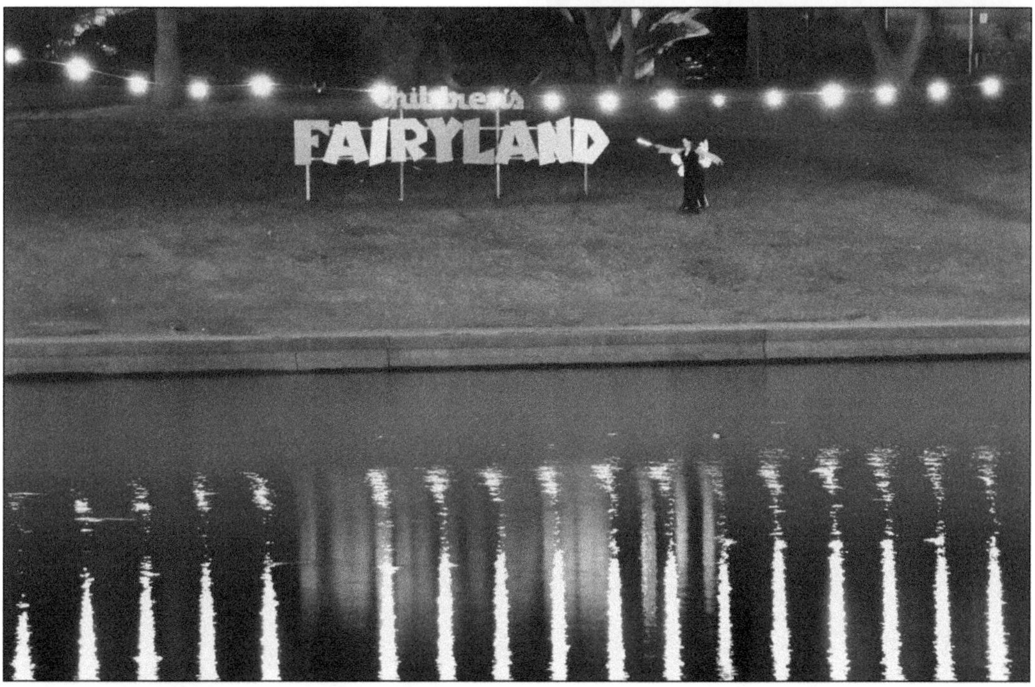

FAIRYLAND BY THE LAKE, 2016. Lake Merritt and Lakeside Park are lit up after dark by an industrious Fairy, while more than 4,000 lamps in the Necklace of Lights encircle the lake. Installed in 1925, the necklace went dark in 1941 because of wartime blackout restrictions. It was reinstalled in 1985 thanks to the efforts of the Lake Merritt Breakfast Club. In 2006, its lights were replaced with energy-efficient, three-watt, cold-cathode bulbs.

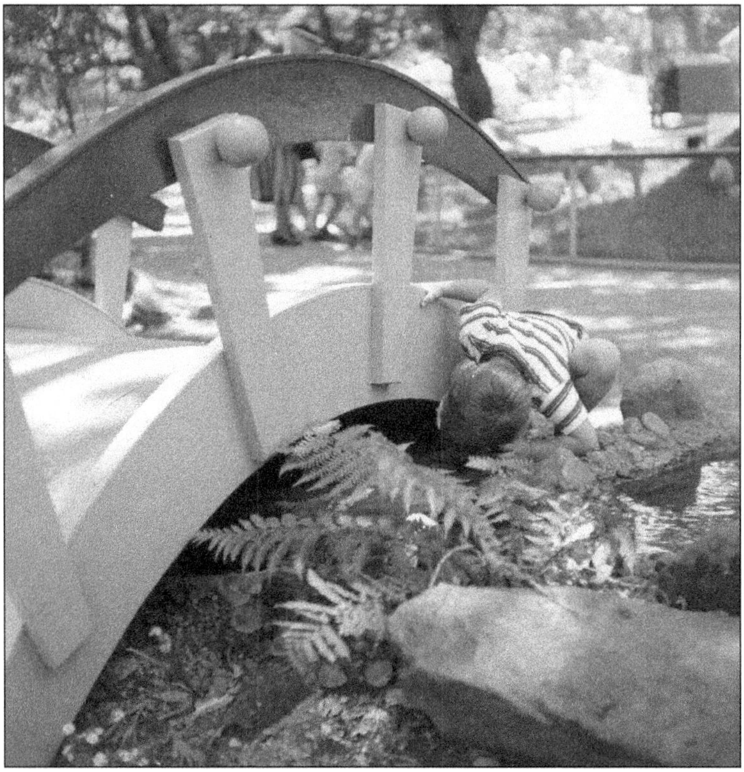

WONDER WHAT'S THERE, C. 1960. An inquisitive young visitor peers under the bridge in search of treasure (or maybe a troll). Much has changed in Oakland, America, and the world since Fairyland opened in 1950, yet children's capacity for wonder and imagination remain the same as ever. And many of Fairyland's most beloved features are still fixtures at the park. Willie the Whale, the Shoe, and the Crooked Man's house—all depicted in a 1953 holiday card illustrated by Alec Stern—still invite and enchant visitors young and old.

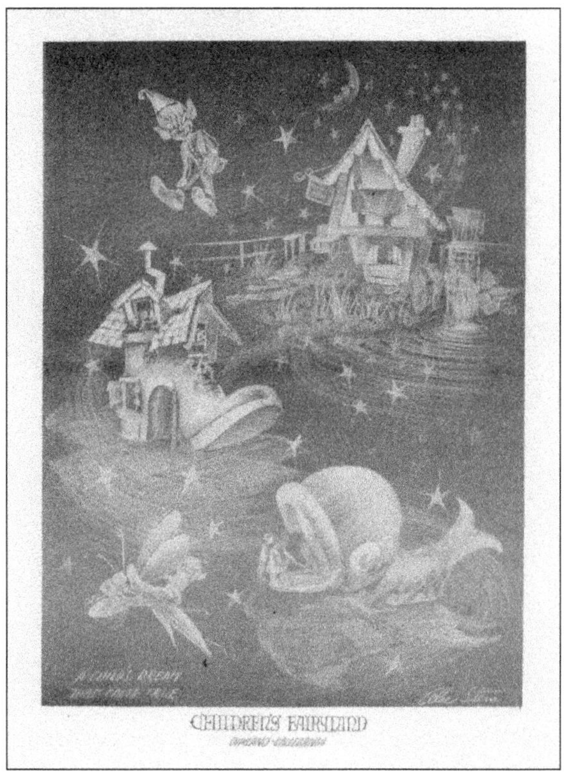

Bibliography

Ad Lib, Oakland Advertising and Marketing Club newsletter, 1949–1955.

Bagwell, Beth. *Oakland, the Story of a City*. Oakland, CA: Oakland Heritage Alliance Press, 1996.

Children's Fairyland archives, 1948–2015.

C.J. Hirschfield, Once Upon a Time in Fairyland, *Piedmont Post*, 2006–2016.

Estes, Michael and Tori Discoe. "53 Years and the Dream Keeps Growing." *Disneyland Line*. July 17, 2008.

Gayton, Sharyn, and Al Kelley. *Lake Merritt Breakfast Club—The Sunnysiders Stylish Story*. Oakland, CA: Anderson Printing, 1992.

Magic Leaf, Children's Fairyland newspaper, 1950–1999.

Metz, Randal J., and Tony Jonick. *Creating a Fairyland: 60 Years of Magic at Children's Fairyland U.S.A.* Oakland, CA: Rappid Rabbit Publishing, 2010.

———. *Storybook Strings: 50 Years of Puppetry at Children's Fairyland's Storybook Puppet Theater*. Oakland, CA: Rappid Rabbit Publishing, 2003.

Oakland History Room archives, Oakland Library

Oakland Tribune

San Francisco Chronicle

"Storybook Playground—Oakland's Children Get Own Private Park." *Life*. March 17, 1952: 95–98.

www.ingramcontent.com/pod-product-compliance
Lightning Source LLC
LaVergne TN
LVHW072040150926
847810LV00055B/441
* 9 7 8 1 4 6 7 1 2 4 1 6 4 *